AF777914

INDIA REVISITED

INDIA REVISITED

Conversations on Continuity and Change

RAMIN JAHANBEGLOO

OXFORD
UNIVERSITY PRESS

OXFORD
UNIVERSITY PRESS

YMCA Library Building, Jai Singh Road, New Delhi 110 001

Oxford University Press is a department of the University of Oxford. It furthers the University's objective of excellence in research, scholarship, and education by publishing worldwide in

Oxford New York

Auckland Cape Town Dar es Salaam Hong Kong Karachi Kuala Lumpur Madrid Melbourne Mexico City Nairobi New Delhi Shanghai Taipei Toronto

With offices in
Argentina Austria Brazil Chile Czech Republic France Greece Guatemala Hungary Italy Japan Poland Portugal Singapore South Korea Switzerland Thailand Turkey Ukraine Vietnam

Oxford is a registered trademark of Oxford University Press in the UK and in certain other countries

Published in India by Oxford University Press, New Delhi

© Oxford University Press 2008

The moral rights of the author have been asserted
Database right Oxford University Press (maker)

First published 2008

All rights reserved. No part of this publication may be reproduced, or transmitted in any form or by any means, electronic or mechanical, including photocopying, recording or by any information storage and retrieval system, without permission in writing from Oxford University Press. Enquiries concerning reproduction outside the scope of the above should be sent to the Rights Department, Oxford University Press, at the address above

You must not circulate this book in any other binding or cover and you must impose this same condition on any acquirer

ISBN-13: 978-019-568944-0
ISBN-10: 019-568944-5

Typeset in Perpetua 12.5/13.7
by Sai Graphic Design, New Delhi 110 055
Printed in India at De Unique, New Delhi 110 018
Published by Oxford University Press
YMCA Library Building, Jai Singh Road, New Delhi 110 001

Contents

Acknowledgements

Of the many debts I have incurred in preparing this book, I would first like to acknowledge the interviewees who inspired me to understand and appreciate India. My thanks to them all, especially those who read the manuscript and provided useful suggestions. I am also thankful to my research assistants, Wasuda Bhatt and Vinita Priyedarshi, for helping me with the appointments, the transcriptions, and the word-processing. I am especially grateful to the Centre for the Study of Developing Societies for funding this research through the Rajni Kothari Chair in Democracy. The funding made possible, among other things, my trips for meetings around India.

I am also grateful for the stimulus and assistance of my friends Ashis Nandy, Suresh Sharma, Peter de Souza, Shail Mayaram, D.L. Sheth, and Rajeev Bhargava. Other people who have helped me in various ways are Raj Rewal, Kapila Vatsyayan, Jasleen Dhamija, Sandeep Ray, Sudhir Kakar, and J.C. Kapoor. I also take this opportunity to express my gratitude to my friend K.C. Singh who was a great help to me and my family while we were in India. I would also like to thank my publisher, Oxford University Press, India, for the invaluable editorial support I received throughout. Finally, my gratitude to my wife, Azin Moalej, for her continuous support. The time she spared for me from our little daughter, Afarin, and from her own architectural work was simply precious.

Making Sense of India

This book tries to make sense of independent India and its evolution over the past six decades. It traces the remarkable transformation of the country from a traditional society to one of the fastest growing economies in the world. It encompasses a full range of subjects—from politics to science and arts—and offers a penetrating analysis of Indian society. Last, but not the least, the aim of this book is to make sense of India through the eyes of Indians. It is a compilation of interviews conducted with twenty-seven Indians about their perceptions of their motherland. Having conversations with Indians can evoke a way of understanding the Indian society. However, India is too complex to be understood in a narrow frame of one or two conversations. Even what Indians say about India is not enough to help us make sense of the country. There is something about India which goes beyond its people. We can call it the 'idea', the 'sense', or simply the 'spirit' of India. This book is a humble attempt to make sense of the country and to capture its spirit. It certainly is not the first and it will not be the last attempt. For thousands of years, Indians have been living in this part of the world with their own way of looking at and interpreting the world. Today, possibly, they are the last remaining 'metaphysical' people on earth who are at ease with both their traditions and the laws of the modern world.

The spirit of India and the very reason for its survival for so long is that it has not been based on any contradiction between the spiritual and the modern. For a nation like India, politically subjugated for centuries by alien conquest and socially unsettled by invasions, the idea of becoming a modern society is no ordinary thought. But even now, the country's national opinion is not uniform on how to become a modern society. What is the lesson for India in our changing world? To pursue the Indian dream without losing foot in the globalized world. Assuredly, India has enough spirit in herself to gain her own measure of spiritual morality, political judgement, and social justice. Indians built India on their own, gradually, imperceptibly, and in spite of global challenges during the past sixty years. The new India has given every Indian in any part of the world the ability to look back and to say proudly: 'I belong to the Indian civilization.' Nations are allowed to occasionally go through self-congratulatory phases, especially when they seek to command respect in the eyes of other nations.

Winston Churchill had once said that India was 'a geographical expression', a land that was 'no more a single country than the Equator'. It is true that no other country in the world embraces so many contradictions. Unlike what many in the West and the East think, India is not limited to one religion, language, caste, creed, or sect. India is the only democratic country in the world with such a large and diverse mixture of traditions and cultures. Yet, at the heart of this nation's diversity lies a great paradox. We have to acknowledge that this is a land of twenty-two different languages. It is also a country where more than 70 per cent of the population still subsists on agriculture. Is this the Mughal emperor Akbar's 'paradise of bliss', in which 51 per cent of the population is still illiterate? Yet, India is one of the leading producers of computer software in the world. It is the birthplace of four major religions and has a longstanding, multi-party, federal, parliamentary democracy, where corruption exists at all levels. So how can one talk about India, keeping in mind all these contradictions?

Jawaharlal Nehru spoke about India as a nation that is held together by a common dream and vision. However, Nehru also knew that there is no such thing as a monolithic Indian nation. If India has any singularity, it is because it is plural. There are as many

Indias, as there are many ways of being Indian. India is the land of diversity and it is impossible to have one fixed idea of it. There is no one answer to the question, 'Who is an Indian?'.

In the twenty-first century, when every sixth human being will be an Indian, this question will arise more often. Yet, even then, when India will potentially be a major economic and political power, poised to emerge as the second largest consumer market in the world, there will be misconceptions about India. This might have to do with the fact that people around the world still have no idea who Indians are. Actually, India will survive as an old civilization and flourish as a great political power in the new millennium precisely because of who Indians are, and not because of what they might aspire to or what others might like them to be. This reminds me of a scene from the famous movie, *The Party*, where Peter Sellers, playing an Indian actor working in Hollywood, solemnly declares, 'In India we don't think who we are, we know who we are.' But do Indians really know who they are? Well, maybe all Indians do not think daily about their situation, but many certainly think about the hard conditions of their lives. Most evidently, the harder their lives, the more difficult are the ways of escaping illiteracy, poverty, and underdevelopment. Poverty exists at the grassroots level in India and income disparities are increasing.

This is no more a cliché, but the bitter backstage of the globalization process in India. It is now clear that globalization and economic reforms have primarily benefitted the rich and the middle classes in India. Inequality has been soaring through the globalization period—within and across India. At a time when there are more billionaires driving around Mumbai in their expensive cars, ordinary urban Indians sleep in their Ambassadors after using them as taxis. Chronic hunger is rising in rural India, reversing trends of the 1970s and 1980s. Recent data shows that this already alarming situation is getting worse, and the number of Indians facing food insecurity is higher than the proportion defined as existing below the official poverty line. Around 320 million Indians go hungry every night. The remedy may well be what Mahatma Gandhi had suggested as far back as November 1928:

everybody should be able to get sufficient work to enable them to make the two ends meet. But the question is: what is left of Gandhi in India today?

The answer is simple: India seems to be distancing itself from Gandhi's principles. Economic reforms have turned the country into a consumer society, a notion that was challenged by Gandhi during his lifetime. Also, the passage of time has led to ignorance and misunderstanding about what Gandhi stood for. Recent Indian governments have neglected his vision and to make matters worse, Gandhians of the past sixty years have not been at the moral and creative level of their leader. They have been Gandhian in words, rather than in acts. However, Gandhi's ideals are not all falling on deaf ears. Nearly everything Gandhi wrote and taught about non-violence, economic justice, and humility are still relevant in today's world. It took India sixty years to become what it is today, and it will probably be another sixty years before India realizes that it should have followed the Gandhian path. From cars to computers, Indian consumers, oriented to the personalization of goods and services, have embraced the allure of a modern society that is uninterested in tradition. To this dichotomy, we may add a second: the gap between the metropolises and the countryside. There is a yawning chasm between the glittering upper-class lifestyle of the cities and grinding rural poverty. It is true that one can see computers and CDs on store shelves, pizzas and hamburgers in restaurants, cola and cornflakes on kitchen shelves, and neon signs and discos in places like Delhi, Mumbai, and Bangalore, but it is also true that rural India is dogged by a number of social evils such as child labour, dowry, and prostitution. India has moved too far along the road to consumerism to be able to turn back now or even stand still. It seems consumerism has led the Indian middle class to become almost a carbon copy or caricature of the Western élite. But this encounter with modernity has also allowed Indians to make serious intellectual and political choices about their destiny. While some Indians say that the modernity that emerged in the West in the wake of the Enlightenment is irredeemably flawed, and that India should turn her back on it and continue with her spiritual traditions, there are also those who believe that modernization has helped the Indian economy, which is growing even faster than the Chinese economy. Certainly, modernization is not a train that one boards and gets off as one pleases. However, there is no creativity in being a mindless imitator of the West. Some Indians now proudly say that India will no longer kowtow to the West, and that with the country going nuclear, the world will now respect it as a powerful nation.

Mahatma Gandhi would certainly not have approved of the use of bombs capable of vapourizing thousands of people as a way of being respected as a powerful nation. In *Hind Swaraj*, one of the earliest critiques of modernity, Gandhi said that the mark of a civilization is the ethical performance of one's duty and the attainment of mastery over passion. He also argued that progress is useless if it is not allied to an internal quest. Gandhi's resistance to Western civilization was actually a resistance to its indiscriminate and thoughtless imitation. But, faced with the rise of techno-scientific globalization, Gandhi's vision of India as a moral civilization has largely failed to materialize. Yet this does not diminish India's spiritual legacy, which encompasses cross-cultural dialogue conducted through centuries of war and peace. The 'dharmic' element has been the main characteristic of the Indian civilization through history. This spiritual orientation can be found today in the cultures of all the regions of India, pervading the folk art of all regions, as well as the minds of many Indians. It is this 'dharmic' element that continues to sustain Indian civilization. The spirit of India imposes on her the responsibility of following her own dharma even if it is difficult and goes against modernity. Gandhi's discussion of India as a 'dharmic civilization' presents us with an idealized version of Indian culture that is completely contrapuntal to Western modernity. Nonetheless, his three-fold foundation (self-respect, self-realization, and self-reliance) for a dharmic civilization appears as a moral basis to the structure of Indian society. For Gandhi, civilization was a mode of conduct which 'pointed out to man the path of duty'. Therefore, Gandhi reversed the modern theory of rights as being legitimated by duties.

In other words, for Gandhi, rights had to be in the interest not only of the individual, but also of society as a whole, and by 'society' Gandhi meant not the state but the collective entity of individuals. This is one of the most remarkable and yet ignored reinterpretations of the theory of rights—a philosophy intended to persuade Gandhi's readers that the unity of humankind as a philosophical principle is ontologically prior to diversity. Inspired by this philosophy, many Indians have dedicated their lives to social and constructive work in India. Popular movements in India have worked independently for the rights of Indians using Gandhian philosophy as inspiration. During the past sixty years, Gandhian ideals have found popularity among social groups and movements in India that seek a more harmonious relationship between human activities and nature, and another world that draws away from the centralization of political power and economic production. The Gandhian legacy of volunteerism spawned a plethora of voluntary agencies working for development in India, particularly after the 1970s. Many city-based professionals have been working in rural areas, helping people with education, health, rural development, water, sanitation, etc., through voluntary agencies.

The Indian government, mostly irritated by the presence of these social movements, has raised the question of the legitimacy of civil society institutions. Indian civil society activists have worked towards the promotion of policies, institutions, and capacities that have strengthened the voice and participation of the poor and the marginalized, by improving their socio-economic status through democratic governance. Indian civil society also has the role of 'ensuring the accountability' of the Indian state in different spheres. Its purpose is to build the framework of a real form of governance, in which both the Indian state and citizens are accountable to each other.

India is today an emerging global player and a potential world power of the twenty-first century. This is not due to the initiatives of the Indian state, but because of India's ongoing democratic revolution, which has invited and intensified dialogue among Indians and with the outside world. Gandhi, Tagore, Nehru,

Radhakrishnan, and many other prominent personalities knew well that unless different cultures enter into a dialogue and understand each other, none can survive and flourish. This has been their message to the world. The Indian way of living and speaking together has been an interactive one for centuries. If Gandhi had been alive, he would have recalled, sixty years after his death, the contribution of different cultures to world civilization.

The unexpected survival of democracy, among a people so diverse as the Indians are, is a miracle. European countries have immense difficulty dealing with their secular multiculturalism and yet, democracy has given Indians an institutional framework for exercising diversity and expressing their dissent. Democracy has acted as an indispensable safety valve for people with different cultural and religious backgrounds, not always democratic by temperament. Thus, Indians, unlike the people of the United States of America or Europeans, are not, as some people like to believe, genetically democratic. They have paid a high price for the implementation and survival of democracy in India.

The essential point is that there has always been a spirit in India that has given unequivocal primacy to the moral imperative in statecraft. Whether it is Kautilya's *Arthashastra*, Manu's *Dharmashastra*, the Tamil *Book of Kural*, Ashokan Buddhist edicts, or Abul Fazl's *Ain-i-Akbari*, they have all been informed by ideas of ethical government. Kautilya says in his *Arthashastra*: 'In the happiness of his subjects lies the king's happiness, in their welfare his welfare. He shall not consider as good only that which pleases him, but treat as beneficial to him whatever pleases his subjects'. The principle that is fundamental to ethics of power in India is the principle of 'dharma'—performing the right actions—and the principle of justice. The *Brihadaranyaka Upanishad* points out that the basic responsibility of the king is to protect dharma. This is because only by protecting dharma can all citizens get equal opportunities so that the weak are not exploited and harassed by the strong. Verse 59.58 in the *Karna Parva* of the Mahabharata eulogizes dharma in the following words: 'Dharma sustains the society, dharma maintains social order, dharma ensures well-being and progress of humanity.' Therefore, dharma is actually the principle that has sustained and ensured India's progress and the welfare of its people through the ages. In fact, the goal of every Indian has been to ultimately find a harmony between the individual, the social, and the spiritual. It is this harmony that provides a meaningful basis for new ethics in the globalized world.

Sixty years of India's existence as an independent nation and of democratic challenges have resulted in one common experience for all Indians. Economic wealth, political power, and technological ambitions are not sufficient to hold a diverse nation together. Something more is needed to tackle corruption, poverty, and inequality. By drawing their inspiration from the spirit of India and remembering beacons of light like Rabindranath Tagore, Sri Aurobindo, Mahatma Gandhi, and many others, Indians can move towards building a better nation and also a better world. As Romain Rolland once said: 'If there is one place on the face of earth where all the dreams of living men have found a home from the very earliest days when man began the dream of existence, it is India!'

Delhi
May 2007

RAMIN JAHANBEGLOO

Romila Thapar

Being an Indian Today

Indian Nationalism and History

ROMILA THAPAR (RT): There have been various approaches to the writing of Indian history in modern times. One was the colonial interpretation of Indian history. Another was based on concerns of nationalism and history. The critique of these gave rise to a more analytical explanation of the Indian past and this has been attacked by the most recent attempt to establish a communal interpretation. Most of these have been selective in terms of the data consulted and its use. However, there has been an expansion in the range and category of sources among those historians who have tried to provide analytical explanations and the questions discussed by them are also more far reaching.

RAMIN JAHANBEGLOO (RJ): But according to you the communalists have made the most dangerous interpretation of Indian history because they have turned history into an important vehicle of indoctrination and by doing so they have put the very fabric of secular India in danger.

RT: I would broadly say that is what I maintain. However, I would like to put it in another way. There has been colonial historical writing and a strong critique of this particularly from a mix of Marxist, secular, and scientific history. And it is this latter to which communal historical writing is strongly opposed. Those who support a communal interpretation are not attacking the colonial structure of viewing history because they borrow many of their premises from it. They are taking some of the aspects of nationalist interpretation to an extreme degree, but the main attack is against secular and rational historical writing, which they uniformly dismiss by calling it Marxist. So it is important to clarify the importance of Marxist interpretations of history.

RJ: Where do you think is the foundation of this school of secular rationalist history writing in India?

RT: Well, I think that these foundations lie partly in certain kinds of nationalist writing which critiqued the colonial, and partly in the very interesting turn which Indian history took in the 1950s and 1960s when it moved from being a branch of Indology to being included in the social sciences. The understanding of history as a field of investigation and one that included sociology, anthropology, economics, and other social sciences, shifted the focus from Indology. The shift also incorporated what was then interpreted by Marxists and non-Marxists as secular rational history. It is this shift that communal historiography has not been able to come terms with.

Plural Histories

RJ: You are among those Indian historians and intellectuals who believe that Hinduism alone cannot be the subject matter of Indian history and because of your public position on this matter you have been accused of offending Hindus. The demolition of Babri Masjid, the communal carnage in Gujarat, the turmoil at Ayodhya, the attacks on Christians, and the controversy about the history textbooks, which have constituted the rubric of the communal agenda in the past fifteen years have put two divergent views on the Indian nation face to face—a vision of an open, democratic, secular, and libertarian society as opposed to the communal, regressive, and authoritarian world view of Hindutva. To what extent have the recent political developments in India broadened the concerns of historical analysis among Indian scholars and academics? Would you say that there has been a general awareness and a radical change at the level of Indian intellectuals in the interpretation of early Indian history, taking into consideration the fact that the study of early Indian history is a complicated process?

RT: What disturbs me the most is not just the reference to Indian civilization as solely Hindu but equally what is included under the rubric of 'Hindu'. I have argued for many years in my writing that Indian civilization is not purely Hindu, and that too upper caste Hindu, but that is has many strands and that it is a multicultural civilization. I have grave reservations about the way civilization was defined in the nineteenth century and we continue to use that definition. If one defines it as a clearly demarcated territory where a single religion and a single language prevailed uniformly, then one obliterates its multicultural form. It is this form that is the uniqueness of Indian history. Other civilizations do not maintain such a broad spectrum of cultural articulation as is the case in India. So my analysis is that instead of, as it were, basking in the glory of this multiplicity and trying to understand how and why it worked, there is an insistence on narrowing it down to one stream.

My second objection is that communal history seeks to legitimize itself by taking recourse to propagating Hindutva, which I think is alien to Hinduism itself. I think that Hinduism is a far more emotionally evocative religion with many dimensions of belief and social attitudes. These produce a complexity of cultures with a range of accommodations and confrontations and this is being destroyed by the concoction called Hindutva, or what I have called in one of my writings, 'Syndicated Hinduism'. I think it is an attack not only on non-Hindu belief and practice but also on the multicultural tradition of Hinduism itself.

The controversy over history has resulted in conceding that a clarification in the discipline was necessary. There was an assumption that history is concerned with only a single correct version of the past. There are facts that emerge from investigations and this produces a definitive interpretation. What is forgotten is that the reliability of the fact has to be constantly evaluated where new evidence surfaces or where the reliability is challenged and that this is based not on arbitrary statements or fantasies but on a rigorous historical method. What is being realized now is that in the social sciences there are no permanent definitive interpretations partly because the analysis itself covers a wider range of sources than were drawn upon earlier. What we regarded as historical evidence when we were taught history as students is only a portion of what we now teach our students. This means that as the range of historical evidence increases the possible range of causation also increases. Let me give you an example. Events in the north-west of the subcontinent were attributed to invasions by foreigners in earlier histories and in the communal interpretation today. We now look at the context of such events. What preceded the invasions in the form of pastoral circuits and migrations, and commercial exchange, which might have motivated an invasion in addition to political factors. What was the nature and form of the invasion since this is not a uniform event in all circumstances. What is meant by 'foreign' since the boundaries of the present day did not hold for the past and people in contiguous areas did not necessarily see each other as foreign. What has now emerged is that either there is a simplistic version that still sticks to monocausal analysis and a tendency to treat historical events as unified monolithic items in their relationship to each other, or else there is the much more sophisticated history which is breaking down the monolithic and looking at it more analytically and searching for causal relationships.

RJ: Has the role of religion in Indian history undergone a major reinterpretation and reorientation or is it still regarded as a major component of Indian history?

RT: As I said earlier, there are historians, and particularly some who write on pre-modern history, who would treat Buddhism, Hinduism, and Islam as monolithic, uniform entities. But there are also those who have done some excellent analytical work demonstrating how they cannot be treated as self-contained uniform entities, neither in the interpretation of their myths, belief systems, and practices nor in their relationship to society through the social institutions with which they identify. The link between religion as a social articulation and the social group that accepts it as such is becoming more evident in recent historical analyses.

RJ: I think you would agree with Amartya Sen to say that the Hindu version of history is sectarian and combative. But would you also agree that India was never a Hindu *rashtra* because the two greatest emperors of India, Ashoka, and Akbar, were non-Hindus—one being a Buddhist and other a Muslim.

RT: History from the perspective of any religious sect tends to be sectarian and combative. Sectarian religions thrive in an ambience where particular beliefs have to be propagated and where sects have to compete for patronage and a following. This is historically as valid of the sects that we have called 'Hindu' sects as those of any other organized religion. As regards the second part of your question I have some problems as a historian with the idea of a Hindu rashtra per se. What some of us are arguing is that unlike Christian Europe or the Islamic states of West Asia, it is difficult to say that the state in the Indian subcontinent pre-modern times could be labelled as Hindu. This is precisely because of the pluralities of cultural articulation and the distinctively different manifestations of religion among those at varying social levels and conforming to distinct social communities. For about a thousand years from 300 BC onwards, Buddhism was a powerful religion in the Indian subcontinent. It competed for patronage at various levels, especially at the level of the state and it was in confrontation with not only common belief systems but also with the most sophisticated philosophical schools. The question often asked is why Buddhism declined in most areas—but not all—in the latter part of the first millennium AD. It might be more interesting to ask the question why and which facets of Buddhism were incorporated into Hinduism and how did these change the layers of the latter. Those who study the history and the sociology of pre-modern religion in India have tended to move away from the package called Hinduism and tend to see it as a range of sects evolving from a variety of antecedents such as Vedic Brahmanism, or Puranic Hinduism, or the Bhakti traditions, and various manifestations of popular religion that incorporated elements of Islam, the cult of Shakti, and a variety of other religious forms. Hinduism itself has undergone fundamental changes which paradoxically accounts for what has been seen as its historical continuity.

There are some who argue that 'Hinduism'—the notion of an 'ism' tagged onto certain religions originating in the Indian subcontinent, is an invention of the colonial period. Prior to about the fourteenth century, people identified their religion according to their sect—Vaishnava, Shaiva, Lingayata, Shakta, or as Jaina, Buddhist, or Muslim, and so on.

Al-Biruni, writing in the eleventh century, stated that there were two religious categories prevalent in India: the Brahmans and the Shamaniyya (the Shramans), and by the latter he meant those who did not accept the Brahmanical precepts. This dichotomy goes back to much earlier times. Megasthenes who wrote in the fourth century BC referred to only these two categories as also did the grammarian Patanjali a little later who described their hostility as innate. In areas like Gujarat, the Jaina Shramans played a major political role.

So I am unclear as to what is the meaning of Hindu rashtra.

Aryan Invasion Theory

RJ: To be effective as a political ideology, Hindutva had to redefine Hindu identity and to do this, it linked the ancestry of the Hindus to a lineal descent from the Aryans. Theories of Aryan arrival to India from across the borderlands or alternatively those proposing indigenous origin have been debated for over a century. For example, Max Mueller was among those who argued in the nineteenth century that Aryans were the foundation of Indian civilization and that they came from Central Asia. However, according to you there is a popular misperception and misunderstanding of the '*arya*s' referred to in the *Rigveda* which has been applied to Indian history and has ended with a theory that equates the Aryans with the authors of the Indus civilization, even though the Indus civilization was pre-Aryan. Are there any archeological evidences for this? Why do many Indians continue to focus on the Vedic corpus as the main historical evidence and emphasize on the question of identity as the central concept of Indian history instead of talking of multi-ethnic migrations and cultural border-crossings?

RT: Unfortunately this is an imprint of the colonial interpretation of history. The notion of the Aryan race in its application to the Vedic texts arises from the confusing of language and race by European commentators in the late nineteenth century. Philology and social Darwinism were brought into play in reconstructing the past. The main language of the *Rigveda*, Indo-Aryan, is a cognate of Old Iranian and they both belong to the Indo-European family. But this does not mean that the speakers of these languages automatically became members of an Aryan race—particularly as we now know that there was no Aryan race. The word Aryan derives from arya in the Vedic texts and *airiia* in the Avesta, where it has cultural and status connotations but these should not be read as race. Max Mueller's reading of the term Aryan as both a linguistic and racial category encouraged the idea of race in the Indian context. The knowledge that we have from linguistics and genetics today questions the theory of race, but this questioning has not become popular knowledge in India. We still tend to assume that there are races. The word race has been loosely used as when we talk about belonging to the Hindu race or the Muslim race, or the Dravidian race or the Bengali race, which contradicts the actual meaning of the term. This confuses biology, language, and religion. Another problem is that of the meaning of arya in the Vedic texts. Does it refer to a distinct people, an ethnic group, speaking a particular language, and/or people respected because they belong to a social group that had status? An Aryan migration would therefore not mean the influx of large numbers of people but the coming of a new language and new culture-ways that merged with and impacted local cultures as indeed the latter made their mark on what has come to be called Aryan culture. The evidence for this is in the language and culture of the *Rigveda* especially when it is part of a comparative study with the Avesta and other sources using Indo-Aryan. The word 'arya' has its own history. The Buddhist monk for example, in a later period, was frequently addressed as arya which was an honorific even though Buddhists did not by any means accept the teaching of the *Rigveda*. In the Ramayana, Ravana, who is depicted as a demon is addressed by his wife as *aryaputra,* literally the son of an arya. So it's a word that is used in multiple contexts. There is a tendency today to collate them and give it one meaning instead of looking at the context and recognizing that the word itself undergoes change historically.

Added to this is the problem that if one insists, as in the nineteenth century interpretation of Indian history, that the foundational culture of India is 'Aryan', then one has to maintain that the origin of Indian culture lay with the Aryans. As a consequence, Aryan is sought to be defined not as a language and culture that evolved in the new borderlands between Western and South Asia, but as indigenous to India with no admixture of any sort. The shorthand for this is the discussion of whether the 'Aryans' came from outside India or have they always been local inhabitants. If they were indigenous then the earliest civilization of India has perforce to be Aryan and equated with the Vedas; whereas if there was an infiltration of the Aryan language and culture into India, thereby creating a new culture subsequent to that of the Indus cities, then the historical questions this raises are of a completely different nature. They have to do with the far more intellectually challenging issues of cultural and social change. Such issues are perhaps a little too complex for those who prefer easy answers of either 'yes' or 'no'. The question of what is meant by outside India poses other problems. What were the boundaries defining aliens and indigenes? Who defined them? In the current argument, the boundaries used to define the outsiders and the indigenous are the boundaries of British India. These are surely a far cry from what might have been the boundaries—if there were ever such notions at that time—in 3000, 2000, or 1000 BC. Boundaries change radically with the shrinking or enlarging of states throughout the past. The aliens of yesterday may well be the indigenes of today.

Indian Nationalism and Religion

RJ: Would you agree that in India there have been two recognizable forms of nationalism, generally distinct but occasionally overlapping? One was inclusive nationalism dating from the late nineteenth century, which kneaded together the segments of Indian society and opposed colonial power and its focus was on the sovereignty of an Indian identity, based on democratic and secular institutions. The second has been the exclusive religious nationalism, either Muslim or Hindu, which has always undermined the secular and democratic values that were sought in India after independence.

RT: Yes, I would broadly agree. But then there is also the point that nationalisms manifest their ideas in different ways and people are nationalistic for a variety of reasons. Indian nationalism was geared towards the creation of a state that was to be secular and the primary identity was to being an Indian citizen. Historians looking back on the national movement realize that apart from exclusive nationalism that certainly existed, whether it was the Hindu Mahasabha or the Muslim League, there was also an inclination among some elements within inclusive nationalism to give some primacy to an identity that was religious. Although Indian nationalism was searching for secularism, in the coming Indian state there was a strand that was not averse to what were seen as the cultural views of exclusive nationalism. The example that has struck me is the stand of K.M. Munshi who was a minister of the central government at independence. His writing on the history of Gujarat was strongly influenced by exclusive nationalism. He maintained a Hindu Aryan foundational identity for Gujarat. This in part motivated his demand for the reconstruction of the temple at Somnath. He tried to involve the central government in the project and Nehru not only rejected the idea of state participation but insisted that the rebuilding be done by a private trustee. The temple at Somnath became the icon with which the Rashtriya Swayamsevak Sangh (RSS) and the Bharatiya Janata Party (BJP) began their journey to the Babri Masjid at Ayodhya, and eventually destroyed the mosque. It was said that this was avenging the destruction of Somnath by Mahmud of Ghazni, even if the revenge was manifested after a thousand years. Some nationalists, when scratched, react as exclusive nationalists. There are few who are genuinely inclusive nationalists.

RJ: Do you think that this obsession with the concept of Indian-ness will continue and that it will continue to be used as a reaction to cultural, economic, and political globalization?

RT: The way in which they define Indian-ness, is in effect a Hindutva identity, and as long as this identity can be used politically, it will continue.

RJ: But don't you think that the tendency to freely interpret history at the street level is going to increase in India with the historically insufficient and distorted role played by the media.

RT: It has got to the point when people, seemingly without thinking, make communal remarks about the past. This refers particularly to comments about the positive nature of the 'Hindu' past and the negative nature of the 'Muslim' past. And the tendency is not to think beyond being Hindu or Muslim. Historical events are explained in these terms since they are easy on the mind and do not require to be thought about any further. People happily pontificate on the basis of virtually no information, leave alone knowledge. History, it is argued, cannot undergo change because it is based on facts and once something is a fact, it is a fact for eternity. That there is such a thing as analysing earlier theories and suggesting new ways of understanding the past is beyond the ken of those brought up on the historical writing of yesteryears when history was easy to read. There is little concession to the fact that knowledge advances, changes, and becomes more complex; and that it is necessary to keep up with recent research on a subject if one is going to pontificate. There is no recognition that historical analysis has become a rigorous intellectual discipline with a defined methodology, which is demanding both in terms of testing the reliability of evidence and the logical basis of the argument. The media makes no effort to question ignorance since it is, with a very few exceptions, equally ignorant itself.

History in the Indian Classroom

RJ: In some ways, the most serious challenge for Indian society is what is taught in the classroom about the Indian past. Would you say that there is enough attention given to breaking the boundaries of Indian history and exploring what lies beyond them with a concern for the present?

RT: Well, I think that has to be done at many educational levels. Most history books in this country are appallingly bad and that was the reason why in the 1960s some of us agreed to write books for the National Council for Educational Research and Training (NCERT). The shift in those days was from political and diplomatic history to social and economic history. This contradicted the pet theory of communal interpretations and that is why the issue of textbooks became such an important issue when the BJP came to power. They realized that the way to control the mindset of the next generation was by giving them textbooks which stated not only their version of the past, but became the bedrock of their ideology for the present, namely, the creation of a Hindu nation-state. How does one tackle the problem of school-level textbooks? One method is through the NCERT textbooks, used in state schools. These, from what little I have seen of the new ones, seem quite sensible. But there are two further problems: one is, who is going to teach them? The teachers who will teach the new textbooks have not been trained in the methods of historical analysis of recent times. What they have learnt at their graduate or university level, is history that is now fairly out-of-date. Teachers inevitably are often open to the influence of the media since they have not been taught to question what the media says. This is why I have been repeatedly writing and urging that more attention be given to the training of school teachers. The other problem is that increasing numbers of schools have been instituted by religious organizations. Some have a front of cultural organizations but teach communal history. There has not been a serious enough attempt by educationists to analyse which textbooks are taught in these schools. When there is a situation where the majority of Muslim parents prefer their children to go to madrasa schools, it is essential that we know what the children are taught in such schools, and the same holds for the RSS-run Shishu Mandirs, or schools run by gurudwaras, or Christian missions. Not enough attention is being paid to this question, perhaps because it is viewed as too volatile. Yet, it is essential to any attempt at creating responsible citizens.

India and the World

RJ: The leaders of the Indian independence struggle felt strongly that India had something unique to offer to the world and they insisted on the civilizational factor of India. In the minds of individuals like Gandhi and Nehru, the civilizational factor was a background that was to be selectively appropriated. Indian-ness required a shared identity, based on a shared conception of what the Indians stood for. Is this 'national philosophy of India' still relevant today or do Indians need a new national self-definition?

RT: I think, in a sense, we have fallen back. It's not that we are not following that path but we have not explored what that path means for an independent nation. What we really needed to do was to discuss and define Indian nationalism not in the context of resistance to colonial rule, but in the context of a nation-state. I have problems with people who dismiss nationalism altogether. Virtually every state that is a nation-state is by its very nature built on nationalism. The question then is to configure the components of a new nationalism, those that we feel are conducive to a creative and positive condition. To insist on constructing an exclusive nationalism negates the future. Contestations over religious identities are in the ultimate analysis rather futile since the real contestation lies elsewhere. I think there are many more dimensions of Indian nationalism today than what the earlier national leaders fought for. The religious contestation has become much more acute and unnecessarily so. The genocide in Gujarat was quantitatively and qualitatively worse than the communal riots of the twentieth century and could not have happened at that earlier time. What appalls me is how quickly it has been either forgotten or else seen as a legitimate ethnic cleansing and Gujarat is now being lauded for good governance. It came and went and Gujarat is admired as the most prosperous state. The echoes of the beginnings of fascism from similar events in modern history are deliberately silenced. The other side of the story, the carnage which should be reckoned with as a kind of counterweight is ignored. Perhaps it embarrasses the media which is busy projecting the image of a shining India. This is not nationalism. This is a poverty of social ethics. It may be fashionable now to throw social ethics out of the window and in this we are following a transnational model. But at some point it is bound to turn around and make us ashamed of what we are doing.

There is also the problem of regional identities and how they force a rethinking of nationalism. This impinges on the perspective of a national history. It is not necessarily a confrontation between the periphery and the centre although this is and can be an obvious way of looking at it. But equally, it involves relationships between the states among themselves, sometimes conditioned by unequal development. It is startling that half or more of the states are experiencing a condition of civil war. There is the clash of identity based on language and ethnicity perhaps, or the fact that some states have more of the good things of life than others. Yet it had earlier been argued that democracy and economic development would bring uniform prosperity. Disparity breeds anger and frustration diverts hatred towards the person who comes from elsewhere, either from the better-off state or a landless labourer from a poorer state who is seen as taking away the employment of a local. There is change but either it is not sufficient or it is of the wrong kind. It is not enough to quote numbers affected by the change. It is equally necessary to assess the quality of the change and to ascertain the degree of effective improvement, if any. This is so apparent in the decisions about education. When we started with the policy of reserving seats for Dalits and those who came from the backward castes, we were told that it would be for a limited period and it would be for those who had been denied the opportunity to be educated. I think elder statesmen such as Gandhi and Nehru would have said that reservations were not the only answer and that the infrastructure of basic education was equally necessary. Further, that the state has the responsibility of educating its citizens and therefore providing the infrastructure in the form of more schools and teachers and a policy of making them effective. The problem cannot be solved merely by increasing the percentage of reserved seats. The parallel infrastructure has to ensure that ultimately reservation becomes redundant and there is an equal opportunity for everyone to be educated. Reservation by itself, without the back-up of support for children who come from deprived economic and social backgrounds, will merely sharpen the cleavages in society. At the same time, there will be a drastic lowering of standards in an effort to expand a system that is at a point of hopelessness as it is. It is glaringly under-financed and under-staffed by qualified professional teachers. The support system even at the level of schools and teachers alone is nowhere near a sensitive solution. I think we have failed to understand the message that we came with at the time of independence and we have gone off in a direction, which for Indians as a whole will be unproductive.

RJ: Would you say that the identity which has wide acceptability among the Indian middle class is an all inclusive Indian identity which gathers together many people, customs, and beliefs or is it only a travesty of what was understood by the founding fathers of independent India?

RT: The basic question is, does the middle class alone define identity and tradition? Both identity and tradition when looked at historically have constantly changed. Identities are never the same from century to century as they are continually reformulated and readjusted depending upon a particular context and its concerns. Tradition is something which is born from the needs of the present but seeks legitimacy by claiming that it comes from the past. So, in talking about identity and tradition the Indian middle class is clear today that it wants certain things and it's going to get them and by-pass the critique of wanting these things by wrapping them up in what it itself has invented as tradition and identity. I don't object to this as this has been a recognized activity in history by multiple social groups, but I do object to the middle class identity not being recognized as an invention, and to the insistence that it is the continuity of a tradition unchanged from the past, which of course, it is not.

Kapila Vatsyayan

Elements of Diversity

RAMIN JAHANBEGLOO (RJ): With about twenty-two officially recognized languages, several religions, including Hinduism, Islam, Christianity, Jainism, Buddhism, Sikhism, Zoroastrianism, and Judaism, various styles of art, architecture, literature, music, and dance, and several lifestyles from the urban and rural to the tribal, India is a melting pot of cultural diversity. What elements do you think are the most essential in Indian culture, and which ones help maintain its diversity?

KAPILA VATSYAYAN (KV): I entirely agree with you that India as a country, is more a civilization comprising a staggering diversity of linguistic (dialects and languages) societal structures, tribes, rural and urban dichotomies, and religions and faiths—Hindu, Buddhist, Jain, Zorastrian, Islam, Sikh, and Judaic and many more. The diversity is reflected in lifestyle, architectural styles, sculptural and pictorial schools, musical family traditions, several genres of dance, cuisine, and much else. So far, India has been able to nurture and sustain this diversity because each of these identities has space and potential for co-existence, not in insularity, but in communication and interaction with each other. This is true of languages, literature, numerous religious movements as also diverse levels of society. Allow me to comment on the metaphor or image of the 'melting pot' you have used.

In my perception, India, so far, is not a melting pot where several ingredients are homogenized into a single solution or paste. In other words, Indian civilization has not demanded the giving up of specific identities; instead it has added a new dimension to an already given identity or situation. The Indian thus comprises a human with multi-identities which he holds together. It would, therefore, be perhaps more correct to use the metaphor or image of a 'kaleidoscope' where single units make different configurations in time and space without any loss of identity, rather than a melting pot. However, let me add that all 'semantic' metaphors are only approximations and can never reflect the complexity of life and certainly not the long history of Indian civilization and culture.

To the third part of your question, that is, 'what or which elements are the most essential in Indian culture and which help to maintain its diversity', I would say that it is difficult and perhaps not possible to identify one or more elements as essential and others as non-essential. It is not so much a question of identifying specific elements, but more a matter of 'ethos' or potential for absorption, assimilation, and transformation without loss of identity, linguistic, religious, artistic, etc. To take an example, India received both Christianity and Islam, and yet in time, there is a distinctively Indian Christianity and a distinct Indian Islam. Also, it was in the fertile ground of India that a very meaningful dialogue could and did take place between and amongst the streams of Hindu, Buddhist, Jain, and Islamic thought and wisdom. This is also true of languages. Arabic and Persian words were assimilated into Indian languages and so were musical structures. In short, organic growth with the potential of 'receiving' and 'transforming' is characteristic. Thus, this diversity will be sustained as long as there is capacity to be both rooted and centred and yet open to change. Any attempt to freeze or isolate particular identities and not allowing fluidity can be a deterrent to the dynamics of the interwoven web of cultural diversity of the country and the civilization.

RJ: India has always absorbed customs, traditions, and ideas from both invaders and immigrants. Many cultural practices, languages, customs, and even monuments are examples of this co-mingling over centuries. Famous monuments, such as the Taj Mahal and other examples of Islamic-inspired architecture and poetry are exemplifications of this inter-cultural dialogue. Do you think that one can say that the Indian tradition is a syncretic tradition that combines elements from different cultures?

KV: I am not sure if I would use the term 'syncretic tradition' for the continuous inter-cultural dialogue that many aspects of Indian artistic schools and styles exemplify. As I said in response to your first question, India has so far demonstrated the capacity to hold together two lifelines—one an original, primal or indigenous, almost immutable line, and the other of 'change'. Thus, no single unit or dimension is totally 'insular' or 'static'. This is true of language groups, that is, Vedic Sanskrit or what is called the Indo-European group and the Dravidian languages, as also Sanskrit and regional languages. In fact, this dialogue was given a beautiful metaphor of *mani-pravala* (pearl and coral) in the context of Malayalam, Tamil, and Kannada. It is evident in architectural styles. Undoubtedly, there was the Greek influence, but the art of the Gandharas and the Kushanas was distinctively Indian, so also was the case in the field of Indo-Islamic architecture. Perhaps, instead of the appellation Indo-Islamic, one should use Indo-Iranian, Indo-Central Asian, etc. While Islam was a motivating factor, the architectural styles of the Lodhi period to the Akbari and Jahangiri and Shahjahani periods are primarily 'Indian', where several factors of both indigenous and the then 'foreign' have played an important part. These architectural styles reflect absorption and rearticulation, rather than a replication or juxtaposing of incongruent elements. The phenomenon is of course evident in other parts of the world, for example, Buddhist stupas in Southeast Asia, and not to speak of monuments like Angkor Vat. While Buddhism and Hinduism were inspirations and there were other Indian models, the monuments are distinctively Indonesian or Cambodian. In the case of India, apart from architecture, the creative dialogue is most exquisitely reflected in music, both what is called classical Hindustani and Carnatic music. The Indian artist appears to absorb and internalize any influence and then transform it to give it a unique Indian identity. Again, fluidity and flux, rather than static insulation or contrived juxtaposition, is the dynamic of the inter-cultural dialogue.

The Indian Diaspora and Culture

RJ: During the last century, a diaspora of Indian émigrés spread their culture to communities as far afield as Johannesburg and Jackson Heights. At the beginning of this century, Indian cuisine, music, literature, and film enjoyed an unprecedented popularity abroad. Therefore, one can say that Indian culture not only competes with but also penetrates the commercial monolith of Western culture. Hindutva 'exclusionism' has not been very successful.

KV: Yes, the Indian diaspora has spread far and wide. Perhaps a distinction has to be made between those who migrated a century or more ago and those others who have settled in different parts of the world, specially the 'developed' world, during the last three or four decades. As far as the first group is concerned, for example, the Indians in West Indies, Fiji, Mauritius, etc., they have preserved the Indian traditions within their own communities while interacting with the culture of the country of domicile. They have preserved languages such as Bhojpuri in their pristine form as spoken a century ago. At one level they have 'frozen' the Indian heritage in time.

On the other hand, the diaspora of the last four decades has had to face the challenge of being 'global citizens' on global terms and yet relocate Indian culture in an environment of very different social mores. Many of them have gone through the trajectory of first intellectually abandoning or certainly not making their Indian identity explicit and then asserting their identity on equal terms in the newly emerging multicultural societies of the developed world, especially in the West. There is a fascinating and sometimes puzzling picture of the diaspora with variations of commitments from the far right or the extreme left; from exclusionist narrow institutionalized Hinduism to the most open-minded intellectuals who can critique both the East and the West. Also, Indians have been able to show that they are capable of relocating cultural traditions without dilution or distortions. There are thus flourishing schools of Indian music in the West and East as also of Indian dance. The seriousness and the rigour of some of these movements are impressive for their capacity to re-flourish in different soils.

Religion and Education in India

RJ: However, some people think very strongly that Vedic culture is not well preserved and protected in India. According to them, the wealthy classes in India often prefer to send their children to schools where English is taught. Unfortunately, in many of the English schools, there is no regard for Vedic culture and Indian history is ignored. Thus, Indian children of the wealthy and influential classes grow up with little regard for their own culture. Therefore, Vedic culture is being lost willingly in India while children of Muslim countries and schools are taught strong respect for the Koran and Islamic principles. So, according to the followers of Vedic culture, India remains the home of Vedic society and to keep itself from certain death, Hinduism must once again enter a phase of self-assertion.

KV: This is complex and difficult question to answer. The first problem relates to the term you have used, 'Vedic culture'. The second problem is in relation to the class of people in India who reject or eschew whatever is understood by the term 'Vedic culture'. The third problem is whether all Muslims in Muslim countries only confine themselves to the teaching of the Koran, and finally, that Hinduism as different from 'Vedic culture' must assert itself as an 'antidote' or reaction.

Pardon me for reformulating your question. This was necessary because implicit in your question is a reference to certain sections or levels of Indian society and not all of India. Now it is difficult if not impossible or erroneous to define 'Vedic culture'; yes, there are certain fundamentals of a world view which are articulated in ancient texts, for instance, the Vedas and principally the Upanishads and the emergent six schools of philosophy. The general appellation of 'Vedanta' philosophy or schools of thought may be more appropriate. Unlike the religions of the revealed word and the single prophet, Vedanta begins by asserting that there are many paths to truth, also that the questioning of the self is the most important. The fundamentals allude to interconnection, interdependence at macro-levels of the primal elements and the micro-levels of body, mind, and soul. The kernel of Vedic thought and Vedanta is 'questioning' and accountability to the 'self' and society with discipline and detachment.

Now, the question is whether this is being rejected or forgotten by a class of Indians who send their children to 'English schools' where there is no regard for 'Vedic culture'. In response to this, I think it is necessary to make explicit that perhaps you are referring to a section of urban middle or upper middle class Indians who are sending their children to English medium and not English schools. The curriculum and syllabus of these schools is not uniform, although it is true that there is a greater emphasis here on immediate contemporary social issues rather than the history of culture or religions. Now the question of curriculum and syllabus is a very complex and complicated issue. It is comparatively easier to teach the so-called value-free subjects, for example, science, and maths, rather than those which invariably have an inbuilt value component. There have been active debates in India on the teaching of subjects like history and controversies, and on whether there should be courses on the history of religions (as different from religious education). Many educationists are concerned about these matters and perhaps a solution will be found when a balance is struck between those who are for totally discarding the study of cultural heritage and others who desire to make education a tool of inculcating religious narrow-mindedness. In the first, of course, there is the danger of de-rooting and uprooting, while in the second case, confining education only to the tenets of particular faiths or denominations would be even more counter-productive because of the potential of bringing up 'bigots' or 'fanatics'.

As I said, this is a very difficult and complex question requiring many chapters of a book to investigate it. Personally, I have been involved in some of these issues at the policy level as also at the advocacy level. Also, the question cannot be answered without addressing the issue of religious education in a 'secular state'. So there are more questions than answers to your question.

Breaks and Continuities with the Past

RJ: Despite the enduring image of India as an old civilization, the Indian population is young and over one-third of it lives today in the cities and probably as many stay in suburban areas. What sense do you think is one to make of this shift towards an individualistic existence? Has India become more modern or more westoxicated, which is reflected in the growing violence, aggressive consumerism, and changes in the moral attitudes of Indians? I remember the saying of Jawaharlal Nehru that: 'Culture is the widening of the mind and of the spirit.' I wonder which aspect of modern culture is more understood by the Indians: instrumental rationality or critical rationality?

KV: Once again, you have asked me a question which has many implicit subtexts. Let me endeavour to respond at a theoretical level in regard to the trajectory of old civilizations and at the realistic level of addressing the problems of the young and of the demographical profile of India. As regards India being an old civilization, there can be no two opinions whether it is old or not, it is certainly an ancient civilization that has survived when compared to other ancient civilizations such as the Mesopotamian, Egyptian, and to an extent, the Greek. Which elements have survived or continued in India so that we can still speak of the continuity of Indian civilization have to be investigated at the level of both theory and practice. Often people have remarked that in India different layers of time are conflated. Also, it is true that age old practices have continued whether in agriculture or in art. There is strong continuity in the family system and in the social structure. The value system also continues to be relevant, although there is questioning at the theoretical level and departures at the level of conduct.

However, all that has to be differentiated from the factual situation of a demographic profile where India has a very large population of the young, in numbers and percentages. Yes, this is true but one wonders whether it is the direct result of either the old civilization or its continuity. It is also true that one-third of the young population lives in the cities and suburban areas. The migration of rural to urban or suburban is accounted for by the compulsions of economic progress as also the real problem of unemployment. The young whether in the suburban areas or in urban areas cannot be grouped together as a single entity who are shifting towards an individualistic existence. More in-depth studies would have to be conducted in order to assess whether family bonds, commitments to the community have either weakened or vanished. Scholars in the field of social sciences have conducted many studies which point at the fact that although the young Indian has become urban, his links with the region or with the family have not been broken. There continues to be a family or community support system. On the other hand, there is indeed a group of young people who have become flotsam in the vast ocean of an urban consumer society. It is these unconnected individuals who are moving sometimes directionless and at other times only attracted to the minimum ephemeral satisfaction of the senses, body, and money. Frustration is evident when they cannot grasp or have ownership of the glittering consumer attractions. Infatuation and frustration affect their moral attitudes and naturally and understandably, if not defensively, there is urban violence. Although there can be no justification, there are reasons for the breakdown of moral fibre. Secondly, one will have to accept the fact that there is a class or section of Indians (not only young) who are pursuing the mirage of aggressive consumerism. This is a situation to which policy makers, educationists, and the civil society have to find answers. Certainly the problem cannot be brushed away.

To your quote of Jawaharlal Nehru: 'Culture is the widening of the mind and of the spirit', and what the Indian understands of modern culture, I would once again reiterate that no generalization can be made in regard to all Indians. There are as many Indians who believe in instrumental rationality as those others who are committed to critical rationality. There is a wide spectrum of differences in approaches, in attitudes, and not only value systems but also mores of social action. If one group of Indians is attracted to only consumer society, there is a small but effective group who by choice and volition is rejecting this model of development. The plea for a model of sustainable development is not only made but is today also being heard. Thus, there is a very impressive group of youngsters who have been spearheading the movement of education for sustainable development and who have been evolving a model of development which will be more suited to the genius of India.

Consumerism

RJ: India's addiction to Western-style consumerism is similar in many respects to addiction to opium in nineteenth-century China. It is very profitable and also extraordinarily unhealthy. Since the introduction of economic liberalization policies and the arrival of satellite television in 1991, Indian consumers and television viewers have been inundated by increasingly violent images of Western culture, which delivers the latest fads and fashions of global consumer culture to the vast Indian middle class. Could one say that the transformation of identity observed in the Indian middle class represents a rewriting of the code of culture, as the traditional idea of Indian-ness is being reformulated?

KV: I believe that what I have said in answer to the fifth question or to your previous question would also apply to the present question. I do not think, therefore, that it is necessary to respond to this in great detail. Perhaps I should add that all technologies are double-edged swords; media can be a most powerful and positive tool as it can also be a very negative one. The satellite television launched in 1991 had an extremely positive aspect of farmers' education, distant education, and much else. The fruits of this can be seen today. However, equally true is the fact that television viewers are inundated not only by an increasing number of violent images of Western culture but, I suppose, also other cultures. The Indian today, unlike the Indian of the past, has to face a new challenge. This Indian looks at these images, rejects them or finds alternates, or do these images really transform, as you say, the identity of the Indian middle class? The situation is in flux and no predictions can be made. However, one can only say that the Indian does have the potential to critically evaluate all that he receives and I hope that there will be a period of maturity. The concern is real and the dangers grave. At a very deep level, Indian civilization is facing the challenge of the fragmentation of a holistic tradition. You know Milton Singer wrote a book called *When A Great Tradition Modernizes*. If and when I write a book the title will be '*When A Great Tradition Fragments*'!

Towards being Indian

RJ: Why do you think that the communal problem in India persists despite the fact that India happens to be secular country?

KV: Yes, there are communal problems in this country. Yes, there have been clashes. Yes, but it is equally true that most communal clashes have political motivations and vested interests. It is not religions which are clashing, it is the religious instinct that is being exploited for violence for either economic or political gains. The nexus of power and politics to fuel tension has been known for a long time. In a manner of speaking, the partition of India is a case in point. Did sharing of power not play a part? As far as the communities are concerned, they have not only lived in harmony but they have supported each other. This history is also known and lived but not acknowledged. In the life cycle it is natural that one community will support the other community at the time of birth and death as also festivals. The effigies of the demon Ravana are made by Muslims, Hindus participate in the *tazias*, Muslim musicians ranging from Bade Gulam Ali to the Dagar Brothers sing songs of Siva and Ram. The greatest musical composition of Hari Om is by Ghulam Ali. People have lived in amity. However, when the fires of anger are ignited by those who wish to exploit the fragile religious identities then there is always trouble. Sometimes balance can be restored, at other times, things are beyond redemption. Communal violence has not been the norm but it has also not been infrequent and this is equally reprehensible.

RJ: In one of your keynote addresses you stressed the liquidity of the Indian *weltanschauung*, with its cosmocentric, rather than anthropomorphic vision of civilization and you emphasized the idea that 'Indian traditions have an inbuilt mechanism of change'. As someone who has been working for a long time to revive the heritage of Indian spirit and art, how do you think this mechanism of change can reproduce itself in an authentic way without the type of education that Tagore had in mind?

KV: I think that I have already responded to this in my earlier answer. I do believe that the Indian vision is cosmocentric and not anthropomorphic. I do believe that at a theoretical level as also at the level of practice all categories are fluid, and not only fluid but reversible, and I do believe that the Indian world view allows for a mechanism of change without total rejection. As I said in the very beginning, there are many paths to a single truth or a single truth can be articulated in multiple ways. This is the kernel. If Indians can have the capacity of holding parts and the whole together like a body system with different limbs, an image that has been used in Indian thought as *purusha*, if India will remember that each part of the body is important and indispensable from the little toe to the head (thus each big or small section of society) and that interconnection and interdependence is fundamental at all levels, then perhaps India could offer a paradigm of a new global world order based on the principles of inter-connectivity, inter-dependence, and complimentarity.

J.C. Kapoor

Post-Independence Evaluation

RAMIN JAHANBEGLOO (RJ): After sixty years of independence, if we benchmark India against other countries of the world, we note that though a lot has been achieved, a lot more needs to be done. India has achieved many milestones, but not enough to eradicate poverty, illiteracy, and other vital issues. If you were to analyse the track record of post-independence India, how would you evaluate its success and failure?

J.C. KAPOOR (JCK): My evaluation is very, very clear that India is one billion people. It was say, 800 million or 750 million at the time of independence. India was moving in a certain direction, which was a mixed economy between communism and capitalism. With the breakdown of the Soviet Union its pressure to move in the market economy became much greater and so also with that the élite, the business people, who could benefit from development of the market economy, they started supporting the idea of becoming a part of the American system. So that is what has happened. Now the question is, is there an emerging conflict between the two phases? One aspect of this is how to make the market system work successfully and second is that if you want to make that work successfully then the message to be delivered to the people will be, look, America was a country of 200 million people and it became a world power. You can no longer develop in the same way, that is, go to the villages and develop like Gandhi said. But then the best thing would be to, let's say, take 200 million people of India and develop a country out of it of 200 million élite. That could be a very powerful and rich country but leave the 800 million who are sitting on the ground where they are, don't touch them and leave them where they are and go ahead with the 200 million people. So if you work on that for ten to fifteen years, you will have a great country. But the international experience reflects that, like the case of America, the economy has moved up but with that the gap between the rich and the poor has become bigger and bigger. Now what does that mean? Hundreds of millions of people are unemployed. The system is breaking down. Now the question, which I am asking, is this. How can the situation in India be different? If you leave the 800 million out and leave them as partial, small beneficiaries in the system, then all the money is not only being pumped to the higher levels in India, it is being pumped to the higher levels in the US and other places.

RJ: Would you agree that the dream of Nehru and Gandhi to give a moral and spiritual basis to India's objectives has not come true?

JCK: It has not come true in the sense in which they wanted. But what is happening in India is unlike in other countries. I see a movement of tremendous regeneration of spiritual thinking. Every evening, there are five television networks, which are religious networks. There are millions and millions of people who congregate to listen to this spiritual discourse. I think this is more than the rest of the world put together. This is the first point and there is a second point. I have seen this from my childhood. There would be Janamashtami, the birthday of Lord Krishna, but it would be a small event. I mean every one would have a little puja and they would go to a temple. But now, there are millions of people involved all over the country. The same thing happens in Ganesh Chaturdashi and other festivals like Deepawali. Now, what is happening? In Europe what is happening? There is a dramatic fall in the number of people going to the churches. There are hardly any people interested in becoming priests anymore. So they are going to Kerala to fetch people to be priests in their churches. It's becoming more like a failing multinational corporation which has to look for markets outside its own country for its products to survive. Now, this market, which is creating that situation of materialism, is hurting them. But in India, what I find is, while this is gradually growing in the US, it is growing at a greater speed here. So what gives me optimism is that somewhere along the line, that way of thinking will have to dominate. Also, our own business leaders are more spiritually inclined and more a part of the Indian cultural system than they are in other countries, at least they seem to be so. But now the threat is from the emerging middle class. When Mr Clinton was speaking to the heads of states of Europe a few months before he left the presidency, they asked him about the threat from Asia and he replied, 'I don't worry. I will do three things. Number one, give everybody a laptop, the young people, give them a telephone set, start giving 100–200 dollars or small notes to millions of people and they will get disconnected with their own country and get connected to ours.' There I see a threat. But I think that the good fortune for India is that their system is breaking down at a time when we are trying to grow. So this will bring the change in direction and when that system breaks down, then this will start growing up.

Contemporary Consumerism in India

RJ: What has the role of the Indian élite been, as the major beneficiaries of the development process in India, in casting aside the Gandhian and Nehruvian visions of India and hoping for a new kind of consumer society?

JCK: It is very true. I agree with you. This is 100 per cent what is happening in India. There is an élite, which spends time on television, sees those channels that show you luxury cars and which joins the millionaire and millionaire clubs, which want to be a part of that system. When you take a symbol and proceed to make that symbol look very good, you see, that becomes the ideal India, that becomes you. Whoever gets there, he is wonderful. So this has changed the ethical and the moral direction of the young people of the country. This has done a lot of damage to the system. There is a dual conflict that is going on. There are families in India who subsist on 700 or 800 rupees per month. Their life is getting worse and the lives of those working abroad are getting better. Second, when they say that they want all the low class people, the scheduled castes (SCs), and the scheduled tribes (STs), and other backward castes (OBCs), to gain equality in matters of education, I think that the intelligence level of India is already very high at all levels. All we need to give to the people is education and health and they will become the brightest people in the world. It is being reflected in another way. India's intellect is being reflected by the Information Technology (IT) industry that I think is the most modernized in India. You take the case of chess or literature, how many Indians are studying English literature nowadays? You take the case of the heads of the political system in America, take the case of the best doctors, take the case of any profession ... just a few days ago, it emerged that the Indian ethnic group has 35 per cent higher per capita income than the all other ethnic groups, including the Jews. So what does this mean? And all this has happened in just ten years. So I am very confident that if they liberalize the education system, a revolution will occur in India of the kind the world has not seen.

RJ: It seems to me that the consumerist attitude in India is transforming certain existing cultural traditions in the interest of expanding markets and constant growth, and after a certain length of time, India will cease to look like India. It will look more like American society. Obviously Indians will still eat different food, practise different religions, and speak different languages, but all the richness and cultural diversities of India will be diminished.

JCK: I agree with you but I would like to make a correction out here. As far as Indian traditions and culture are concerned, as I told you, parallel forces are running in the country, but the issue is that it is confined to 200 million people. The bulk of the country's population, which constitutes 800 million people, is totally unaffected and their pressure on this is great. Now the question is that they have opened large department stores, as they have done, say in China. Do you know that 80 per cent of these large stores are slowly closing down? I don't know of any who are actually doing well except a few. Why? This is because of the attitude of the small shopkeepers. My wife has never entered a big store. She purchases whatever she wants from the small shopkeepers. Now the cultural vision of India is very strong, much stronger than any other country. I agree with you in what you said that there are dangers that India will start looking like the US one day but today after seeing the whole world scene, I came to the conclusion that this system cannot go very far.

Now there is one very subtle diference that is going to answer the question you asked. In China, there is a linguistic limitation. First, the Chinese language enables you to think only at a certain level. Indian languages enable you to see the abstract. Therefore the cultural strengths of China are much weaker than those of India. Second, the Chinese have been seeking something and now the Chinese have started remodelling the Buddhist monasteries, hundreds of them, all over the country. There are now fantastic Buddhist monasteries, so they have now started going to the monasteries.

In India, even at the highest level, there is a difference of attitude. Take the case of one of the richest men in India, a man who built Infosys, Narayan Murthy. He has assets worth millions of rupees. Ten years ago, he used to live in a small house with three rooms. Today, in spite of having so much wealth, he still lives in a small house. People asked his wife, why did they stay there? She said, 'I like the people out here; my neighbours are so nice, they are so friendly. What will I do if I go and start living in a big house all alone?' Now Murthy is famous because his success story is well-known. People marvel at what he has done. What does this signify?

I graduated in America and learnt technology there, yet for the past fifteen years I have been trying to understand India. I spent all my time trying to grasp the deeper India. While I am impressed, I don't know how to deal with the consumerism occurring in India.

RJ: In your book *Our Future: Consumerism or Humanism*, you compare the operative paradigm of armament-protected consumerism to what you call monoculturalism and monopowerism. But Indian national identity is defined with reference to a composite culture not solely associated with any of India's religious groups. This is in contrast to say the Israeli state that is concerned with Judaism alone.

JCK: I will explain it to you. First I will take the case of monotheism. You see, all the attempts of monotheistic religions such as Judaism and Christianity tend to congregate around certain ideas. Out of the same monotheistic approach emerged colonialism; first powerism through industry, then the industrial revolution, and then colonialism. When they came to India, they first began converting people. The point I am making is this: monotheism helps to concentrate power.

India is a highly diverse society. Each one of us worships Durga on the eve of Dussahara, Kali on the eve of Diwali, and so on. Over the centuries, what I would call identical discipline or psychic movements have transformed religious practice and all religions followed in India are in one form or the other, linked to cosmic reality and to nature. Consequently, what is happening is that if somebody is immersing Ganesha in Mumbai, or Shiva in South India, or if somebody is worshipping Lakshmi in his house, all of them are doing exactly the same thing at some point and they are together. There is a diversity of the kind that is totally unimaginable for people in the West. Now take another instance. When I went to a temple like Rameswaram in South India, which is an 2000-year old temple, a puja was going on and the priest was reciting

Sanskrit shlokas. I was surprised to learn later that he was reciting the same shlokas that his old great-great grandfathers used to recite. He belongs to the same family, reciting the same shlokas. He is carrying the entire tradition of India and linkages with cosmic reality on his own. Where else do you see this in the world? Now you see Durga is here, Saraswati is here, Ganesha is here, Laksmi is here, Kali is here, even Christ is here.

RJ: So are you saying that India has been saved by polytheism?

JCK: Polytheism, yes, and what I am also saying is that when the Jews were persecuted, they came to Kerala, when the Christians were persecuted, they came to the east coast of India, when the Parsis were persecuted in Iran, they came in and settled in the Gujarat region. So when you have thousand of gods, it's a fantastic way to make place for one more god. The whole attitude is different because if you have one god, as it is in the West, anybody who doesn't fall in line is not included in that society.

RJ: But in the past India has been suffering from a sectarian politics, which has not only threatened Indian secularism but has made the lives of minorities less secure. What has led to this kind of 'jehadization' of politics in India?

JCK: I don't think of that as a religious process. It is a political process. About 90 or 95 per cent of Indian Muslims today draw their inspiration from the same political culture and the same spiritual contexts as every other Indian. Now that is the concern of Islamic fundamentalism. People with political and religious interests, in order to consolidate their position and to keep their identity separate, are propagating this. You just take such forces out and see what happens.

RJ: You are an industrialist and have studied abroad. While India has considerable industrial activity, it is still an agricultural country in terms of the development of its population. Has the use and development of technology been in balance with the local needs and made an impact on the lives of ordinary citizens. Is there any success in the development of indigenous technology appropriate to national priorities and resources?

JCK: This technological development that is taking place is to create a country of 200 billion who are enjoying the highest standards of life while 800 million people remain totally unconnected, this is my point. When I came to India and started my career I wanted to build an ideal village of the twenty-fifth century using renewable sources of energy. But when I built it, I found that there were forces that were leading this village in directions, which were different from what Gandhi wanted or what Nehru wanted later on. There is little support from the intelligentsia and from writers for such projects and neither is there much criticism of how Gandhi and Nehru's ideals no longer guide rural development in India. So I fully agree with you that technological development should be at a level that will not destroy the environment, which is happening now. High-energy technology is ruining mankind today and we need to find ways to reduce this. The technology that we use in this country must have a relationship with the needs of the large mass of people of the country, not with the products to be produced for an urban mass market. People must produce for themselves, and for their use, and create employment.

RJ: Indian leaders believe that affluent nations can build the country. That is why practically every field has been opened up for foreign investors. But what will happen to Indian sovereignty five years from now if the trend of globalization in South Asia remains unchecked?

JCK: I am very seriously opposed to this form of globalization. This globalization is being done to protect and serve the interest of certain financial oligarchies that are operating in Europe, London, Amsterdam, and the US. Today, they are running the world system. They are the ones waging the war in Iraq. They are planning one in Iran too. They are the ones who are playing the game. So we are dragged into that system and that is where we are now.

RJ: Do you think that a South Asian Economic and Political Union could be the answer to the problems of backwardness and poverty in the Indian subcontinent?

JCK: I have said this in one of my speeches that somewhere along the line we have to stop all this and the first thing that we need to do is to stop the violence that is killing people. In the US, the think-tanks suggest that the only way you can stop this violence is by having weapons that are more powerful than others'. So they have produced thousands of weapons ready to destroy anybody, including India, Iran, and China. Thousands of these weapons are lying in Diego Garcia. Now what has happened? There is an energy crisis. The oil prices have gone up. Environmental pollution is getting out of control. We need new energy resources if the system has to be maintained.

They are now looking for nuclear power that has the potential, but for the last forty years, the US has not built even one nuclear power plant successfully using new technology. If you make a list of the ten advanced nuclear-enabled countries, the US comes in the ninth position, while India and Japan figure at number three. So now they have come to sign an agreement with us, a nuclear agreement to procure Indian equipment and to control the Indian seas. You know, one of the central concerns of the foreign policy of the US during the negotiations was that India should not vote in favour of Iran.

There is a problem brewing within this system. The US, at one point, became the controlling boys sitting in the middle to transfer the dirty work, the production work, to countries like China and India. These countries produce goods at half the price while the multi-nationals will then sell it at a higher price. So a thing that is sold for a hundred dollars in China is sold for 300 dollars in the US. The US economy is growing at 300 dollars while the Chinese economy is growing at a slower rate. So the fact is that unemployment levels in the US are very high!

So the point is that India will soon deal with the things that are going wrong. There is an inbuilt strength for recognizing our priorities and the process has already begun. And we will see the consequences in no more than five or ten years. India will straighten its path, go in the right direction. I predict China will be running into serious complications and difficulties if the policies there do not change course.

Partha Chatterjee

Modernity and Indian Nationalism

RAMIN JAHANBEGLOO (RJ): In your book *Nationalist Thought and the Colonial World*, you show that Indian nationalism produced a discourse which, even as it challenged the colonial claim to political domination, accepted the very intellectual premises of 'modernity' on which colonial domination was based. In other words, from your point of view, Indian nationalism attempted what Sri Aurobindo called a 'selective assimilation'. How do you see the evolution of these contradictory elements in the evolution of the nationalist discourse?

PARTHA CHATTERJEE (PC): As a matter of fact, I think that these contradictory forces were present not only in the period of the nationalist movement but they also exist in the present. There was a challenge made then to the assumption that only colonial powers could bring modernity to India. Keeping in mind the framework of modernity in the Western world, the Indian nationalists made a distinction between the spiritual and the material aspects of modern life. Their argument was that as far as the technologically enabled material side of modernity was concerned, there was no option but to imitate Western modernity. But as far as the spiritual aspect of modernity was concerned, in the sense of language, of arts and culture, the family and social life, etc., they thought that they needed to be original and there was no need to copy Western practices. This is the formula through which the parameters of nationalist modernity were defined. Of course, the actual production of Indian modernity has gone through various phases from the nineteenth century onwards, but still this was the formula with which the contradiction pointed by you between the adoption of Western modernity, while challenging it, was resolved.

RJ: Can one argue that Indian intellectuals sought to forge their own narrative of Indian national modernization by focusing more on Nehru as the towering figure of modern consciousness rather than on Gandhi as a charismatic figure who turned his back on history?

PC: This is how this history has been written since independence. After independence, when the task was to use the power of the state to build a new modern nation, the Gandhian ideology, which was completely opposed to Western industry and technology-driven modernity, was considered to be backward-looking. Of course, there was still the problem of retaining the Gandhian legacy within the framework of the Indian national movement. So what was done was to incorporate Gandhi into the history of the modern nation by erasing several of the critical elements in Gandhian ideology. Gandhi was opposed to the modern concept of the state, but this Gandhian idea was discarded in the history of the new nation. But other aspects of the Gandhian ideology were incorporated, such as the ideas of non-violence, tolerance, and social harmony. Thus, even Nehru remarked in the 1950s that it was wrong to assume that Gandhi was against machines and that if he were alive, he would have blessed us. The truth, however, is that many critical ideas of Gandhi were discarded in the journey towards making India into an industrialized economy along the lines of Western countries. Philosophically, Gandhi was an anarchist, since he believed that the modern state as we know it was not needed and that the whole object of political struggle should be to get rid of the state. He believed in the powers of social beings to govern themselves. He thought in terms of self-sufficient economic localities or neighbour-hoods. On many occasions, he said that history was only a record of violence and that change was not always good or essential.

RJ: So through his readings of Tolstoy, Ruskin, and Thoreau, Gandhi borrowed from Western heritage resources that he thought necessary for the deconstruction of that heritage itself.

PC: He considered the critics of modern Western society as useful and borrowed many of their arguments. Many of these thinkers like Tolstoy or Thoreau were anarchist thinkers.

RJ: The main issue with Gandhian thinking is that it has presented itself as a non-modern critique of modernity and of bourgeois civil society, but it has never been able to suggest a strong alternative to the modern state. Maybe that is why Gandhism remains more of a moral ideal rather than a practical solution to the problems of today's India.

PC: That is correct, even though Gandhi himself believed that a practical solution was possible and he tried to create it through his vision of a self- sufficient society that would be need-based rather than based on the idea that consumption is limitless. In this sense, the limits on human desires and social needs would have to be moral ones. It is through a moral exercise that we must decide whether we really need something, and whether we must produce it. He really believed that it was possible to construct a society in which everybody participated in labour and produced only that which was needed. For example, his khadi programmme tried to bring into existence a different kind of economy based on limited exchange and need-based production. But it failed even in his lifetime. Gandhi himself realized that the khadi programme was going nowhere.

India and Western Forms of Modernity

RJ: Could we talk today of an Indian modernity or did India fail in finding a thematic for its modernity?

PC: I think that in the history of the past sixty years of independence, during which the project was undertaken to use the powers of the modern state to create a new form of modernity in India, many new things have emerged. Earlier Indian nationalists may have thought that there was nothing for Indians to innovate in the material sphere of modern life because the West had far greater technological resources. But since then, many institutional innovations have been made in India even in the domain of modern economic practices and political institutions that are completely alien to Western modernity. There are many new institutional practices that have emerged in Indian democracy, which are completely modern and yet which cannot be found in Western democracy. Even when one looks at economic transactions, many institutions have emerged in India in the economic sphere that are not part of modern economic life in the West. And if you move to the cultural domain, like Indian cinema, for example, you will find that though the technologies used are the same as in the West, the results are quite different. Thus, the technology of the photograph or cinema was used to produce an aesthetic that is not dominated by realism as in the West, but has quite a unique character. There are many such instances that prove that an Indian modernity has been produced which is different from the forms of modernity of the West.

RJ: In your long essay entitled 'Our Modernity', you say that: 'Modernity is for us like a supermarket of foreign goods, displayed on the shelves: pay up and take away what you like. No one there believes that we could be producers of modernity.'

PC: When I say that no one takes us seriously as actual producers of modernity, I also mean that even we do not take ourselves seriously as the actual producers of modernity. The example I gave of Indian cinema would often be interpreted by many Indian intellectuals as an example of a corrupt or distorted form of modernity. They might even say that this is a poor modernity because Indian cinema cannot reach the standards of Hollywood cinema. I think that it is a matter of attaining a certain cultural self-confidence. This is beginning to emerge but still it is not that strong. As far as our assumptions of modernity are concerned, the old assumptions still continue. In fact, when I say that nobody takes us seriously as producers of modernity, one needs to separate explicit articulation of ideas and concepts from practices. If one makes the distinction between ideas propagated by intellectuals and what happens in actual practice, one would find a great gulf between those two things. If one thinks about actual practices, whether the political practices of democracy or cultural practices, many new and innovative things have emerged without there being an adequate language to describe them. The only language available is the Western language of modernity. When one tries to describe them using that conceptual language, the actual Indian practices turn out to be inferior or not quite modern. But if one is to avoid the limitations of the Western language of modernity, one must develop a new language by which this different modernity can be articulated.

RJ: In this challenge of India with modernity how do you analyse the failure of Indian élites and the rise of popular politics?

PC: In the entire history of Indian nationalism, there has been always a suppressed conflict between popular initiative and élite control. In the last twenty-five years before independence, this conflict was crucial in determining the course of the Indian national movement. Since then, quite contrary to other postcolonial countries, the Indian élite has managed to retain its control and yet evolve a political process in which there has been an expanding degree of popular participation. That has been a huge achievement, I would not give the credit only to Gandhi or Nehru, even though they played a very important leadership role. But more important was the popular participation that was able to pressurize the élite to make space for popular initiative within the political process and for the government to respond to those popular initiatives. With the recent phase of urban development and the expansion of the new consumption sectors, people talk of the top 20 per cent of Indians as constituting the new middle class. There is among this middle class a general distaste for politics and a growing disenchantment with government and the procedures of the state. I do not say that this would necessarily lead to authoritarianism. Yet these tendencies are already here. This, I think, is the real danger for Indian democracy. There are some very uncomfortable signals that one gets from recent developments in Southeast Asia, where also there was a very rapid development and urbanization that created a new urban middle class totally devoted to the new modern consumer society. Thus, we have the example of Thailand where the elected government was overthrown by the army largely through pressure from the middle class. This, I do think, is a real danger. The authoritarian tendency would be born out of the feeling that India could grow much more quickly and become like a Western country, since we have the manpower and the resources and it is only politics that is holding us back. This is a feeling that can be sensed in the urban middle class in India today. This is the point where the élite leadership has to be very innovative and socially responsible to actually manage the social and political consequences of this kind of rapid growth. The 9–10 per cent growth in China and India involving millions of people has not happened before in the history of the world. So the leadership has to be innovative and responsible in dealing with the social, economic, and political consequences of such rapid developments.

Ashis Nandy

Gandhi and the Indian Identity

RAMIN JAHANBEGLOO (RJ): Mahatma Gandhi gave contemporary India an identity, perhaps both in a national and political sense. Indians from across the subcontinent began to think they were one; Indians, many of whom spoke of Gandhi as Bapu, sensed India's nationhood. Sixty years after independence, do you think Gandhi is still at the core of the idea of Indian nationhood, in the minds and hearts of the young generation of Indians?

ASHISH NANDY (AN): Yes and no. Yes, because Indians still adore him. A recent survey shows that he is way ahead of all contemporary politicians in popularity and is still considered an ideal person by nearly three-fourths of Indians. There is not even a close second to him. However, if one looks at the country's ruling culture of politics, one finds that the space he occupies has shrunk and survives mainly as an underground consciousness that often clashes with or defies the priorities of the Indian nation-state, particularly in matters of security, foreign policy, science and technology policies, and full-scale capitalism. Gandhi has also become an embarrassment to many Indians. He has become like an aged, much-loved grandfather who has gone slightly gaga and by mistake sometimes strays into the drawing room where a roaring party is going on and the guests are entertaining themselves to death.

RJ: The critical difference between Gandhi and the other Hindu political figures was that, while Gandhi used his Hinduness to build bridges with Muslims, the others sought differentiation and at times conflict. The contrast with Savarkar, the ideologue of the Hindu right is particularly striking. In direct opposition to Savarkar, who sought to politicize Hinduism, Gandhi urged to spiritualize political life and institutions. Gandhi was pleading for transferring spiritual elements into the political domain in order to transform it. In which way do you think this Gandhian view of 'spiritualizing politics' or 'finding ethical grounds for the political' could help us today to face different forms of religious fundamentalism around the world?

AN: This is a critical question; I am glad that you have raised it. There are two kinds of people in the world now: those who think that the desacralization of the cosmos and everyday life has gone too far and we must resacralize at least human life, nature, and the principle of reproductivity as opposed to productivity. There are others who fall sick the moment someone uses the word 'spirituality'. If, for the moment we bypass this issue, you have to confront the fact that, in a democratic order, a majority of the people prefer to use the language of religion and you can do nothing about it. Unless you are willing to wait a few hundred years for them to shed their faith, you have to learn the language to reach out to the people. Gandhi's attempt to provide an ethical basis for politics took him to Hinduism and to religious traditions in general.

Also, he would have denied that he was trying to establish an understanding between Hindus and Muslims because this understanding had already been built over a thousand years. He wanted the hard-hearted moderns to access that understanding. Gandhi was afraid that in the name of building a nation and a state, in the name of building a sustainable political community, some like Savarkar were using religion instrumentally, while holding in contempt the religious world view and, in the process, destroying the age-old understanding—social, cultural, and political—that the Hindus and Muslims had established at the ground level.

Savarkar was an out and out nineteenth-century European modernist and he had the zealotry of the newly converted. His core political ideas were picked up from the dustbins of Europe's history. Gandhi was in line with the entire tradition of spirituality that had grown up in medieval India. He was an out and out critical traditionalist.

Unlike in Europe, where medieval times are viewed as the darkest period of European history, in India, medieval times were one of the most creative phases of Indian civilization. The idea of India as a territorial-cultural entity, Indian dance, music, and literature as we know them today, revitalized traditions of non-canonical, cross-religious spirituality—they all got constituted during medieval times. It is to this tradition that Gandhi belongs. During the medieval period two forms of vibrant spirituality emerged: Bhakti and Sufism. They were close to each other and constantly in conversation. Gandhi tried to bring these strands and sensitivities in to politics. To that extent he was not a secular politician. He was a person who, like many others in our times—Martin Luther King, the Dalai Lama, Ali Shariati, Desmond Tutu, and the liberation theologians—was trying to resacralize the world. The Gandhian world view may have gone underground but it remains a powerful world view and seductively relevant. It does not allow us to talk glibly about separating religion and politics.

Gandhi's Relevance

RJ: Gandhi believed that the future of mankind depends on non-violence. Looking back at the spread of the concept and the movement around the world in the past sixty years, would you say that the principle of non-violence still has an impact on social and political changes in India or has it been transformed into a political slogan in the hands of Gandhians and Indian politicians?

AN: If one talks of Indian politics, then it has merely become a slogan. Commitment to non-violence, either on the part of the state or of the law and order machinery is not easy and seems to flout the canons of political realism. To that extent, non-violence is not salient in Indian politics. Political violence is actually growing in the country. But as the major actors in world politics checkmate each other by new weaponry, as we reach more and more dead-end like Kashmir and Palestine, the debate on non-violence will open up and widen. Gandhi was far-sighted enough to realize this. I am optimistic enough to believe that the new generation will be less burdened by the older traditions of statecraft, which do not leave much scope for non-violence. Younger Indians will recognize, as the disciplines of political science and international relations have already done, the limits of political 'realism' and will not be hamstrung by pre-Second World War textbooks, as many in Indian bureaucracy and security community are.

RJ: A debate about the application of Gandhi's ideals in India today has been the subject of many books, seminars, and lately Hindi films. Gandhigiri has become the new buzzword against Dadagiri among ordinary Indians. Don't you find it strange that the reawakening of an interest in Gandhi in India is done through Bollywood and the concept of Gandhigiri?

AN: Bollywood caters to and cares for popular psychology; its survival depends on that. Bollywood doesn't look into political or cultural theory and doesn't care for conventional political sagacity, maturity, rationality, objective truths of history, and other such worthy totems. Popular cinema in India grapples with the 'truth' of public emotions and it has sensed that in India people are sick and tired of violence, that there is a subterranean yearning for going back to some of the older values of the freedom movement, which, despite all predictions to the contrary, succeeded much better than some of the violent means deployed to overthrow the imperial regime and, later, to advance the cause of the Indian state.

I find nothing strange in the rediscovery of Gandhi by Bombay cinema. Its commercial interest in what people feel and value has freed it to touch the raw sense of being an Indian in India. It cannot afford to take an expatriate Indian's view of India or accept the

Indian establishment's views of India, obsequiously imported from Europe of the 1930s and from mediocre American universities.

RJ: The neglect of Gandhi's ideas in India is also evident from the fact that there is not one serious academic institution in India doing serious research on Gandhian philosophy and the institutions that were built in his memory, like Gandhi Peace Foundation in Delhi or Mani Bhavan in Mumbai are suffering from lack of funds and public indifference.

AN: It's not lack of funds but the huge mass of unimpressive, shoddy research done in these institutions that should be the cause of our concern. Naturally, such research doesn't have much impact. The kind of sensitivity Bollywood has intuitively displayed, even if driven by the market and not backed by academic research, is not usually evident in the institutions of higher learning in India.

On the other hand, specialized institutions for Gandhian studies, I don't think, are the answer. More important are the many creative researchers in India who have rediscovered Gandhi and are working on him in new ways. Look at the writings on Gandhi by a whole range of persons—from Bhikhu Parekh, Ramchandra Gandhi, and Jit Singh Uberoi of the older generation to younger scholars like Raghuramraju, Vinay Lal, Akhil Bilgrami, Leela Gandhi, and some of the subaltern historians. In many ways they have done better than the specialists on Gandhi. I think that their work will have a better impact in the long run, since its reach is not confined to a cultish few and has opened new kinds of possibilities. For me it's a very healthy development.

Even more important for our political culture have been two other kinds of political initiative. First, there are those who, even when not studying Gandhi or Gandhism, have explored the potentialities of Gandhian values and cognitive frames. They may be writers like Ananthamurthy, literary theorists like D.R. Nagaraj, or playwrights like Prasanna. Second, there are also the diverse, often-anarchic, advocatory intrerventions from activist-scholars like Vandana Shiva, Sunil Sahasrabudhe, Corrine Kumar and her associates, Claude Alvares and the multivarsity group, Murari Ballal and Rathabeedi Geleyar Samskrutika Sangha at Udupi, and Madhu Kishwar. In a subtle way, often unwittingly, they have changed the landscape of activism as well as knowledge in India. A Medha Patkar or a Rajendra Singh would not have been possible without them. I would not have been able to write many of the things I have without interacting with such disreputable figures. You may foam in your mouth about the retrogressive romanticism, irrationality, and nostalgia in their 'action-writings', as one academic once contemptuously described their work to me. But you will have to grapple over the next few decades with the movements and sensitivities they have unleashed in the public sphere.

RJ: Gandhi's name is often dragged into partisan quarrels and battles in the Indian political arena, unrelated to his values and his non-violence. Would you say that Gandhian principles have been better understood and applied outside India in the past fifty years?

AN: On the whole, yes, for even when they, those pursuing Gandhian values outside India, don't invoke the name of Gandhi, they use some of his core principles and techniques. Look at the way Aung San Suu Kyi is fighting against the Burmese military junta against all odds, whereas the Indian state is collaborating with it. Or the way the Dalai Lama has made Tibet an issue of moral choice without once raising his voice. If one looks around, one finds many such instances. Even in India, remember the way Jayaprakash Narayan sought to intervene in the unending conflict in Nagaland or secured the surrender of hardened bandits.

RJ: Presently, as a world community, we tend to respond to conflicts through violence—we have created a culture of violence. Do you see any encouraging sign that in the twenty-first century this will change and that non-violence will become more understood and more mainstream than it is now?

AN: Even though predominance of violence in the public sphere is age-old, the present style of using violence as a political tool for settling differences has come to us largely as a remnant of European dominance and the colonial times. It is also a style that was directly copied by the American state in the post-Second World War world. I distinguish it from the earlier forms of state violence and wars because the new violence is more bureaucratized, more impersonal, and more assembly-line. The genocides in the twentieth century have made us more aware of this difference.

This style of conflict management is losing its sheen after 250 years. We are now entering an age when the kind of violence we have seen in the last century is becoming more difficult to justify. As we have seen in Vietnam, Palestine, and Iraq, it has already become more difficult for powerful states to actualize their policies, goals, and interests through the use of armed might. The psychological profiles of the countries and the people have changed. It is an indicator of things to come that public demonstrations against war and human rights infringements are stronger in societies that dominate the world through their military and economic might.

RJ: Do you agree that Gandhi remains one of the main historical figures who has the disturbing capacity to unsettle our fixed thought categories, to shake our inherited conceptual habits, and to let us see our world in a new light?

AN: I consider that to be the crux of Gandhi. He tries to unsettle settled patterns of thinking about politics and cultural life and, in the process, he opens up for us pathways that were not previously thought of. That opening up is bound to have a long-term impact. The process of democratization is releasing new energies in societies all over the world, particularly in the South. Communities, groups, and individuals that could never think of climbing the higher rungs of power are now within striking distance of power. In India, these people are not a part of the traditional national consensus on foreign policy, diplomacy, and strategic concerns. And they are least concerned with the nineteenth-century's bloodthirsty ideologies of the Right and the Left. These newly empowered sectors are looking for new ways in which they can handle, negotiate, or survive in politics.

To these groups, many of the Gandhian principles will be much more attractive than the values of cosmopolitanism that nineteenth-century Europe foisted on the rest of the world. Mostly, they will not opt for these principles for moral reasons, but on grounds of convenience and familiarity. Political figures like Mayawati, Lalu Prasad Yadav, and Mulayam Singh Yadav come from the margins of society and have moved centre-stage. I feel that the Gandhian world view and its capacity to unsettle settled ways of thinking will allow them to have more self-confidence and—this they will like—more manoeuvrability. They will not feel handicapped by the fact they have not been trained and tamed in the globally respected citadels of knowledge and learned their politics from there. Rather, they are likely to look at the Gandhian world view as something that is home-brewed, that has worked in earlier times, and as something on which they can depend upon to rethink issues and reconceptualize politics according to their own visions of a desirable society.

Soli Sorabji

The Indian Constitution: Strengths and Weaknesses

RAMIN JAHANBEGLOO (RJ): Sixty years in the life of a developing nation such as India is not a short period of time. The experience of the working of the Indian Constitution during these sixty years should be enough to ask questions about its strengths and weaknesses. Do you think that the concerns that shaped the making of the Indian Constitution are still relevant today?

SOLI SORABJEE (SS): Talking about the weaknesses of the Constitution, one is reminded of the fact that the Constitution in its working has proved to be more pro-centrist but that is one aspect. The other is that the ideals of the founding fathers regarding the advancement of the SCs/STs was not meant for infinity but it has continued till date. For example, the empowerment was for ten years and even the reservation was not to the extent of 69 per cent as has been the case in Tamil Nadu. Politicians use the Constitution and never take pains to analyse that excessive reservation is causing reverse discrimination and this creates problems. The third thing is that institutions like that of the governor have not lived up to their expectations. No doubt they have few discretionary powers to be exercised in their individual capacity, but even then they should not act as the rubber stamp of the centre. We have had good governors like Gopalkrishna Gandhi and T.N. Chaturvedi, but the institution as a rule has suffered. The speakers in the state believe that if a certain government appoints them then they owe their allegiance to that government. When their impartiality comes into question, particularly when they have to decide the question of dis-qualification on account of defection, then my experience has led me to believe that these speakers, especially of the Northeast, do not have this background of independence and they think that they owe it to the chief ministers. Then certain conventions have developed like the exercise of the imposition of President's rule. It was thought that it will be used in the last resort but that was not to be. The situation got so bad that finally, the Supreme Court in the S.R. Bommai case said that they couldn't use it so often as per their whims and fancies. The worst case was the imposition of Emergency on the pretext of a threat to India's internal security. But it was not a threat to the internal security of India, rather it was a threat to Indira.

As for its strengths, the greatest strength has been the guarantee of Fundamental Rights enforceable by an independent judiciary with the power of judicial review. The judiciary has upheld the rule of law and the Constitution. Whenever they have found that some law went against the basic provisions of the Constitution, then they have not hesitated to strike it down and that has been the greatest strength and that has happened because of the temperament of the judges and their background.

RJ: During the course of the sixty years that the Indian Constitution has been in operation, many new avenues of work and responsibility have come up which were not there earlier. The government was responsible for the maintenance of general law and order apart from implementing certain governmental programmes of economic development. But the executive machinery failed the basic aims of the Constitution to eradicate mass poverty and illiteracy and to improve the standard of health and general well-being. It seems that the government has forgotten its own purpose as it has failed to live up to the expectations of the Constitution to give real substance to the policies designed to promote social well-being. According to you, which of the two have failed: the institutions provided by the Constitution or the people who work these institutions? Gandhian principles should have been in the list of Fundamental Rights instead of being among the Directive Principles. Would you support the idea of giving Directive Principles more importance?

SS: Nothing is wrong in the institutions and only the people who work them are responsible for their failure. Many of the Directive Principles have been given the status of Fundamental Rights through the interpretation of the judiciary like right to live with dignity that includes proper health and there is nothing wrong in it.

RJ: In the past sixty years, Indian political, social, economic, and cultural facets and the needs of the Indian population have changed radically but there has been no attempt to rewrite the Indian Constitution. Do you think it's time for the Indian constitution to be re-written?

SS: I think only certain aspects of it need attention and debate, but not the entire thing. There has been a debate regarding the efficacy of the presidential and parliamentary systems but I think that in our system the parliamentary system is the best despite its deficiencies. The problem is not with the Constitution but the problem is corruption. The Lokpal Bill has not yet been implemented. Social justice, which is the signature tool of the Constitution, has not yet been realized. The disparities in income and wealth have to be removed. The politicians are not inspired by the same ideals as the founding fathers were. Politics has really become a business, a game of numbers. One thing that requires serious amendment is the electoral law. I believe that once charges have been framed against a man, he should not be allowed to contest elections and then a speedy trial of the case should be ensured. Another thing is that the state should finance elections. All the black money is used for election purposes. The worst part has been the rise of communalism. The remedy lies only in education, the way you educate the coming generations about religious tolerance. No doubt the Constitution gave not only the right to preach and practise but also propagate religion, but with the changing times one needs to find out a way to practise it. I am sorry to say this, but the madrasa cannot expose Muslims to the outer world. They need to understand the importance of universal knowledge.

RJ: The Constitution asks the republic to re-work traditional society, which is structured along caste lines, with categories of outcastes. But whose interest does the judiciary serve when faced with a clash between the spirit of the Constitution and the interest of traditional society? I am referring notably to the Dalit problem in India. Even if the father of the Indian Constitution was a Dalit, in rural areas in most parts of the country, Dalits are still unable to battle the arrogance of the upper castes.

SS: The present chief justice of India is a Dalit. Of course, in the rural areas, Dalits still face discrimination but this is also the case with the OBCs. With this in mind, the concept of the creamy layer was introduced but it should not be perpetual as then people will have vested interests in being backward, they will say that they are backward to take advantage of the reservation system. Caste is playing a more divisive role in society than religion and yet the strength of the Indian people is that there will never be a military takeover in India. We had it for a short period during the Emergency and it was thought that Indira Gandhi will win thumpingly, but she was thrown out and the entire Congress Party was wiped out. The reason is a free and rigorous press and media. So despite everything, democracy in India wins and it is not a myth.

RJ: The Indian Constitution does not recognize the right to privacy as a Fundamental Right. However, according to the Supreme Court, this right is inherent in Article 21, which says that no person shall be deprived of his life or personal liberty except according to the procedure established by law. Does this mean that the state or the media can violate the right to privacy with impunity?

SS: I know the Supreme Court does not recognize the right to privacy, but the court of the US does. In the US justice system, the right to privacy is from other provisions, as it is not mentioned in the Constitution. In India too, judges have done the same thing. Right to privacy is a Fundamental Right by judicial interpretation. Similarly freedom of press is not there in the Constitution but it is implicit in the freedom of speech and expression. So these judicial interpretations may change and yet the fact is that no Fundamental Right is absolute.

RJ: Since the founding of the Indian Constitution more than five decades ago, public awareness of the problems with death penalty and prevailing international legal standards has evolved significantly and the emergent international consensus against death penalty has been reflected in recent international instruments. However, currently, capital punishment is included as a penalty in a number of legislative acts such as the Indian Penal Code, penalty provisions of the national security legislation, and anti-narcotics legislation. Attempts to abolish death penalty through legislative actions have repeatedly failed. The previous president, A.P.J. Abdul Kalam, has said that a comprehensive policy should be laid down for all aspects relating to death penalty. When do you think India will be ready to abolish death penalty?

SS: The Supreme Court has said that death penalty should be given in the rarest of the rare cases but does not elaborate on what constitutes rarest of the rare circumstances. Today the Indian public and judiciary is against death penalty and it has reversed judgments of death penalty into imprisonment because evidences may crop up later to prove the innocence of the person and by that time it might be too late.

RJ: While the Constitution prohibits discrimination on grounds of race, caste, creed, sex, etc., it does not specify sexual orientation. Section 377 of the Indian Penal Code reads: 'Of Unnatural Offences. Whoever voluntarily has carnal intercourse against the order of nature with any man, women, or animal shall be punished with imprisonment for life or imprisonment of either description for a term, which may extend to ten years and shall also be liable to fine.' However, Section 377 does not define what the 'order of nature' is all about and has left it to the discretion of the courts leading to a lot of controversy. Further, this section does not differentiate between consensual and coercive sex. Don't you think that it is time for India as a democratic country to legalize homosexuality?

SS: The court believes that if sexual intercourse between the same sexes is through consensus and within the confines of privacy, it is fine. Article 377 has been challenged and it is in the court. People can say that they are homosexuals but if they are found indulging in homosexuality they will incur the wrath of the court. American Supreme Court defended it but three years back it reversed it.

ADDENDUM: Our founding fathers were aware of the vast disparities in wealth and income of our people. Their anxiety that the operation of the economic system does not lead to wealth is reflected in Directive Principle 39 of the Constitution, namely 'that the operation of the eonomic system doesn't result in the concentration of wealth and means of production to the common detriment'. While winding up the debate in the constituent assembly, on 25 November 1949, before the Constitution was finally adopted, Dr Ambedkar pointed out the perils of what he described as a life of contradictions in these memorable words:

> On the 26th January 1950, we are going to enter a life of contradictions. In politics we will have equality and in social and economic life we have inequality. In politics we will be recognizing the principle of one man one vote and one vote one value. In our social and economic life, we

shall by reason of our social and economic structure, continue to deny the principle of one man one value. How long shall we continue to deny equality in our social and economic life? If we continue to deny it for long, we will do so only by putting our political democracy in peril. We must remove this contradiction at the earliest possible moment else those who suffer from inequality will blow up the structure of democracy which this constituent assembly has so laboriously built up.

Rajni Kothari

Indian Democracy and Pluralism

RAMIN JAHANBEGLOO (RJ): Modern India represents the largest democracy in the world with a seamless picture of unity in diversity unparalleled anywhere else. India is the only Asian country where the democratic form of government has survived for more than half a century. Actually most of what is right about Indian democracy lies in its basic cultural, political, philosophical, and historical background. There is the splendid tapestry of a mass movement, the freedom struggle, embroidered with the finest idealism of social reform, non-violence, secularism, and egalitarianism. There is the historical democracy of Indian society, making space for every religion known to man. India is all about pluralism. It is as if India and democracy were made from each other. Could we talk about the miracle of Indian democracy? How do you explain such a harmony between India and the idea of democracy?

RAJNI KOTHARI (RK): It is a mistake to think of our adoption of the democratic framework as something that came out of British (or Western) influence. In reality, the very notion of a pluralist perspective arose out of our own historical and cultural background. The modern framework of democracy arose out of our own heritage of a pluralist society, not something we borrowed from the British!

RJ: India has gone through a massive change, involving political, economic, and cultural transformation. Do you think that this process of change endangers the Indian democratic way of life? Let me put it more clearly, do you see a decline of democratic virtue in India? Is India still disposed towards democracy as it was in the post-Nehru era?

RK: The very process of social change and transformation arose out of our very basic idea of democracy, as conceived by our leadership and broad acceptance by the mass of the people.

RJ: In your recent book *Rethinking Democracy*, you characterize India as an apolitical society because you affirm that India has been unable to construct a viable political authority. Is this political authority crisis in India due to the lack of charismatic figures like Gandhi and Nehru or related to the weakness of mechanisms by which people, considered to be free and equal, allocate authority to make decisions on their behalf?

RK: I don't think of this as some kind of a failure to construct a modernist framework of political authority. What I was laying out in the book was that historically, an apolitical society led to a process of politicization through which we constructed and asserted a political structure. It was a new creation, a new structure. Gandhi and Nehru arose out of this process of politicization.

RJ: Indeed, the riddle of democracy in India is not whether Indian democracy can generate democratization, but whether Indian democracy can itself survive the democratization process in India. One can say that despite the robust democratic system in India, nobody can take for granted that its party system produces the kind of growing prosperity and opportunity that form the only real foundation for long-term sustainable democracy. Does this mean that Indian democracy is facing erosion because of a huge social and economic inequality between the richest and the poorest? India is politically much richer as a result of its democracy, but does it pay an economic price for it, as it has sometimes been alleged?

RK: The two aspects grew simultaneously—democracy as an institutional framework and democratization as a bottom up process of political transformation. Hence my whole idea of grassroots upsurge, both through a political leadership and stirring, and in the long run involving the mass of the people, including the marginalized, the poor, and the underprivileged—the Dalits, the tribals, women, and the underprivileged.

RJ: Many Indian thinkers consider that there is an inseparable link between democracy and secularism in India. From this point of view, secularism is a compulsion for Indian democracy. But today, after sixty years of independence, communalism is still a powerful force in India. It seems that Indian secularism finds itself increasingly challenged at every level of society. I believe that communalism, as a political mobilization strategy, is the principal challenge to Indian politics and to the Indian Constitution. Do you agree that communalism can tear apart the closely knit fabric of Indian pluralism?

RK: The basic challenge facing the country and its people is the persistence of poverty and the deeply ingrained structure of injustice (arising out of the pervasive structure of poverty) and, as a consequence, the deep divisions between communities and classes. Communalism is an outgrowth of this interface between poverty on the one hand and inequality-cum-injustice on the other hand. Out of this has arisen the basic challenge of the deeply laid out system of inequality and injustice.

RJ: The development and maintenance of democracy has frequently been traced to the role of the Congress Party. The democratic infrastructure provided by the Congress has diminished the ability of the political system to manage disputes in a democratic manner and has contributed to the intensification of the civil conflicts in India. Also it looks like Indian democracy is producing a pattern of coalition politics rather than a political system with a majority party capable of providing democratic functions at the national level.

RK: Indian democracy all along is coalitional. First, within the Congress and then with the assertion of 'Hindutva' and its institutional assertion through the BJP, the RSS, the Vishwa Hindu Parishad (VHP), and its demand for the 'Mandir'.

RJ: The decline of the Congress was further assisted by the way in which it was 'deinstitutionlized' under Indira Gandhi's rule, creating a vacuum in Indian politics that was filled by the Hindu nationalist BJP. One has to remember that the biggest weakness of Indian democracy is that the BJP is a mere political front of the RSS and that the RSS and its progeny like the VHP, Bajrang Dal, and Vanvasi Kalyan Ashram are extra electoral bodies, not accountable to the electorate. Today, the BJP is no more in power and the party seems to have a weak leadership. But could we say that India was weakened by the BJP rule in the last decade?

RK: This whole issue needs to be looked at in terms of the polarization between the RSS and its progeny as argued in this questionnaire—this includes the BJP!

RJ: Democracy in India has always been a space of dissent and contestation. Its mobilizational dimension has always influenced Indian politics. In the face of the declining legitimacy of the Indian state and the continuing development of civil society in India, do you think that the political discourse in India is still a dissentful discourse or has abandoned its grassroots civil initiatives?

RK: I have always argued that the core of the democratic process is dissent. I would add that now the dichotomy between the grassroots upsurge within civil society and the growing decline of democracy in the framework of the state provides the rationale of the 'crisis' that faces the functioning of the Indian state.

T.N. Madan

Critiquing Secularism

RAMIN JAHANBEGLOO (RJ): Secularism, originally a non-Indian term, is now part of the everyday vocabulary of Indian politics and society in a way that others could embrace. However, secularism in India had to define itself in relation to a multi-religious reality. How did Indian secularism equip itself politically and philosophically to deal with the reality of multiple religions in Indian public life?

T.N. MADAN (TNM): I think that the politics of this country overshadows everything else for a whole lot of reasons, and this is true of secularism also. I think that we have a political ideology of secularism in India. There is a particular argument, which is essential or necessary in our multi-religious type of setting, that the state should be neutral in its relation with the citizens, that the rights of the citizens should be defined irrespective of their religious identity, and so a secular state is one that is supposed to make no distinctions constitutionally. But the philosophical argument, as far as I can see, to answer your question, would be, is it possible to treat all religions as being of the same moral value? Suppose there is a religion that promotes sacrifice. Those practices of Hinduism, which involved animal sacrifice, appalled Gandhi. What I find is that we have in this country a clear political ideology which suffers in the process of being operationalized: what might have been a political stance of the state being politically detached from all religions often results in the state being equally close to the religions, like when religious subsidies for pilgrimages and financial support to temples and mosques are given. The constitution never used the word secular except in a sub-clause of Article 25 to describe the worldly activities of the religious institutions like their ownership and estates. It was only in 1976 that Indira Gandhi, by an amendment passed by the Parliament, introduced the word 'secular' into the Preamble of the Constitution. Otherwise when the Constitution was in the making, the framers thought that religious freedom was the issue, and so you will find the Constitution supportive of the idea of religious freedom, but if we think of secularism as a world view, then there were difficulties because as I have said before, most of the people in India are religious. Sikhism, Islam, and Hiduism do not separate the sacred from the secular, even when they may be distinguished, in the manner Christianity does. So the cultural roots of the notion of secularism as a world view are not there. One may look at the argument of Romila Thapar where she looks at certain medieval developments like the guru and pir religions, Bhakti and social movements, which could be supportive of the idea of pluralism; but I would rather say that basically we have a political ideology and we have a constitutional guarantee, all kinds of laws have been made but the roots have been political, ideological, and judicial. It has not been that the people have been taught the philosophical implications and therefore I would make three distinctions: first, secularism is a political ideology, and that is what we have, it is there in the Constitution; second, secularism is a world view but we don't have that and we have to do something about it; we could have had a better educational policy because there are people who believe that if you want to have secularism then you must teach comparative religion to the masses at the appropriate level, may be at the college level; third, secularism is a philosophical question and I think that this has gone totally unattended. I have often posed this question to myself, 'can I consider all religions as equal?'

Gandhi was a person who critically evaluated this question when he analysed that there are aspects of Hinduism, like the animal sacrifice, which have to be taken out. If one eliminates these then one may come to the core, which could be the same, but this needs to be worked upon.

Religious versus Non-religious State

RJ: It is interesting to note that the creation of a secular state in India marked a break from the institution of caste in India but it was not accompanied by a secularization of beliefs. Secularism in India did not reject all sense of the sacred that transcends the profane world. Also, it is notable that the word 'secular' did not appear in the Preamble of the Constitution when it was adopted by the Constituent Assembly in 1949. The only place where the word 'secular' appeared in the Constitution was in Article 25 (2b) where it refers to the sense of 'non-religious'. Do you think this omission was deliberate on the part of the constitution-makers in India?

TNM: If you look at the constitutional debate at the time of the making of the Constitution then you would come to know that there were people like K.T. Shah (an economist who worked with Gandhi), who wanted the word secular to be included in the Constitution, and like H.V. Kamath (who wanted the Constitution to open with the words 'in the name of the God'), but they did not get support from other members. So there were individual members on both sides of the debate—those who wanted to give a religious colour to the Constitution and those who wanted to make the Constitution secular—and neither of them won. The majority opinion was that the issue was freedom of religion. At that time the notion of secular state did not seem to be the central idea. My own feeling about this is that when people like Amartya Sen say that we need to go back to Ashoka and Akbar to get the idea of secular state, they are perhaps going too far back in time. I have often said that the concept of secular state has been the gift of the Indian mutiny. The mutiny of 1857 was over the perception that the British were challenging the religious beliefs of the soldiers by asking them to bite bullets, which were supposed to be greased by the fat of cows or pigs. When the mutiny was controlled, Queen Victoria came out with a proclamation in the year 1858, which inter alia said that while Christianity is a superior religion, her government was committed not to discriminate between people on the basis of their religious identity, or to interfere with their religious activities. So I think that the immediate source of the notion of non-interference lies perhaps in the policy of the colonial government. In the national movement all this was a part of the dialogue between the nationalists and the communalists.

Issues were not conceptualized in terms of secularism. I can't be hundred per cent sure, but I have tried in my own limited way to find out the earliest use of the word secular in the Indian political discourse, and found it in the presidential address of Jinnah to the 1916 annual conference of the Muslim League; and Nehru used it in 1930 in one of his letters to his daughter, but he was talking about Turkey. Jinnah was talking about 'our common secular interests' in 1916. So my view is that in the national movement, the whole rhetoric was of two nations and one nation and nationalism but never of secularism as such. So only as we moved into the process of nation-building, the issue of secularism came to the forefront. Until 1946, Nehru ridiculed the idea of partition saying that having a state based on religion is like having an army using bows and arrows in the nuclear age. But when the partition came (it is my surmise), one of the men who had considerable influence on him, namely Radhakrishnan, whom he chose as vice president, advised that it would be odd for India to make secularism in the Western sense the state policy. So this idea of secularism as an attitude of respect for all religions was not framed till then; rather issues were framed in terms of communalism versus nationalism. Now, by hindsight, people are saying that the debate was between religious nationalism and secular nationalism, but one does not find the term secular nationalism used. There is also this point of view that people like Nehru, who led the national movement, grew in an educated upper middle class setting in which religious tolerance was something that was part of their daily life. I would say that being part of a Kashmiri family Nehru had imbibed many of the Muslim aristocratic ways like the clothing style and food. The Kashmiri Pandits have always been very adaptive. When they came to Punjab they started identifying themselves with the Sikhs, started growing beards and when they went to the east in Uttar Pradesh they came closer to Muslim culture. People like Nehru came from that background which you could call composite culture. Now these were the people who thought that partition having been accepted, those who wanted to go to Pakistan had gone, and those who had stayed behind would remain as citizens of India. You would be surprised to know that there was one Muslim member from Bihar in the Constituent Assembly who moved a resolution for banning all external symbols of religious identity such as personal names and dress.

RJ: Many people around the world consider the legacy of secularism in India as a great achievement, but it seems to me that the Nehru-Gandhi consensus on the secular state, which was grounded in the necessity to deter the persecution of religious minorities, has performed its functions rather poorly. The destruction of the Babri Masjid on 6 December 1992, and the communal violence that followed across the country, especially in Gujarat in 2003, and the claims and activities of the Hindu and Muslim political extremists have all been threats to secular India. This is mainly the reason why a number of critics in India point out that the concept of secularism in the Indian context is an 'obscure' and 'empty' concept and is based on an arbitrary distinction between what is religious and what is non-religious. Would you agree with that observation?

TNM: I would never say Gandhi was secular. For Gandhi, politics ideally had to be rooted in religion. The state had to be secular in a particular sense. When he was asked the question, not very long before his assassination, what his conception of the idea of state was, true to his long-held view that has been discussed in Bhikhu Parekh's book, *Gandhi's Political Philosophy*, he said that he would like a minimalist state. He would like a state that had nothing to do with private life and was only concerned with communication, transfer, currency, and secular welfare. Nehru's state was all embracing and he wanted it to do everything. Gandhi was for civil society. But I think that both agreed on one fundamental issue that the state should not interfere in the private lives of the citizens.

Now regarding the second question that, when we have established a secular state why have we been witnessing these riots, I think we have not attended to all those things which could have promoted mutual understanding, notably education and the economy. Very often religious riots are due to one community rising at the expense of or in competition with another: this creates a fear in the minds of the other community of being overwhelmed by them. A single fact or explanation for the riots in India arising from the religious differences is not correct because we have not done enough fact finding on the causes of riots. One can also say that in the Christian religion there is the notion of two domains, sacred and secular (God and Caesar) and Luther's notion of the individual being in charge of his fate, to mention just two notions. These make it easier for the people generally to accept the idea of a secular state. It has been said that secularism is a gift of Christianity, and I agree with that. I am not saying that because we are not a Christian society we can't make a success of the secular state, nor I am saying that we have to accept all Christian ideas; what I am saying is that if common people can't make sense of such ideas as the 'privatization of religion', it becomes harder for them to accept the exclusion of religion from everyday life and the public domain. There is no concept like Luther's notion of the 'compact between the individual Christian and his God'. Such ideas narrow the scope of institutionalized religion. I am not for one moment saying that there is no compatibility between Indian religious traditions and the idea of secularism in the sense of a this-worldly ethic and tolerance: what I am saying is that if we know that the passage towards secular society is not going to be easy because the separation of domains is not a familiar idea, then we ought do something about it. If we simply sit and say that secularism is India's destiny, which is there in India's Constitution and people will realize it, then I think we are fooling ourselves. I think that the answer lies in, among other strategies, educational programmes that include the history of secularism and comparative religion. Both Ashis Nandy and I believe that we should look at the resources within the religious traditions for spreading the idea of tolerance among the different religious communities rather than saying that all religions are essentially mutually hostile. As Romila Thapar has recently said, there is a live syncretistic guru-pir tradition in India. I too drew attention to this syncretism twenty years ago. We need to do more in the classrooms, more in the education policy, more in the civil society initiatives, and more of philosophical discussions.

RJ: Should I draw the inference that secularism in India has been élite driven and we need to have a non-élite driven secularism.

TNM: Not only that, we need to spread knowledge about religious tolerance among the masses. You go and ask ten north Indian Hindus whether a Hindu temple with a Hindu God can have a Muslim concert and they will laugh at you, but in the south there is this tradition. We need to spread such information among common people. I do not want to minimize that there are certain fundamental differences between Islam and Hinduism but what I am saying is that if we realize how in real life people have worked out understandings, then a lot could be achieved by way of inter-communal harmony. I often say that people don't know about the composite culture of the Kashmir valley. Being a Kashmiri, I grew up in a marvellous atmosphere. We knew that the differences between Hindus and Muslims were basic but we also knew that that was not the basis for the conflict between them. I remember many of the Muslims saying about a Hindu that 'he is a good Hindu as he does his daily puja'. I grew up learning the *fateha*, as the house next to ours was that of a maulavi and he used to teach Muslim children the Koran: I could hear it all from my own home. The notion that they would come and eat with us or the notion of inter-marriage was not there. The notion that they would celebrate Holi and we would celebrate Id was not there but we knew what Id and Holi were, and we lived a harmonious life until politics invaded our lives. So I think that we Kashmiris had developed this notion that you could build up agreement over differences and that you need not be culturally or religiously similar to live in peace. I feel concerned when people say that secularism is India's destiny and have nothing more to say or explore. We need to work for it and to struggle for it. There are threats all around us. In Kashmir itself the emergence of militant jehadi Islam has virtually finished off the composite culture I just spoke about.

RJ: The Indian model of secularism was a hybrid product of secular humanism and neo-Hindu revivalism. On the secularist side were democratic socialists like Jawaharlal Nehru and B.R. Ambedkar and radical humanists like M.N. Roy who believed that a rational reform of the Hindu world view was a prerequisite for social progress. As for the revivalists, they were inspired by neo-Hindu ideas of Swami Vivekananda, Sri Aurobindo and others, who believed that a regeneration of the supposedly tolerant and benevolent Vedic 'golden age' was a prerequisite for social progress.

TNM: Yes, I agree with all that you have said. I have not studied Aurobindo's work so I can't comment on that, but I have read Vivekananda. He had the notion that if you are a Hindu rooted in Vedic knowledge then you would automatically be respectful to other religions. His notion of reformed Hindu and Hindu revivalism included the notion of the spirit of religious tolerance. But I don't agree that he was a secularist or that he regarded the Vedas to be of the same moral value as the scriptures of Islam or Christianity. He said that Vedanta is the most perfect religion and that it not only includes the best of all religions but also possible developments within itself, a strange idea. Similarly, Maulana Azad said that Islam is the most perfect religion. But while making such statements they asserted that the notion of differences among different religions was in the detail, not in the core. So all these people, like Vivekananda, Radhakrishnan, and others, quoted a particular verse from the Vedas, which says that the truth is one but the learned state is in different ways. It only meant that if you were an aware Hindu or Muslim, then you would be more tolerant towards the other religion. I have argued that Gandhi was more tolerant than Vivekananda, that he was a genuine pluralist and respected religious diversity. Gandhi in fact believed that he was incomplete simply as a Hindu, and that there were certain religious truths, which he had learnt from other religions, such as social egalitarianism from Islam. I thus think that his pluralism was different because there was humility in it, which is the distinguishing characteristic of Gandhian thought on religion. There is perfection in every religion but my human intelligence and capacity does not allow me to realize that which is not explicit in my religion, but if it is explicit in other religions, it is accessible to me and enriches me.

RJ: According to Amartya Sen, there are two ways of understanding secularism. One is focusing on political neutrality between different religions, and the second is political prohibition of religious associations in state activities. Sen believes that Indian secularism has tended to emphasize neutrality in particular, rather than prohibition in general. In other words, there is a concept of tolerance of religious diversity, which is implicitly reflected in India's secularism as a shared home for Hindus, Buddhists, Jains, Jews, Christians, Muslims, Parsis, Sikhs, and atheists.

TNM: Yes, I agree with the use of the word 'shared home', but then that should not mean passivity: we should live in our own home mindful of what is happening in other rooms because that is what participatory religion is all about. Secularism is a world view no matter how we try to define it in the Indian context; Nehru said that secularism was based on scientific temper and also mutual respect between different religions. Orthodox secularism places human reason and not faith in the centre. So I would say that orthodox secularism basically remains a world view that is not friendly to religion but in the process of adaptation its scope is widened. A rationalist would say, fine, you are a Muslim and worship your god and I being Hindu will worship mine, and rationality is not opposed to that. Faith and reason are not antagonistic: they do different things. A fundamentalist, who insists on unalterable religiosity and even resorts to violence to impose his views on others needs to be told that the God hates evildoers, quoting the scriptures back to him.

RJ: In the words of Ashis Nandy: 'Secularism is not communal amity; it is only one way of achieving such amity. As an ideology, it is not even 300 years old ... Modern India, till today, has not produced a single hero of secularism except for that fading star, Jawaharlal Nehru.' According to Nandy, 'Despite the consistent failure of secularism to contain the growth of both Hindu nationalism and Islamic, Jewish, and Christian fundamentalism in recent years, both in India and elsewhere in the world, only a few seem to have the courage to look beyond it.'

TNM: I do think that things are changing. A number of political theorists have recently written about the limitations of secularism and about its arrogance. The few, who look beyond the present certitudes will, I think, become many before long.

RJ: What kind of secularism is best suitable to deal with this Hindu and Muslim problem?

TNM: I think that good relations between communities must have multiple sources and must encompass improvements in economic status and life chances of the communities, through, for example, affirmative action pursued sensibly (and not quota-based reservations). Second, there is this need for social and cultural transformation that would require time and it will not happen in a day. I would like to quote M.N. Roy, who said that secularism can't be enacted as it is an 'atmosphere'. Marx has cautioned that secularism after displacing religion could itself become a religion. So secularism has to be subjected to critical evaluation constantly. If you think that it is like scriptural revelation then you are stuck. So I would say that it would take time, as we have to instill the spirit of plurality and multiplicity in society. Secularization of society has been going on ever since man developed tools to hunt and did not wait for the food to fall from heavens. If you go to a doctor to seek treatment for your illness, and not to an astrologer, then you are a secularizing your outlook. Secularization is an instrument of realizing how to do things efficiently.

RJ: Do you think that the concept of secularism in India has produced a viable governmental policy because I have a sentiment that secularism in India means different things to different people and because of that it has become a paradoxical notion. When I look at the future of the Indian state then I find that India is going to have a big problem with the notion of a secular state.

TNM: I think that from the point of view of the state the basics are there in the Constitution, which is defined in terms of freedom of religion and Fundamental Rights. If these principles of the Constitution are implemented sincerely, then things will improve. But if we hold the state as primarily responsible all the time for the cure of all ills, then we are sticking to Nehruvian policy. I would rather say that civil society is more responsible for harmony in society. The state has its limitations. In a society like ours that is so diverse and big, with provision for federalism and decentralization of powers, why do we look at the state to solve all our problems? Nehru was very worried about the issue of reservation and in one of his letters he wrote that secularism is not only about religious identity, and that the way forward did not lie in perpetuating such identities. But, see how we have complicated the whole issue of caste. True, there are things to be done, but the way reservation has been invoked is not the way. I think that we talk more about minority rights and less about human rights and that perhaps is a mistake: the truth is that, whether I am a Christian, or a Hindu, or a Muslim, I have certain human rights. This realization and its implementation are needed for making the society more pluralistic and just and humane.

D.L. Sheth

Caste in Modern India

RAMIN JAHANBEGLOO (RJ): When we think of India, it is hard not to think of caste. In common parlance, caste has become a central feature of India, indexing it as fundamentally different from social classes in other places. Caste has been as always there in Indian history and is one of the major reasons why the sense of history in India is different from the historical vision of other nations. The history of discourses on caste cannot be separated from the full institutional history of British colonialism. Significant changes took place in the caste system during the colonial period with the process of urbanization and modernization. What was the impact of these changes after Independence?

D.L. SHETH (DLS): Colonial history is crucial to our understanding of caste today. A number of issues around caste, crowding Indian politics today, have their origins in the discourse of the independence movement and policies of the colonial regime: the two were operating in some kind of a dialectical relationship.

First, almost suddenly after the 1857 uprising, caste and religion began to be seen as a key to understanding any and every aspect of Indian society. In the British 'discovery of caste' everyone—the colonial ruler, the Christian missionary, and the English-educated Indian—found a generic principle that rendered the complex realities of India in facile terms by which virtually every Hindu Indian was seen as occupying a specific, unitary status in a fixed, religiously-sanctioned social hierarchy. Caste was seen as a system resilient to any change or progress. The ethnographically inclined British administrators, Orientalist scholars, and the missionaries, together, although differing among themselves in their goals, acquired a perspective on caste by which every aspect of Indian life was seen, analysed, and problematized through the prism of caste.

This of course doesn't mean that there was no caste before the arrival of the British. It was very much there, but it was now seen as if caste from its inception was a fully formed system, enacted and structured at one go in some distant past, and has since been functioning in the same manner, that is, unidimensionally as a hierarchy of ritual statuses. But, this was not how the Indians saw or experienced caste. The ritual hierarchy, in reality, functioned as a plural, multidimensional status system in which groups could acquire a significant degree of social and economic power, despite their lower ritual status and, in effect, could move upward in the status hierarchy. Ritual hierarchy was not the only governing principle of caste. Differences, mutual repulsion, and a degree of political-cultural competition among groups always prevailed, constituting 'difference' as a principle of caste, along with ritual hierarchy. In the colonial perspective, however, caste was seen and treated reductively as a unitary building block of the vertical hierarchy, the proverbial Indian pyramidical social structure. Even more, it was seen as the sole determinant of Indian culture and personality. Many other aspects of the lived life of Indians which co-existed with caste but were different in their socio-cultural constitution and were even in opposition to the idea of ritual purity and impurity, were all seen and problematized undimensionally in terms of rituality.

Second, this construct of caste was structurally reinforced by the decennial census operations instituted by the British in 1881. With this, the colonial state permanently fixed a unidimensional identity of every Indian as having a specific caste/tribe status and a unitary religious affiliation. The fluid and shifting social cultural matrix of India was frozen in a permanent order of social precedence. Even more, the British administrator/civil servant assumed the role of a super Brahman who located and relocated statuses in ritual hierarchy by acting as an arbiter of all disputes relating to status claims by different castes. In this process, *hierarchy*, as against *difference*, was administratively and politically established as a singular, universal feature of caste. It must be emphasized here that caste, and even the religious identity of an Indian has always been multi-layered and even multi-caste, and multi-religious. This is reflected even today in the practice of hypergamy in Gujarat in which marriage liaisons are made across castes extending from the higher Rajput/Kshatriya castes to the lower Shudra castes of the Kolis. Several agricultural and artisan communities in Gujarat as well as in other parts of India identified themselves simultaneously with different varna categories or different occupational-caste categories. The examples that come to the mind are the Saisuthars and Brahma-Kshatriya of Gujarat and the Bhandaris and Charis of Konkan. It is conveniently forgotten that even in censuses and official surveys a substantial number of people reported themselves as simultaneously belonging to Hinduism and Islam. One of the several examples is the Piranas of Gujarat. Similarly, religious identifications as of being Hindu-Vaishnav and Jain, or a Hindu and Sikh in a single family, even between a husband and wife, were not uncommon until recently. In short, caste and religious identities of Indians have always been multiple and overlapping, but they remained unaccounted for in the colonial theory of caste. It was forgotten that there was life outside caste.

Third, I do not wish to suggest that caste did not have a durable structure and systematic continuities. Far from it, caste has had a formidable, long-lasting social structure. It survived powerful anti-Brahmanic and anti-ritualistic movements like the Shamanic (Buddhism and Jainism), the Tantric, and Bhakti. What I wish to suggest is, first, that caste has primarily been a power structure (political organization), regulated and perpetuated historically by its sanctification in (Brahmanic) religious terms. Second, what the earlier movements could not do to caste has been done by modernity and democracy. These forces have destroyed the *ritual* (sacrilized) status system, and have pushed the traditional power structure into the secular, horizontal space. With different groups competing in open spaces for power, those with inherited resources have an edge, but this is now being balanced by social policies of the state and the numerical power of 'lower-caste' groups.

RJ: Did the new ideological discourses on individual rights and social justice, which took shape with the independence movement, succeed to interrogate and revise the idea of ritual purity and impurity, according to which the traditional stratificatory system endowed entitlements?

DLS: There is no doubt that the idea of ritual purity and impurity has totally lost relevance in the allocation of statuses and entitlements in society. But it took quite sometime, three decades after independence, for the new discourses of rights and social justice to gain political ground and for the Indian state to formulate and implement social policies that could shake, let alone destroy, the caste-based power structure. As I said earlier, the caste structure of power was never fully subsumed by or became coterminous with ritual-status hierarchy. So, the caste power structure survived—survives even today even if in severely attenuated form—even after the collapse of ritual hierarchy. It survives in the form of status-resources (accumulated social capital) that the upper castes (the dwijas) inherited thanks to the monopoly they collectively enjoyed among themselves for centuries of the epistemic, political, and economic power. The lower castes (Shudras and the outcastes), on the other hand, inherited meagre social resources and enormous status-liabilities. They were all along subjected to an elaborate system of reward and punishment as well as to coercion whenever they resisted dwija dominance—and such resistance was not so infrequent in history. In short the Shudra and the outcaste communities were conditioned as well as coerced into acceptance of their given stations in life. This didn't leave much scope for them to accumulate any social or economic capital. Thus, historically, caste was governed simultaneously by two different principles: the ritual-status principle and the power principle. The dialectics of status and power operated in such a manner that power remained with those *communities*, which held, acquired or could credibly claim (not always inherit) the dwija status. There are many examples in history of non-dwija communities acquiring political and economic power and being accorded the dwija-ritual status, as also the dwijas falling off to the non-dwija status.

If we focus on the initial decades after independence from the theoretical-historical perspective of the interplay of status and power principles, it becomes clear how caste power could prevail under democracy. During this period, the power of the upper-status castes, which was embedded in their higher ritual statuses, began to be transmuted into secular hegemonic power of a new élite. This élite ruled by electoral consent of the hitherto socially subjugated and populous communities of the middle and the lower rungs of the caste system. Although it had a clear caste character, the élite operated with the self-consciousness of a 'casteless' and 'caste-blind' people who generally identified themselves socially as belonging to the 'middle class' and politically as constituting a secular and democratic leadership in the government, bureaucracy, and professions. All this did not come in their way of securing and using their inherited status recourses for establishing, rather renewing, their power in the changed political context of a liberal democracy. This élite, thus lost privileges attached to their traditional ritual status, but not the power they had acquired in the old system of stratification. Obviously, they now sought legitimation of their power in new, non-ritual terms supplied by the ideology of a modern nation-state, that is, secularism and development.

The other aspect of change in caste was more structural than ideological or discourse-dependent. This was caste's incarnation in politics. This aspect of caste was, in fact, suppressed during the colonial period, which privileged ritual hierarchy as the only principle of caste. What I have in mind is the *community aspect* of caste, which materialized in politics, giving social content to the democratic principle of political equality. From its inception caste was not just a hierarchical arrangement of statuses but also a world of numerous communities who among themselves were fairly autonomous and competitive and interacted in horizontal spaces. Democracy revived this aspect of caste, and the electoral politics brought it in full play. Consequently, the hierarchical aspect of caste became both ideologically and structurally subdued, foregrounding the competitive nature of castes *qua* communities. By and large after independence, caste became more like an expanding ethnic type community, acquiring a new *political-cultural identity* in place of its social-ritual identity. The interrelationships between caste-communities were no longer expressed in the conventional language of subordination and superordination. Instead, we now hear castes articulating their aspirations, cultural assertions, and resentments in terms of economic interest, political equality, ethnic pride, nepotism, and chauvinism. In any case, castes have discarded the language and practice of hierarchical obligations or of superiority and inferiority in terms of one's ritual-status. People may have a private thought, a self-appeasing idea about themselves being 'high' and others being 'low' in ritual status. But in public life, that is, institutionally, legally and in social intercourse, the hierarchical aspect of caste has become defunct.

RJ: The Congress was a Brahmanical umbrella party that held power for over four decades. Though it refused to publicly identify itself with Brahmanism, it did encourage and sustain it in its own way. Could we say that the Congress Brahmanism was basically a bureaucratic kind of Brahmanism as opposed to the BJP one, which has been a societal one? Also, don't you think that there lies a link between the two parties in securely leaving the spiritual space to the dwija castes, particularly to the Brahmans?

DLS: It is not as simple as that. When it is about assessing the influence of Brahmanism, the political and social realms are not that neatly separable. Congress was and also was not a Brahmanical party. It incorporated a large following of peasants, landless labourers, Dalits, and Muslims during the independence movement under Gandhiji's leadership. And these groups served as a durable support (electoral) base of the Congress after independence. The bureaucratic power during the Congress regime was indeed overly Brahmanic. Brahmans and some upper castes dominated the civil service, nationally as well as at the state level, till the late 1960s. The lower caste presence was more like an exception proving the rule. More importantly, the bureaucracy was Brahmanic in its attitude and approach to economy and development. It was as if capital accumulation and wealth creation by 'unofficial' non-state actors and agencies polluted the sacred arena of the state. The bureaucrats and generally the ruling élite revelled in ideological debates and procedural wrangles rather than giving concrete programmatic content to the planning and development process. So there were two Congresses, the 'pre' and the 'post' independence Congress, the movement and the party. On the whole, the Congress can be described as an umbrella party, which brought in its fold people of different castes, religions, and income groups. Ideologically and politically, it tried, and succeeded, in preventing for long any type of polarization: on caste, class, or communal lines. It ideologically emphasized secularism and national integration, but socially and economically served the interests of the upper castes. The policies were consciously or unconsciously framed accordingly. It is, for example, not accidental that for decades after independence, during the Congress rule, the Indian state didn't implement the constitutionally promised policy of universal primary education. Large resources were allocated to higher [college, university, and professional] education at the expense of primary education. This is because the ruling upper-caste/class élite was all, hundred per cent, educated. Their children were already receiving primary education of good quality. By making investments in higher education, they facilitated the social and physical (international) mobility of their children. In brief, one can say that the Congress movement led by Gandhiji was cross-sectional, non-Brahmanic. And the post-independence Congress regime could be more appropriately described not as Brahmanic, but as upper-caste élitist.

The RSS began and for a large part remained a Brahmanical organization. But as it fanned out in different sectors of the society with proliferating members of its *parivar*, especially after the formation of the BJP from its earlier incarnation as Jan Sangh, its Brahamanic character became more inclusive Hinduist. Its conscious effort to retain Brahmanic values did not last for long. Massive inductions of the backward classes and the Dalits as well as the tribals took place through its various social, cultural, and political organizations like the Bajrang Dal, the Vishwa Hindu Parishad, Durga Vahini, Vanvasi Seva Kendras, Shishu Mandirs, etc. The BJP as a political party in a liberal democracy could not grow and succeed in garnering viable political support by retaining Brahmanic hegemony of power within the organization. A party wanting to create majoritarian Hindutva politics can't afford to remain Brahmanic in its organization or in its scheme of distributing power. You will find that today the BJP has fairly visible numbers of OBCs, tribals, Dalits, and women in positions of power in its organization compared to other parties, including the Congress and the parties of the Left. The primacy it has lately given to Hindu unity has not just eroded Brahmanism, but has led the party to strongly support such policies as of affirmative action and creation of smaller ethnic states. Its politics of building coalitions with regional parties also constitutes a part of this larger and long-term strategy. The short point is that the BJP and the RSS parivar as a whole is now working for politics of Hindu unity and for that they are prepared to dilute or even give up the symbols and politics of Brahmanic hegemony. It is as a part of this politics that they emphasize polarization vis-à-vis the religious minorities. This politics of Hindu inclusivism versus minorities-exclusivism or majoritarianism is aimed at making religious majority concomitant with political majority. Narrow Brahmanism has little scope in such politics. In brief, the BJP's ambition is to be a mass Hindu party outgrowing its Brahmanic image originally derived from the

RSS. As for spiritual spaces, they have vastly opened up for the non-dwija castes. This has to do not only with Hindutva politics but also with changes in the organization and practices of Hinduism. There is ample evidence of Hinduism becoming a deritualized mass-based religion, inclusive of all communities of the Hindus, especially of those from the lower rungs. This has facilitated much greater congregational participation in religious and spiritual activities of the non-dwija castes along with upper castes.

Ambedkar's Relevance

RJ: Do you think Ambedkar was correct in his thinking that the caste system must be 'annihilated' if untouchability is to be genuinely eliminated? Is he still relevant for the oppressed sections of India?

DLS: Ambedkar saw caste almost exclusively as a ritual-status hierarchy. As such, he associated, and rightly so, untouchability with the Hindu ritual practices. Untouchabililty is integral to rituality in so far as it defines physical distances among individuals and groups in terms of purity and pollution. Such distances were indeed observed even within a family, between husband and wife and even between mother and child, for example, in the case of a menstruating woman. Some scholars mistakenly see such a practice of temporary and contextual 'untouchability' as comparable and qualitatively similar to the practice of caste Hindus treating the entire group of people as untouchables for centuries. In the case of untouchability of an untouchable caste, it is a permanently fixed attribute that is meant to be inherited from generation to generation. This untouchability has little to do with the physical cleanliness or uncleanliness of the so-called 'untouchables'. In their case, untouchability is treated as inhering in the bodies of untouchables. It is not the work they do which is defiling, but what an untouchable does, becomes defiling. Whatever object he/she touched or on which he/she cast a shadow of their body was considered and treated as untouchable. In this sense, untouchability has been an extreme form of rituality (ritual practice). Traditionally, the arena of ritual practice was considered sacred and the observance of ritual purity was seen as endowing the practitioners with magical powers making them pure bodies. Rituality, thus, constituted its own sacred sphere and that space was monopolized, in different degrees, by the communities of dwijas (the Brahmans, the Kshtriyas, and the Vaishyas) who were supposed, literally, to embody purity!

It seems that historically, it was when observing ritual purity began to be associated with the gaining of magical powers by its practitioners (roughly, the period of epistemic predominance of the Mimansakas and Smritikaras) that the exclusion of the non-dwijas became institutionalized. Observing ritual purity and, consequently, untouchability acquired even a 'moral' justification—a behaviour that earned merit. Those among the Shudras, considered the 'inassimilable' vanquished, for example, the Chandalas of the ancient times, began to be despised, and treated as the outcaste and untouchables. Since then, the numbers of 'untouchable' castes began to proliferate with the growing obsession of the dwijas with ritual purity. This resulted in attaching impurity to an increasing number of economic—productive and service—activities and occupations and their practitioners began to be treated as 'polluting' *in their persons*. Several groups of people and individuals were not admitted into (for example, the Chandalas for resisting subjugation), or were pushed out of (for example, groups of people who ate dog meat or skinned dead animals) of the caste system as a punishment for intransigence as well as for deviance and transgressions considered serious and violative of the basic ritual codes of caste organization. In the creation of untouchability, the dimension of *rituality* was, thus, intertwined with that of *power*.

Thus seen, Ambedkar was right to associate untouchabililty with the caste system. My point is that the ritual aspect of caste having been extremely weakened, almost defunct, the practice of untouchability, which we witness today, has lost any ritual-moral justification. It is used as an instrument of the powerful to subjugate the powerless. The conflict and violence we witness toady on the issue of untouchability is theoretically more understandable in terms of changing relations of power, rather than the reinforcement or assertion of any ritual practice associated with untouchability. The dominant castes often use 'untouchability' as a means to subjugate, even humiliate, the Dalits so that they can have them as a source of cheap and perennial labour. The Dalits, on the other hand, having recovered their self-respect and achieved a degree of well-being, thanks to the rights movements and the policies like reservation, resist and protest upper caste dominance. On the whole, atrocities are committed on Dalits by the upper castes, particularly by those among them who have either felt acutely the loss of traditional social power or the castes who have been able to establish their dominance in villages, using their economic power and the political power of numbers. All said, so far as Dalits are concerned, it can be said that some elements of rituality still survive in their relation to the savarna castes. Among the non-Dalit castes, however, as I argued earlier, ritual hierarchy has by and large lost relevance.

Beyond the issue of untouchability, Ambedkar has become relevant today for another reason also. This pertains to the issue of Dalit unity. Ambedkarian politics practised by the Dalit movements have enabled Dalits to project political unity nationally—across castes, regions, and economic classes. This politics has unified Dalits like it never did when Ambedkar was alive. In fact, it is the movements and politics spawned by Ambedkar's thought that have brought together ideologically disparate and numerous castes of the ex-untouchables. In this process, the category 'Dalit' has emerged as an ethnic or ethno-class type political-cultural entity. This entity, the Dalits, cannot be described as a simple, political conglomerate of castes, or as an economically homogenous class. It is a new, post-caste formation that is structurally more tentative and more open-ended than a caste.

Hierarchies in the New Economy

RJ: Could one say that there is a new stratification system in India today, no more characterized as a hierarchy of ritual statuses, but based on economic and political power?

DLS: Yes, it will be a mistake to characterize caste today as a ritual-status hierarchy. The structure of stratification that has emerged in India, especially after independence, is in many ways quite different. First, the new stratificatory system has acquired a pan-Indian macro structure, which is radically different from the local ritual-hierarchy based caste structure. The macro structure of caste, if it had one, was more like a theoretical reference, a conceptual scheme used for identifying the mobile and migrant communities of different castes in general terms of ritual status, so that some sense could be made of their place in the new local hierarchy they entered as migrants. This was the scheme of varna categories. Whereas the stratification system that has emerged after independence has acquired a structural character at the national-society level. This is because, for the last fifty to sixty years, a national economy and market have grown in India in the course of economic planning by the state. Lately, with the freeing of markets from the state control, the process of structural delinking of the national economy from the caste economy—characterized by the *jajmani* system, hereditary occupations, and local systems of food production and distribution—is now complete. At the national and regional levels castes have entered a new political economy of the modern nation-state. In this process, caste is fast losing its identification in ritual status terms. Castes which functioned primarily as units of a vertical system of local hierarchies of ritual statuses, have been transformed into larger social-cultural conglomerates and ethnic type formations, each representing commonality of political interest. These new formations occupy spaces at regional and national levels and cannot be identified in old caste-status terms. They will have to be identified in new social and political-cultural terms. I mean, they would make little sense if one attempts to identify or classify them in ritual hierarchical terms. This is why survey researchers and the social analysts face an unsurmountable problem (in fact, they get into an irrelevant and infructious exercise) of codifying and classifying castes today in ritual hierarchy terms (as 'upper' 'lower', etc.). In fact, such expressions as 'high castes' and 'low castes' have lost meaning. This is why they are often prefixed with terms such as backward, forwards, non-backward, dominant or poor, middle class, and rich.

Most interestingly, the means, avenues and even aspirations for upward mobility in the society as well as the reasons for downward mobility of individuals and groups have fundamentally changed with the collapse of ritual hierarchy. No one can rise or fall in status today by adopting or discarding virtues of rituality or attributes of ritual status. For example, in the new stratificatory system, sanskritization has lost relevance. People at the lower rungs of hierarchy no longer care to adopt Brahmanic or upper caste ritualistic behaviour or symbols for upward mobility. Today, they rather emulate the economic and consumerist lifestyles of the upper classes. This is because economic and political power, rather than ritual status, is a surer means for upward mobility. With the loss of economic power, many an upper caste persons have experienced downward mobility, despite their higher ritual status. In the caste system, aspirations of different castes were conditioned and structured differently. Today, people of all castes and communities have common aspirations and they are all related to economic lifestyles. It is another matter that some can and some can't realize these. But in this process, social mobility is increasingly becoming an individual pursuit rather than a collective group pursuit. Of course individuals use group-collective politics as a means to individual end of achieving 'higher' status in the society. A large part of caste politics is thus related to individual aspirations of the members of the lower castes to enter the middle class. This is why leaders of several lower castes pursuing upper class life-styles are often blamed as deserters of the cause of their castes or as those who have been 'co-opted' or 'sold out'. One hears such complaints more frequently in respect of Dalit and tribal élites pursuing improvements in their economic and social status.

So you have today a stratification system in which the central category is the middle class. It is a new middle class and not the one of the pre-independence period, which was a euphemism for a conglomerate of upper castes (the dwijas). In reality also, members of upper castes had almost exclusive access to modern education, professions, and even politics. Even as late as the mid-1960s about 70 to 80 per cent members of the higher civil services and the managers in public and private sector companies belonged to the upper castes. Today over 50 per cent of the middle class, according to the Centre for the Study of Developing Societies (CSDS) surveys come from the non-upper (the non-dwija) castes.

RJ: So there is a close relationship between the enlargement of the Indian middle class and simultaneously the new social and political configuration of Dalits and OBCs.

DLS: Yes, the middle class is a heterogeneous category comprising of communities who occupied different ritual statuses in the caste system, including the Dalits, the tribals, the OBCs and also the members of religious minorities. As members of the middle class, they are all subject to a politically and culturally homogenizing process marked by modernity and democracy. Of course there is also a working class, but not of the Marxian type. Empirically, it is preponderated by members of the erstwhile lower rungs among the OBCs, the Dalits, the tribals, and the Muslims. Their politics, however, is tuned to their ambition of entering the middle class. In this working class you also have a substantial numbers of the erstwhile upper castes who still remain bound to their traditional occupations and could not effectively take to modern education or who lost assets like land wherever land reforms were implemented. Also, the structure of opportunity today is generally more open to urban and metropolitan residents, which means that children of a lower caste person in a metropolis has better life chances than a similarly or even better placed upper-caste person in a village. In brief, education, urban/metropolitan residence, social policies of the state like land reforms, affirmative action, and democratic politics have all, in their different ways, caused structural changes in the society effecting a massive reshuffling of statuses. What we witness is the emergence of a new stratification system, which, of course, also represents some continuities and transmuted forms of the old.

Politicization of Caste

RJ: How has the process of the politicization of caste taken place in the past sixty years? It seems that during elections, the caste phenomenon is still used as vote bank.

DLS: The politicization of castes is a continuous process of expanding the participation of people in democratic politics; especially those groups and communities who were structurally denied access to political power, the knowledge system, and even occupational mobility. The so-called caste politics has brought together many castes occupying similar structural locations in the caste system and who were historically subjected to conditions of social and economic deprivations. It is a dialectical process through which a number of castes forged for themselves a broader cultural identity, and share and pursue common secular interests. Thus viewed, the politicization of castes has led to the collapse of the caste-hierarchy on the one hand, and on the other, to intense competition among communities for power and resources in society, made possible by the operation of democratic principles of political equality.

RJ: Could you identify the central issues facing Dalits today? Is it possible to see the Dalit movement in a national/pan-Indian sort of way at all, say like the Hindutva movement?

DLS: First, the real problem today for Dalits is the growing incidence of atrocities committed on them by members of upper castes. No one can deny that even today, as I have already pointed out, there are remnants of relations of ritual status surviving in villages of some Indian states, in so far as some upper caste members seek to force Dalits in their traditional social and economic roles. Although such role expectations have no legal or even wider social sanction, members of upper and middle castes, wherever they are in dominant positions, use their power to subjugate and humiliate Dalits who are usually a small minority in a village. Strictly speaking, this is not as much a manifestation of ritual-status relationship as of the assertion of power by a dominant caste in the village. Whichever way one looks at it, this is a real issue facing the Dalits, viz., their vulnerability to local power exercised by the dominant castes. The issue of atrocities on Dalits is, in fact, about the failure, often even deliberate neglect, of law and order machinery at the local level. But it is also related to the improved social and economic condition of some sections of Dalits. This development of Dalits is envied, resented, and not tolerated particularly by those sections of upper caste who have lost social power due to almost complete irrelevance of ritual status as a means of power.

The second issue about which some Dalit leaders are concerned is the educated middle class Dalits losing identification with the problems of ordinary Dalits and, in the process, not engaging with issues raised by Dalit movements. This, in fact, is a real dilemma. Seen from the perspective of normal process of social change, this is an expected and even a welcome development. Like everyone else, an educated middle class Dalit has a right to exit from the pulls and pressures of the community and opt for the life of anonymity offered by modernity, that is, exercise the option of joining the so called 'mainstream'. This phenomenon is more like what was seen and criticized in the Marxist movements as 'bourgeois individualism' or the bourgeoisiefication of the working class. But considering that a very small number of Dalits have achieved professional and middle class status, such dysidentification may adversely affect the movement, which anyway has a small and socially undiversified leadership. This issue is not sufficiently articulated for the contradictions between the politics of identity and interest to be reconciled or resolved in the Dalit movement.

The third issue, which remains shrouded in the discourse of Dalit movement, is the condition of scavenging community or the so-called sanitary workers known as 'Bhangis' or Valmikis in the villages of western and northern India and their equivalents known by different names in other parts of the country. These are the unseen and forgotten Dalits who, in some villages, live in sub-human conditions. Even the upper rungs of Dalits practise the ritual distance kind of exclusion and even untouchability vis-à-vis them. Although the Dalit movement thrives on projecting imageries of such exclusion from which a large and articulate section of upper and middle rungs among Dalits have moved out, the movement has yet not evolved significant programmes—mobilizational or welfare and uplift-oriented—for the Dalit castes of the 'Bhangis' and Valmikis. Of course, there are few exceptions of Dalit leaders and organizations that I personally know in Gujarat who have taken up issues on behalf of the 'Bhangi' communities. On the whole, however, their existence and identity remain submerged and unarticulated in the politics of demands and protests, which the Dalit movements address at the national and regional levels. The most inexcusable is the practice of carrying night soil (human excreta) on heads by the officially employed sanitary workers of the scavenging castes. The origin of this practice is, of course, in the ritually polluted and polluting status assigned to them in past. But persistence of this practice today has little to do with rituality. It has more to do with the cynical neglect and non-recognition of this section of Dalits, both by the state and the movement. This non-recognition has made the untouchable also an unseeable! If recognized, the problem is simply of deploying resources and harnessing technological equipments to abolish this inhuman and also a legally criminal practice adopted officially by the civic administration of several small towns and large villages. Let me explain my point as to how this practice today has little to do with the ritualistic caste relations. In towns where the sanitary workers have been freed from the practice of touching and carrying night soil physically, employment as scavengers is being sought and obtained by members of the upper castes. In some parts of Uttar Pradesh, even the Brahmans, along with other upper castes, have enrolled themselves as sanitary workers. Even though it is true that the upper caste sanitary workers unofficially contract out their work to members of the Dalit castes the fact remains that the formal recruitment of members of different castes, including of the upper castes, as sanitary workers, frees the work of a scavenger from the odium of untouchability. To put it differently, with the increase in educational, economic, and occupational opportunities for the Dalits at every level and technological development that makes dignified labour universally possible for the sanitary workers, the issue of untouchability is likely to become totally irrelevant in public discourse and in practice.

Fourth, in every region of India, there have been growing divisions among Dalits on socio-economic and cultural dimensions. About a hundred years of Dalit movements and the social policies of the Indian state after independence, accompanied by such forces as modernization and urbanization, have remarkably improved the socio-economic conditions—consistently and uniformly—of certain Dalit communities. They have been able to receive the impacts of changes more effectively and positively because they had acquired receptacles to receive them in the form of education and urbanization. These upper sections, for example, are identified with the Jatavs in Uttar Pradesh, the Mahars in Maharashtra, the Mahyavanshi, Vankaras and Chamars in Gujarat, and the Malas in Andhra Pradesh. There is another section who lack the receptacles and cannot receive the impact of policies. They are lagging behind and feel that the advantages of policies are cornered by the upper sections. This issue of how to distribute scarce assets and resources among different communities of Dalits will have to be politically resolved for the Dalit movement to attain coherence and unity.

Finally, there is almost a complete divergence between Dalit movements and Dalit party politics. The movements articulate their politics in moral, righteous terms. They have a kind of disdain for electoral and party politics pursued by Dalit leaders like Kanshi Ram who founded the Bahujan Samaj Party or by his disciple and successor Mayavati, who expanded the party electorally and became the chief minister of Uttar Pradesh, the largest state in India. The movement activists look down upon party politicians, who, in their view, have no patience for pursuing long-term programmes for the educational and economic development of Dalits. Further, by making social-political alliances with upper castes, and by entering into political coalitions with not-Dalit parties, the Dalit party-politicians, in the view of movement-activists, blunt the ideological edge of the movement. The political leaders themselves see the movement activists as impractical idealists who can't recognize the tremendous role electoral and party politics can play in empowering the Dalits. In my view, these two can become complementary to each other and there is a need for dialogue and interaction between the movement-activists and party politicians.

Now, your question about how comparable are the Dalit and the Hindutva movements. In my view, these two movements are not comparable. The Dalit and Hindutva movements are two structurally, ideologically, and organizationally different movements. The Dalits are more like an ethno-class category within which there are populations belonging to these different religions: Hinduism, Islam, Christianity, Sikhism, and Buddhism. Although it is true that Dalits belonging to different religious affiliations share a common problematic arising from their historical exclusion, they face different specific problems, depending on the region of India they live in. This is why there are different organizational patterns and varying priorities of issues of Dalit movements in different parts of the country. It is not possible, nor probably necessary, for these Dalit movements to become *one* national movement, keeping itself in a permanent state of political-emotional mobilization. National level mobilizations do indeed take place even today, but those are episodic and intermittent in response to such events like atrocity in some part of the country. While such events generate widespread condemnation and protests nationally, they do not and cannot sustain a massive, long-term mobilizational politics. And yet, there is a *national* character to the Dalit movement, which is primarily ideological, and expresses itself in a number of advocacy-related issues and which find a collective national level articulation of injustice and humiliation that the Dalits may experience. But these expressions remain confined to intellectual-activist arenas in the urban areas and lack a long-term organizational basis. This is not to deny that such articulations have an impact on the national level discourse and also on state policies. What I am trying to say here about the nature of mobilizational politics of Dalit movements was evident in activities during the run up to the Durban Conference as well as at other national and international forums. Dalit movements do not have a single-movement national leadership and organization; what they have are national and even international *platforms* and *coalitions* which emerge during campaigns on issues. The ongoing struggles of Dalits are carried out by myriad regional and micro movements addressing specific as well as generic issues of Dalits, all expressing a commonality of perspective and even ideology, but diverse political preferences and organizational forms.

The Hindutva movement on the other hand is of an entirely different character. First, it is primarily a non-local, that is, locally unrooted 'national' movement. To express itself politically, it manufactures and propagates national level symbols for everyday Hindu-ness, which is otherwise confined to diverse local milieus. Moreover, the Hindutva movement has politics of targeting religious minorities who in substantial numbers constitute the category Dalit (and tribal) along with the Hindus. This obscures the Hindutva politics of communal polarization, aimed at forging the unity of *all* Hindus. A movement like Hindutva requires the continuous inventing of issues, which can keep its followers in thrall, in a permanent state of emotional mobilization. It is for this reason that the Hindutva movement continuously and fervently woos the Dalit, the OBC, and the tribal Hindus for their political as well as social and cultural inclusion. But in this respect, the Hindutva movement has yet not succeeded nationally, although it has made significant advances in some states of India, such as Gujarat, Rajasthan, and Madhya Pradesh. On the whole, the Dalit movement as well as the movements of backward classes and tribals have so far acted as a counter-veiling force against the majoritarian-communal politics of Hindutva. This, for example, manifests in the electoral politics of the states like Uttar Pradesh, Bihar, and the south Indian states, except probably in Karnataka and Goa.

RJ: Is there an emerging Dalit cultural space in civil society?

DLS: The communities that have been identified as Dalits today have a long history of developing a variety of fine arts, crafts, music, folk songs, folk literature, poetry, use of special musical instruments, martial arts, etc. These elements of cultural life of the Shudras as well as the communities treated as the outcaste in the past, were only rarely recognized as such because the recorded social and cultural history of medieval India is by and large an account of upper caste achievements. This is not surprising in view of the fact that this non-recognition forms a part of the institutionalized exclusion of the Shudras and the outcastes. Although some trends of non-recognition continue, large and significant cultural spaces have now become not just visible but are influencing the cultural scene in larger society. This is especially true in the field of literature. In almost every major Indian language, Dalit literature and poetry have made their own place. They have enriched the literature in these languages even as they challenge and interrogate literary norms and conventions. In some of the languages, new literary forms have also emerged through the contributions of Dalit creative writers. Similar contributions are being made in the fields of fine arts, folk music, sports, etc. Today, there are several Dalit NGOs and movements using creative art forms, stage and street plays, and other cultural means to raise awareness among their compatriots, and for articulating and advocating issues concerning Dalits. Cultural spaces are created and widely used by the Dalit movements. This is specially the case with Dalit movements in western and peninsular India, where cultural and political spaces overlap widely. These developments have lent significant cultural content to Dalit identity today.

A Moribund Caste System

RJ: To sum up, would you say that today, sixty years after independence, both the ideology and organization of the traditional caste system have become vastly eroded?

DLS: Yes, the organization of caste has imploded, and the ideology has become defunct, it has ceased to perform any legitimating function for sustaining the caste hierarchy. With this loss of legitimation, it is as if the caste system survives like a patient on a deathbed, surviving on the artificial system of life-support. Caste that we witness today is not the *system* it was. What we have are disparate, individual castes surviving, at one level as primary a community of inter-related kinship groups and at another as politico-cultural communities competing, conflicting as well as cooperating in horizontal social spaces. In this process it has become increasingly possible for individual members of any caste to exit or outgrow the ritual status in which they are born by acquiring modern education, professional careers, political power, wealth, and other such attributes privileged by the new stratification system. The old organization of castes where individuals inherited generationally given occupations, that is, occupations ritually attached to their castes has almost collapsed. Today a vast majority of members in every caste have quit ritually ordained hereditary occupations and have taken to new, modern occupations or those belonging to other castes. In fact, the occupational structure of a community can be seen/used as an index of the survival or non-survival of ritual relationships between castes or in a certain context of their social and economic backwardness. For example, those agricultural and artisan communities in which the occupational structure remained insufficiently differentiated and their members in significant numbers follow traditional-hereditary economic activities (cultivation, crafts, carpentry, pottery, etc.) are also the socially and economically backward communities. It should however be noted/emphasized that a traditional occupational activity in itself does not suggest the continuity of rituality/ritual relationships. For example, the occupation of a barber in the ritual hierarchy of caste is located in a jajmani context, where the barber regularly visits the houses of his patrons for giving them a hair cut and he as well as his wife (who is usually the mid-wife of a village) perform many other roles for their patrons. In fact, in the jajmani system, entire families of the service communities of Shudras were attached to their patrons.

The barber opening a hair-cutting shop, for example, marked the end of ritual relationships. Likewise, many such occupational and economic activities, for instance, of a washerman, a carpenter, a blacksmith, or a potter have all changed from a barter-based, ritual jajmani type to a contractual type of relationship based on monetary exchanges. The other important principle of caste organization relates to marriage. Though today, empirically, only a minority of people marry outside caste, it is important to note that the very idea of caste boundaries has changed. First, the idea of marrying within caste would mean marrying in any caste of the same varna. For example, there have been numerous castes among the Banias, the Brahmans, and the Khastriyas, or among the OBCs and Dalits. In most parts of India, these inter-caste, inter-community differences among these categories are being increasingly ignored and marriage alliances are made across such castes. More importantly, many a self-arranged or parentally arranged marriages take place between castes even *across the varna boundaries*, specially among the savarnas, that is, among the communities of the erstwhile dwijas and Shudras. Considerations for making such alliances, as a rule, are about matching economic status, political position, professional background of the families involved, and education and income of the prospective spouses. The only barrier is sometimes observed in negotiating the across varnas, inter-caste marriages is the vegetarian–non-vegetarian divide.

Where some degree of the ideology of purity and pollution survive, as a last bastion of rituality, the relationship of the savarnas (caste-Hindus) and certain (not all) castes of Dalits remains, and that too in some rural areas. This is expressed in the form of untouchability, about which I have already talked earlier. As I have already pointed out, wherever it is observed, it is more through physical enforcement than acceptance of ritual status relationships. Another ideological basis of caste, the ideology of karma, which provided justification for caste inequalities and induced acceptance of one's undignified and stigmatized existence, say as an untouchable, is no longer accepted by the victims. The CSDS survey data show that a vast majority of people belonging to the lower rungs of social hierarchy do no longer accept that their lower social economic conditions has anything to do with their deeds in the past birth. The demise of the caste ideology of purity and pollution, in my view is best illustrated in the recent assembly elections in the Uttar Pradesh. It is a pity that the political pundits have yet not got much sense of how democratic politics has created a social revolution in India. Electoral victory of the Dalit party led by Mayavati, like many such events of Indian politics, is seen by many an analyst as a 'victory of caste politics'. In my view it represents a complete repudiation of caste ideology. What with the ritually *pure* Brahmans aligning with Dalits occupying the *polluted-end* of the ritual hierarchy, and even more, accepting a Dalit woman's leadership! It has made the 'twain'—the two ends of purity and pollution—which according to the colonial theory of caste were supposed never to meet, meet in Uttar Pradesh politics, the politics which, ironically, is dismissed as caste politics.

This organizational and ideological erosion of caste system has however not yet resulted in the individuation or independence of individuals from communities. It still remains politics of *communities*. It is true that communities have ceased to be a part of a vertical ritual hierarchy. But individuals still remain, at least in villages, bound to the norms and rules of the communities they belong to. India on the whole still appears as a society of communities—though the communities are multi-dimensional and open-ended—and Indian democracy is more a democracy of communities than of citizens. This is caste's challenge to democracy.

Surendra Prasad

Science and Society

RAMIN JAHANBEGLOO (RJ): India's first prime minister, Pandit Jawaharlal Nehru, realized the importance of science and particularly its end application to Indian society. He once said: 'What is planning if not the application of science to our problems?' Do you think during the past six decades, science and technology have received a major emphasis in all five-year plans in India?

SURENDRA PRASAD (SP): I think it was based on Nehru's vision that everything else was planned, like the setting up of the Indian Institute of Technology (IIT) was a major step undertaken by him at that time. The leadership at that time was very clear that the development of science and technology would be the basis of a progressive India. The spirit sought at that time is still there; perhaps we have lost some ground at the level of implementation. If you ask me to analyse the progress made by India over the past sixty years, I would say that it has achieved a lot. Whether you look at defence or the nuclear field or the research undertaken by the public sector companies, the achievements are commendable. The public sector research bodies have produced results of which we can be proud. But there is also a negative side to all this and I don't disagree with that point because the pace of development of science and technology has not picked up, as it should have in a country like ours. Until recently hardly any research was being done in private companies. It is only in the past five or ten years that it has started to happen in a big way. I think that this has partly to do with the type of economy which we began to work with. Earlier, there was controlled regime where exports were not encouraged and so competition didn't exist and so there was very little need and motivation for companies to undertake research. For science to surface and to come up to a certain level, young people should be able to see a career in it. To some, there are career options available in defence, in space, and in atomic research, but that is in very small numbers. One needs science as a vocation in general and that will only happen if there is intensive capital investment in it and that can only happen in the private sector.

RJ: So this is how you explain the brain drain in India, which costs the country a loss of two million resources every year. Could India channel the scientific-minded in the right direction?

SP: I think that we can and I think that perhaps we are now at that stage because now we have knowledge-based industries coming up. Young minds should think that science has a career and they can choose it as a lucrative career option. Once that realization comes, the brain drain problem will automatically be solved.

RJ: Are you telling me that the implication of science and technology has made a great impact on the lives of the people of the country?

SP: It has made an impact, but it should have had a greater impact. We have not, to some extent, been able to reach out to the masses as far as science and technology are concerned. The very fact that we have a large number of poor people residing in our country shows that we have not been able to harness science and technology to alleviate the impact of poverty on the masses. There has been improvement in the standards of living of the people but what we have achieved is a small fraction of what we should have achieved in reality.

RJ: Has the government of India been able to set up coordinating agencies at national, regional, state, and university levels to monitor research and development in India? Are you telling me that the implications of science and technology have made a great impact on the lives of the people of the country?

SP: I think that the government has been trying its best to set up a scientific system, be it in the form of laboratories or universities, but we have a large mass of manpower to be trained, for which huge resources are required. The government is trying but still what we have achieved falls short of what is required. So it is the private companies who are in a position to invest a lot in research and thankfully, there are things that have been achieved by the private companies and things are improving.

RJ: Do the members of the scientific community in India keep themselves acquainted with developments in the scientific domains of physics, medicine, and biotechnology?

SP: I would say that in any country one can divide the scientific community into several levels, levels at which they pursue science. The persons who teach science in schools, of course they have to keep themselves abreast of new things but therein, a relatively slower pace is required. But for the person who teaches in colleges or in universities . . . as you go higher up in the ladder, you will find that the need to keep abreast of newer scientific findings becomes more and more important. Also it is not a matter of pride that we have not emphasized our scientific publications enormously in the past two decades as compared to, say, what has happened in China. So there is a lacuna somewhere and I would say that it is a mixed sort of yes and no. By and large, people are engaged in scientific activities but the type of output is not commensurate with the kind of country and the kind of population that we have.

RJ: According to a recent survey India's rank in the world output of scientific papers has slid from the eighth place in 1980 to the fifteenth place in the year 2000. How do you explain this regression?

SP: Somehow we have been ignoring the nurturing of scientific activities and the reasons for this, I think, I have already answered.

RJ: It seems obvious to many that a country the size of India needs independent space research capabilities. However, some critical opinion is sometimes aired questioning the relevance of the Indian Space Research Organization (ISRO) in the light of the low per capita income of the average Indian citizen, usually from foreign observers. In response to this, defenders of the Indian space programme point to the fact that ISRO is unique amongst space programmes for its focus on developmental applications such as educational broadcasting and remote sensing. With its ambitions to put a man on the moon, how far ahead is India in terms of the scientific and engineering aspects of satellite technology?

SP: I think I don't have much knowledge about this and you should ask people who are much closer to research in space. From an outsider's perspective, it appears that we are doing well. Here is a body that has proved in the past that we can do it and that has infused confidence in the people that through science, we can make and do world-class things. It is thus important to take up challenging research like space research. We have challenging missions ahead of us and the fact that a part of the scientific community targeted something and was successful in that mission gives a message that we can also do equally relevant and fruitful things. I don't think that space research is irrelevant because it develops industries around itself and develops the applications that have social values for the community.

RJ: Can India become a scientific power in the next twenty-five years?

SP: I would say that it is even possible earlier but then that would be a wish. But it can, and not only it can, it has to be, because this realization is very strong today and the will power of Indians will take us there.

RJ: Science and technology have been an integral part of Indian civilization and culture over the past several millennia. Few are aware that India was the fountainhead of important foundational scientific developments and approaches. These cover many great scientific discoveries and technological achievements in mathematics, astronomy, architecture, chemistry, metallurgy, medicine, natural philosophy, and other areas. Indian science today is very westernized, because the scientific knowledge taught in the universities lacks a connection with the spiritual and never mentions India's ancient tradition of scientific inquiry. Do you think scientific research and technology development in India could benefit from Indian traditions of uniting science and spirituality?

SP: What I would say keeping myself on the ground rather than taking myself into the spirituality realm is that we have to find ways so that science reaches the common man all over the country and not just in the current urban centres. We need to generate many more urban centres in what are presently numerous small clusters of villages so that the local population out there can also benefit from science, so that they have job opportunities through which they can raise the standard of their lives. This is because agriculture is not going to meet the job requirements of the entire country and thus we need to set up industries, whether in the small sector or in the big sector, which somehow have to be linked with private sector capital investments, somehow generating industries at the village level. I don't know how this will be achieved but a massive industrialization programme is required if we have to raise the level of life of people. About spirituality, I can't say much because I am not an authority in that field. We at IIT are making specific efforts to reach out to rural people and we are trying to reach out to them in a number of ways, in whatever way we can think of. One way is to go to them and look at their current ways of doing things, to look at how they use technology to produce things that the community in their neighbourhood requires. This is because their technologies are centuries old and one immediate task that I can think of is whether they could be made to use technology in such a way that whatever they do, it increases their capacity and they are able to produce the things in a better way and in more numbers. If we could build a management system through which we could sell their products outside the village, then the economy of the country could also be boosted. This is the aim that we are aspiring to achieve in rural India.

Amit Bhaduri

The Indian Economy: Challenges and Uncertainties

RAMIN JAHANBEGLOO (RJ): When India as a newly independent nation set out on the path of rapid economic development within a democratic framework, it aroused great expectations. Today, sixty years later, the record is a mixed one. India is the twelfth largest economy in the world with a Gross Domestic Product (GDP) of Indian Rupees 25,238 billion in the year 2003–04, which is equivalent to US$ 550 billion and it is also the fourth largest in the world as measured by purchasing power parity (PPP), with a GDP of US$3.611 trillion. The GDP growth rate was 8.2 per cent higher than the preceding year. GDP growth has been on an average over 6 per cent per annum during the last decade. The number of listed companies in India is second only to the USA and Foreign Exchange Reserves of India, by August 2004, had crossed US$ 122 billion. But, according to the World Food Programme, nearly 50 per cent of the world's hungry live in India. How do you explain this contrast?

AMIT BHADURI (AB): By standards of development, India has certainly performed better and has maintained a steady growth rate. But one thing, which India never tried, was growth from below. It never tried to integrate the economic process of growth with the way in which wealth was distributed among the different sections of the economy. The role of the state was to redistribute and promote growth as separate agendas. The two was never brought together and the most classic example is the lack of emphasis on the growth of employment for the poorest. After liberalization, things have really gone from bad to worse. Economic growth has accelerated but it has become more dependent on corporations and has become more dependent on giving concessions to the large corporations, both domestic and foreign, but the question of integrating the poor has receded to the background, except at the level of slogans. The result is that the growth of employment despite high output growth is lower today than the growth of employment was during the 1950s and the 1960s.

RJ: During the post-independence era, India was well known as an agrarian economy with a weak industrial base, very low level of employment opportunities, and serious regional imbalances. The public sector was forced to play a dominant role in developing the economy because the private sector neither had the necessary resources nor the will to undertake risks involved in large investments with a long term perspective. Is the agrarian sector still at the centre-stage in the Indian economy?

AB: It depends on what the emphasis is on. In human terms, certainly, and that is the tragedy of the current state of development that more people will be affected if agriculture does not do well, rather than if industries do not do well. The worst thing is that the most vulnerable will be affected if agriculture does not do well. It is not a case of statistics only, but it is the question of leaving out the poorest and the most vulnerable out of the developmental process. This is the reason that India is witnessing so many suicides and the Naxalite movement and all kinds of extremism. Yet, instead of dealing with the problem of rural credit or employment generation on a war footing, this government wants to corporatise agriculture which will take away many more livelihoods from the small and marginal farmers than it will create.

RJ: Why is it said that the Indian economy is monsoon oriented?

AB: The Indian economy is not monsoon based if you think in terms of the regional distribution of food grains produced, because most of the food grains produced under high yielding varieties and other modern techniques require relatively controlled water inputs. This controlled water, from the colonial times, has been biased towards Punjab, and to a lesser extent, towards western Uttar Pradesh and some other parts of India. About 40 per cent of cultivated land has reasonable control of water and the rest depends to varying degrees on nature and on the monsoon. These are the areas where if nature fails, the poor agriculture-dependent households will have almost nothing. More days of work are created in an area under controlled water. If there are three crops, you get on an average about 200 days of work. But with one crop, if the monsoons fail, there is less than a hundred days of work for agricultural labourers and near landless peasants. So they have to migrate to other areas when the monsoons fail.

RJ: Indian economic policy after independence tended towards protectionism, with a strong emphasis on import substitution, industrialization, state intervention in labour and financial markets, a large public sector, business regulation, and central planning. Jawaharlal Nehru expected favourable outcomes from this strategy, because it involved both public and private sectors and was based on direct and indirect state intervention. The economic liberalization of 1991, initiated by the then Indian prime minister, P.V. Narasimha Rao, and his finance minister, Manmohan Singh, in response to a balance-of-payments crisis ended many public monopolies, allowing for the automatic approval of foreign direct investment (FDI) in many sectors. Today we are witnessing a new phase of globalization of the Indian economy. What is your analysis of this new turn in the political economy of India?

AB: I will answer your question in three distinct steps. First, factually, it is not correct to say that the Indian economy took a dramatic turn in 1991. Policies took a dramatic turn because of a balance-of-payments crisis, but liberalization had started in the 1980s during Rajiv Gandhi's period. If you take a statistical look at things, you will find that there has not been a distinct break in the trend rate of the growth of the economy from the 1980s or 1990s, but there has been a gradual acceleration of growth. Actually, the dramatic rise in the trend rate of the growth rate, which constitutes a structural break with the past inertia, came somewhere around the early 1950s itself. In this sense, the policies followed by Nehru and his advisors can hardly be called less successful. Second, you cannot judge the performance of the economy only in terms of the growth rate. I have already pointed out that the dramatic turnaround in the economy came right after independence, and probably, that strategy was more effective than the present liberalization policy. Even in terms of benefits, India derives today from globalization in areas like IT, the base was set during the Nehru period through massive state intervention in higher technological education. So the most criticized aspect of globalization, namely, state intervention, was done during the Nehru period; the IIT and Indian Institute of Management (IIM) were upgraded through state support during the Rajiv Gandhi period, while the current 'wisdom' is to privatize education. It was the state's intervention in promoting so-called human capital, which gave India an edge in certain sectors. With the privatization of education and the weak development of the public schooling system, except for a small section of our population, it will become more difficult to integrate to our advantages with the rest of the world, as only people who can privately finance education will get this chance. It is said in defense of liberalization that the people who went to IIT and All India Institute of Medical Sciences (AIIMS) belonged mostly to the middle class and upper middle class. This is true, but to counter this we need to strengthen primary and secondary education, broaden the base and the catchment area. Signing up with the World Trade Organisation (WTO) or attracting direct foreign investment will integrate us in a lop-sided manner with the world, without giving an opportunity to most Indians;

we need instead to build up our capacity on a broad and not a narrow élite base. There has been almost no expansion in public-funded primary and secondary education in remote areas in the last fifteen years. And India will be the land of the largest number of illiterates in the twenty-first century. Is this strategic integration with the rest of the world? Third, things have gone wrong in at least two other ways. First, it is not a question of opening up to FDI. The strategy of development needs to integrate the poor by increasing the purchasing power of the poor so that they, rather than a privileged upper and middle class, can spend money on goods they need. These goods are mostly produced efficiently at home. This means expanding the domestic market for consumption by ordinary people. This is something that this government has not done. Second, increasing the efficiency of domestic production and attracting foreign investment should be viewed as complementary, not competitive strategies. This has not happened mainly because the domestic market involving the poor has not expanded at the rate required. Giving concessions and holding down wages is a wrong strategy. The strategy should be to expand the domestic market by involving the poor, and to open this domestic market to competition between foreign and domestic firms by inviting both to produce under Indian conditions. Foreigners would come because they would want the expanding Indian market, but the types of goods produced would be what the poor mostly needs. This should be our perspective on the link between the internal market and foreign investment.

RJ: Were there any external reasons for these reforms initiated by Manmohan Singh? Could we refer to the collapse of the Soviet Union and its economy whose central planning was the model for the Indian economy and for the phenomenal success of China since the opening up of its economy to foreign trade and investment in 1978?

AB: As far as external factors are concerned, I would say that there are two types of liberalization. One is strategy driven and the other crisis driven. In the latter case, you have little option. In the Indian case, for Narasimha Rao and Manmohan Singh, liberalization was crisis driven; in contrast, Rajiv Gandhi's liberalization was strategy driven. When you are driven by crisis you are more affected by external forces like pressure from International Monetary Fund (IMF), World Bank, etc. The Congress government under Rajiv Gandhi, was more accountable to the people in so far as it had clear single party majority. The government was more clearly accountable and they realized that liberalization has to proceed at a slow pace. Since then, we have had coalition governments and nobody wants to be clearly accountable. So it is best to pretend that the market will do the necessary job for development, and all parties follow this as the most convenient ideology. However, they are promoting policies that the IMF and the World Bank want, apparently to be on the side of the powerful. But people are more powerful in a functioning democracy, and these policies have repeatedly been rejected by the people. So you find the liberalizing Narasimha Rao-Manmohan Singh government losing elections to the BJP, the BJP crashing with its 'India Shining' slogan, and perhaps, most tellingly, Chandra Babu Naidu losing elections in Andhra Pradesh that was supposed to glitter with IT industries. Market-oriented liberalization and reforms are not a popular strategy in a poor country.

RJ: One would expect to see a healthy flow of foreign capital to raise the Indian investment rate much above Indian domestic savings rate. It is no mystery that FDI inflows to India are less than what the much smaller economy of Thailand has received. And yet between 2000 and 2004, India's savings rate increased from 24 per cent of the GDP to 29 per cent.

AB: The Indian savings rate is largely the saving rates of Indian households. The dramatic increase in savings came when the government invested. Today, what has happened is the expansion in financial markets have taken place through an emerging middle class that has a higher propensity to save. The rich save more than the poor out of their income and if you have more rich people, then the savings rate would usually increase. India now has a middle class, which saves a larger amount of its additional income through financial institutions.

RJ: One of the reasons why the Indian economy has been in the spotlight more than usual is the phenomenal growth of the Indian IT sector whose output has been doubling every eighteen months. India already has a global market share of almost 20 per cent in software development and customized software.

AB: One of the defining features of the modern phase of globalization through multinational corporations is intra-firm trade. European Union (EU) estimates show that around 40 per cent of world trade is accounted for by trade between the subsidiaries of the same firm. Perhaps the first developing country to take advantage of this was Singapore. It produced almost no final goods, but it had the largest number of multinationals which produced something in Singapore in their intra-firm chain. The same applied later to much of Southeast Asia with Japanese and Taiwanese investments. India has an advantage in the IT sector that originated partly in the double advantage educated Indians have of knowing English and a better mathematical training than in many other countries. This combination gave us the initial advantage to enter into the chain of intra-firm trade. To contrast, Russia certainly has a better advantage in the mathematics training, but is worse placed in the language part. The Indians also came to know better the tricks of the trade through their jobs in US multinationals. It is said that even today, Indians do not develop mostly routine software and do work outsourced to us because it is cheaply done in India. We are less at the innovative end of IT industries. This has limitations and one of the most well-known Indian science journals *Current Science* wrote that Indian IT workers are becoming science coolies for the USA. It brings me back to the same point. Without a more imaginative and broad based education policy at different levels, many of the current advantages of globalization will be transient for India. Our mindless privatizers are only ensuring that in the name of market reforms.

RJ: Many sectors of the Indian economy such as power, ports, telecommunications, and transport have not received adequate attention so far. It is critical for the Indian manufacturing sector to grow significantly and focus on export-oriented manufacturing. Also for long-term growth to be sustainable, India will have to do a great deal in the social sectors, especially health and education.

AB: The reason for this is that the government has been waiting for this public-private partnership. The government has decided not to be very active in the social sphere or any other sphere because the government wants to cut down expenditure. In the Indian economy, it is very difficult to raise taxes fast and so the government is going for large-scale borrowing in various forms for infrastructure development. However, the government can spend in social and other sectors and these investments can act as a multiplier to expand the domestic market several times the original investment. The more we do it in a decentralized manner, the more we will be successful in including the poor in this expansion of the domestic market. Instead, the IMF, the World Bank, and this government want to do it by bringing in the corporations. It will fail. We will have the growth repeating the story of 'India Shining' but the poor will be left out. This is bad economics, unsustainable politics, and simply not just. All political parties are following this path, but instead, we must have three things together. We must have social investments on a large scale, we should have decentralized infrastructure to promote broad-based growth, and we must keep in focus the strategy to include the poor. These three aspects can be combined by adopting simple infrastructure development in rural India. We have no option but to do it, unless we want to create more misery and inequality in the name of development. If we do not try this, it will be the development of the corporations, not of the people!

RJ: To sum up, one can say that even those who are not euphoric about the state of the Indian economy today think that now is the time to initiate 'second generation reforms' to enable the Indian manufacturing industry to capitalize on global opportunities and drive the growth of the Indian economy to the next level.

AB: To me, public versus private sector is not the issue. The issue is how to include the poor and to do it immediately; not in twenty years because children will grow up as a generation of illiterates in twenty years and the poor will not have enough to eat for twenty years. Now the private sector, nowhere in the world, has done anything to include the poor and the marginalized. So we need to mark out a massive area where the state can intervene. There are certain areas where you cannot include the poor, like if you want to develop atomic energy. But where there is a possibility, we must do it and that is why emphasis needs to be given to employment generation for the poor, linking it with rural decentralized investment. First generation reform was regarding the de-regulation. Today, if you do more reforms it means pro-corporation reforms, as are happening right now. This is something that is not correct. The government should not be subservient to corporate interests, purchasing land for them, getting the labour law changed for them, etc. We need instead to find out where the maximum employment generating capacities are for including poor people and then the government should go all out to promote this without thinking of what the IMF, the World Bank, and other financial pundits say. Fiscal deficit is not a problem that should thwart this strategy; unemployment is a much more serious problem than fiscal deficit. So the reforms should be more towards de-centralization through fiscal autonomy to *gram sabhas* and *panchayats*, where the poor can participate to some extent. This is the time to redefine our democracy by really creating a kind of economy where the poor can participate. We have the framework for that because India has the three-tier election system and we can decentralize through them. With this we must have accountability and transparency at all levels by strengthening the right to information while reforms should give financial autonomy to the panchayats. Our government hijacked the term 'reform' as if reform merely means reform in favour of the market and the corporate sector. We want every memorandum of understanding, which the government signs with corporations to be made public automatically. We want reforms, faster and more of it, but of a different kind. While the social investments in health and education would prepare our poor majority for gradual strategic integration with the world market to our advantage, all reforms should be employment-oriented, focussed on the expansion of the domestic rather than the external market through rapid employment growth, and employment must be made productive through decentralization and accountability at all levels. This is the real challenge for reforms in India.

Krishna Kumar

Evaluating Education

RAMIN JAHANBEGLOO (RJ): India has one of the largest higher education systems in the world with 185,000 upper primary schools, two million colleges, a quarter of a million non-formal education centres, 110 million students in primary classes and three million teachers. However, with 35 per cent of the population under the age of fifteen, India's education system faces numerous challenges. Successive governments have pledged to increase spending on education upto 6 per cent of the GDP, but actual spending has hovered around 4 per cent for the last decade. Why is it that the BJP or Congress-led governments have not been able to improve the standards of education in India?

KRISHNA KUMAR (KK): The question of standards is a complex issue because any perception of quality in education is related to the aims of education and the conditions under which these aims are pursued. The higher education system in India evolved under colonial rule in the later half the nineteenth century and it has continued to operate largely with the same norms and procedures, which had been established in colonial era. The idea of knowledge embedded in this system needs to be recognized. In any colonial relationship, the colonizer denies the validity of the knowledge which the colonized owns and has the capacity to enhance. In addition to this denial, colonization also means imposition of knowledge—both its idea and body ... Thus, alienation from the knowledge one is compelled to receive and master is an essential aspect of being colonized. Learning under colonial conditions also means deriving a supposedly moral benefit from knowledge received, which essentially means that the colonized start to behave and act like their colonial masters. The idea that education creates the capacity to think for oneself and to produce or create knowledge is still quite alien to the system of education in India even though we have achieved political independence. Change in the concept of knowledge is a cultural process, which has proved difficult. One reason is the absence of a sustained reform effort. Another is that the emphasis placed on the moral benefits of education found a resonance in other indigenous ideas as I have explained in my *Political Agenda of Education* (Sage, 1991). The picture remained confusing and did not allow a reform agenda to crystallize. Certain reforms in curricular and pedagogic practices have been initiated at the school level and if they are sustained for a sufficient length of time, they might begin to influence the higher education system. The size of the system has expanded a great deal since independence in 1947 without any improvement in curricular planning and the methods used for teaching. To some extent, educational opportunities have expanded, among the lower socio-economic classes, but the overall proportion of the young who enroll in higher education of one kind or another is still no more than 10 per cent of the total age cohort. The system's inability to reform itself, in terms of its concept of knowledge and teaching, has triggered the argument that excellence can only be achieved in a few islands. Such islands have been maintained at a high rate of investment while the rest of system functions at rudimentary levels of public spending. It is not surprising that general standards of achievement have remained quite low even as a handful institutions pursue higher goals and prepare students for globally competitive roles.

RJ: Nehru envisaged India as a secular democracy with a state-led command economy. Education for all was seen as a crucial tool to unite India divided on the basis of wealth, caste, and religion. But despite Nehru's visions of universal education and the intentions of the Kothari Commission in the 1960s to provide all young children with free and compulsory schooling, a significant proportion of India's young population still remains uneducated. Although enrolment in primary education has increased, it is estimated that at least thirty-five million and possibly, as many as sixty million, children aged 6–14 years are not in school. How do you explain these statistics?

KK: It is hardly true that political leadership and educational planners of the early decades of independence were concerned about educational reforms. If budgetary allocations were seen as a measure of concern, it would be difficult to prove that education was given high priority in Nehru's government, even though it is true that his personal vision of India's progress carried the assumption that education will spread to all sections of society and will create a new sense of confidence. A similar confusion prevails over the Kothari Commission of the mid-1960s. It is true that this Commission recommended universal schooling, but if we look even slightly deeply, we will find that Commission's report was steeped in the ethos of its time, which projected militaristic progress as an immediate priority. Any probing of the voluminous report of the Kothari Commission will show that it marked the end of the Gandhian experiment to use education to release India's productive forces. Gandhi's emphasis on rural education imparted in the mother tongue and centred around the knowledge of a culturally-significant, local, productive craft had begun to make a social impact, which might have meant a long term transformation of caste-based social relations. The Kothari Commission's report diluted whatever little stress there still was in the educational policies of 1960s on experiential learning and reinstated book-based conventional pedagogic practices. It is true that the Kothari Commission also recommended several other measures which could have sped-up certain systemic changes and pedagogic modernism, but the kind of financial investment this report had envisaged never became available. The Commission's Member-

Secretary, late J.P. Naik, himself came to the conclusion towards the end of his life in 1981 that there was a lack of sustained political will and, on the other hand, there was also resistance to the transformative potential of education. The statistics of enrolment and retention you have referred to are hardly surprising, given the continued problem of an absence of consensus in the élite sections of society about the importance of educating every child.

Addressing Social Disparities through Education

RJ: Severe gender, regional, and caste disparities also exist. There are dramatic differences in literary rates by place of residence, with rates in rural areas lagging behind rates in urban areas. By 1971, only 22 per cent of women and 46 per cent of men were literate. By 1991, after Rajiv Gandhi's new education policy, the National Policy on Education, which was intended to prepare India for the twenty-first century, 39 per cent of women and 64 per cent of men were literate. Has there been any real progress in improving educational attainment for both sexes in India over the last decade?

KK: Yes, there has been significant progress in terms of the spread of literacy among women. Regional and caste disparities in the context of gender do persist and we cannot expect them to immediately vanish. In the northern Indian Hindi belt, bias against women has not faced any resistance from a wider cultural movement. The only positive influence has been the devolution of power to women under the Panchayati Raj, which has begun to show some impact in parts of northern India. In the context of *Sarva Shiksha Abhiyan* (SSA), participation of women in the process of community mobilization for better supervision of primary schools has increased. These larger processes indicate a slow change in the ethos, which will effect the enrolment and retention of girls in schools. In southern India, the spread of education among women has taken place far more speedily, benefiting from the egalitarian cultural movements, which had begun to soften the social climate from the late nineteenth century onwards. Stereotypes about the lower castes, women, and tribal groups do exist in the mind of the urban middle class, but the situation has begun to change. There has been a considerable amount of educationally-fuelled upward mobility among the lower-caste groups in several regions of the country, especially the southern states. Policies promising justice to a vast section of middle and lower castes on the basis of positive discrimination have been in operation in the southern states for a long time and these have indeed shown visible results in the social structure. The fact that these states are among the leaders in economic development has challenged the stereotype that reservation for the lower castes leads to inefficiency.

RJ: This idea that the lower castes are not deserving of education is so deeply rooted among the Indian middle class that it has hampered the Nehruvian idea of the universalization of primary education.

KK: The idea of the universalization of primary education predates Nehru as Gopal Krishna Gokhale first mooted it as a bill in the Imperial Legislative Assembly as early as 1911. Still earlier, Jyotirao Phule had forcefully argued in Maharashtra in the late nineteenth century that the lower castes not only deserve education but also that without educating them the overall society cannot make significant progress. It is no surprise that in western and southern India this long struggle has to a large extent removed the middle class stereotype. However, the stereotype does persist in northern India, especially in the Hindi-speaking states.

RJ: Every year, India produces 2.5 million graduates and this figure is only lower than the US and China. However, in terms of quality, India is falling behind the developed world. In fact, many of the graduates cannot find jobs, as they are not up to the mark.

KK: Quality is a complex concept. As I said earlier, it is linked to the aims of education and the conditions in which education is imparted. I suppose you are using the word 'quality' in an everyday or conventional sense in which it means the dependability of a product and the efficiency with which it is produced. In this sense, the quality of graduate level education varies a great deal across different Indian universities, but the same is true in almost in any country, including the US and China. It is also difficult to say that our graduates cannot find jobs because they are not up to the mark and we must notice that the present-day economic policies prevalent in most parts of the industrialized world do not promote steady employment. Rather, they discourage careers and stability and encourage the casualization of work. This tendency has found its way into the Indian economy as well, and it is one of the factors responsible for putting college and university education under a convoluted kind of stress. In the name of job-orientation, many institutions of higher education are being forced to promote narrowly vocationalized courses, which can hardly be called higher education. In China and the US, this kind of fragmentation of 'higher' education has been growing for a considerable length time, and the same is now happening in other parts of the world.

RJ: There is also another problem. Teaching is an ill-paid job in India. As a result, many brilliant students are not joining teaching. Some Indian teachers and scholars prefer to migrate to the Western countries for better facilities. Have there been any measures at the level of education funding in order to stop the brain drain in India?

KK: It is true that teachers are not well paid in India, but this problem is normally discussed mainly in the context of university teacher, and the point of brain drain mainly applies to this sector. If we look across the education system, we find that teachers serving in institutions of early childhood and school education at the elementary and secondary levels are much worse-off in terms of the salary they receive than college and university teachers are. The situation has indeed gone from bad to worse, especially in the context of the structural adjustment programme which started to influence social sector priorities from early the 1990s onwards. If we look across the world, we find that India is not alone in treating its teachers badly. In many countries, salaries of teachers have declined in real value and the profession has become unattractive for the young. Also, working conditions of teachers have worsened because the teacher has to handle the consequences of stress and other distortions visible in the lives of children, originating in the larger economic and cultural policies. We can say that the teacher has assumed the role of a healer that often makes professional training of teachers inadequate, if not entirely irrelevant to the kind of challenges that contemporary life presents. This is an issue, which rarely attracts attention of the so-called civil society. I would like to refer to an editorial article published by UNESCO's official journal, *Prospects*, which was entitled, 'Where Have All The Teachers Gone'. It analyses the reasons that have made teaching globally unattractive.

RJ: It seems as if the labour market policies and predominance of public sector employment opportunities did not put enough pressure on the educational system to change as the degree has been more important than acquired knowledge and skills.

KK: Craving for a degree has been a common feature in many colonized countries. Knowledge and skills do get sidelined when the 'Diploma Disease', as Ronald Dore has called it, spreads. It is not merely labour market policies and the predominance of public sector employment, which can be held responsible for putting insufficient pressure on the system of education for demanding knowledge and skill. The inherent logic of education in colonial societies is a historical force. A generalized idea of employment does not permit us to recognize the kind of resistance that education as a system displays in a nearly spontaneous way. Now that public sector employment is diminishing quite fast, one would have expected that the education system would respond to the demand for skills and knowledge required in the market. It is evident that the system of education is still resisting this demand and we must ask ourselves why. It is not useful to see education in isolation from the social structure, especially from the constraints on justice, which a sharply stratified social structure poses. Public perceptions of what is important in education—knowledge or the degree—are shaped by the possibility of justice and the symbolic means associated with the pursuit of mobility. The market of employment opportunities alone cannot fully explain how a system of education behaves in response to people's expectations.

RJ: How do you evaluate the problems of education in primary schools for Muslim children in India? I believe no government has ever dared to provide Muslim children with proper educational infrastructure.

KK: The recently published report of the Sachar Committee has given an elaborate analysis of the problems of education faced by Muslim children. This analysis is quite sound and it points to numerous policy deficiencies as being responsible for reinforcing cultural constraints within which a Muslim child grows up. Your point that no government has dared to provide proper infrastructure for the education of Muslim children is a bit strange, considering the fact that the educational infrastructure available for rural India as a whole and for the urban poor has remained neglected. As we discussed earlier, education has been a victim of state neglect and systemic problems inherited from India's colonial history. The Muslim child has, of course, suffered from a special neglect, which needs to be understood along lines that the Sachar Committee has indicated. It has pointed out that economic stagnation, cultural constraints, lacklustre social policies, and non-specific development goals form a complex whole in which the poorer sections of Muslim community and its children have been living.

RJ: As you said previously, higher education in India is basically a state-funded sector. The share of the state varies in total funding from 70 per cent to 90 per cent, excepting the very few private unaided colleges that charge heavy donations and very high rates of tuition fees. Many believe that given equity considerations and resource constraints, financing higher education mostly from the general tax revenue may not be a desirable policy in the long run. Is it possible to evolve a model of funding higher education in India that could provide a mix of the various methods?

KK: The perception that higher education requires private investment is growing as a corollary of the discourse of state withdrawal from all social sectors. If you look at higher education in India historically, you will find that private initiative played a significant role in creating infrastructure and providing opportunities for higher learning and research in a colonial context marked by extremely poor funding by the state. Quite a few important institutes of science and technology have a history of private initiative. In the arts and social sciences also, personal initiative taken by men of imagination and reformist zeal played a major role. However, this spirit of initiative had no commercial interest behind it. There was no question of making a profit from an educational institution in that era. It is a indeed ironical that the philanthropic spirit witnessed in the colonial era did not grow rapidly after independence, and over the last few decades, we are witnessing a contrary development, namely, the rise of education as business. Recently, even the judiciary has put its stamp on the use of education as a means of earning a livelihood in cases where someone wants to establish an institution. The new situation is steeped in the belief that privately-run institutions provide better quality than what government-run institutions can provide. The use of the word 'quality' in education has taken an entirely commoditized meaning, carrying the notion that teaching is a professional service comparable to services, which industries like tourism provide by packaging an experience and turning it into a purchasable item. Under the ideology of neo-liberalism, knowledge is being brought under property laws. This kind of ethos is very suitable for arguing that instead of providing finance to higher education from the general tax revenue, the government should encourage private providers to create a market of educational services. The mixed model you are talking about was in operation in pre-independence times and has continued to operate till quite recently in a reasonably healthy way, although, given the scale of the provisions higher education requires, the contribution private institutions could play was quite limited.

Lessons for the Future

RJ: I recently read an article written by you in *The Hindu* on 'Green Schools in a Greying World'. This challenge of softening Indian education through environment-related learning is an idea, which was already put forward by Mahatma Gandhi and Tagore more than seventy years ago. How do you see the relevance of the Gandhian or Tagorian theories of education in the framework of the rigid bureaucratic procedures of state directorates of education in India today?

KK: Gandhi and Tagore are just as relevant today as they were in the first half of the twentieth century. Indeed, the National Curriculum Framework (NCF), 2005 starts with a long quotation from Rabindranath Tagore in which he explains what it means to respect the child's free and active spirit. Gandhi proposed a radical scheme of education in which children and teachers were expected to engage with the productive forces of their environment. I quite agree with your point that environment-related activities can help us soften the rigid system of education. Under the NCF, twenty-one focus groups were appointed, one of which was on 'Habitat and Learning'. This report suggests that children can serve as an active resource for the collection of data about environmental changes. This kind of idea has been tried in some countries and it has helped the creation of a strong awareness among the young about protecting their natural environment. A debate recently held among the senior environmentalists in a journal called *Curriculum Inquiry* focused on the question of whether education can save the earth. One of the participants responded by saying: 'perhaps not, but it must try'.

I think education is a key arena in which the future of human relations with nature can be shaped. The policy concerned with sustainable development, as the slogan goes, can at best help us to cope with disasters like climate change, deforestation, and pollution of water and soil by poisonous pesticides, not to forget the terrible dangers lurking in genetically modified seeds. Education is not about coping with circumstances. It does not deserve to be called education if it does not shape life and circumstances. Taking charge of destiny is the only way that we can define the goal of education, but we must avoid the dangers of being excessively obsessed with human comfort and safety. Nature is a much wider category and education must treat nature as a responsibility, at least to the extent of healing the terrible damage we have done to nature.

M.J. Akbar

Politics and Democracy in India

RAMIN JAHANBEGLOO (RJ): I will start with political developments in India since independence and the fact that it has often been analysed in terms of state-society relations. The explicit form of the Indian nation-state created by the Indian Constitution was that of a modern liberal democracy. It is often said that the reason why liberal democratic institutions have performed towards bettering India is due to the strength of its civil society. Do you agree with this idea?

M.J. AKBAR (MJA): Yes, but it depends on which India you are talking about. Are you talking about the India of 15 August 1947, or April and March 2006? Civil society—I am afraid I can't agree with a very unfortunate connotation or environment—assumes that there was no civil society before. All nation-states and all civilizations have had civil society. That is the meaning of civilization. Iran has one, Egypt has had one, and the Arabs have had one. 'Civil', a variation of civilization reminds me of the story of Mahatma Gandhi. He was only half joking in London when he went for the first or the second Round Table Conference, and the reporters asked him what he thought of the Western civilization. Gandhi replied that it would be a very good idea. Civil society is not a modern concept and civil society has always existed, and in India, it has existed for a long while. In fact, colonization brutalized us in many ways. Just before the anguish left, nearly four million people died of famine in two or three years in the vicinity of Calcutta and it was a man-made famine. In fact, there was a great collapse of civil society towards the end of the British rule. They left this country impoverished, hungry, and demeaned, in many senses. The great strength of the India that emerged after 1947 was the very strong conviction in the idea of Indian state; extraordinary leaders were determined that it should not be a sectarian state, it should be an inclusive state, a liberal state. People forget that India was the first country to emerge out of European colonization. And there were no role models. For many other countries India became a role model. The real strength of India lies in the culture and the convictions of its people. Because even liberalism cannot be imposed from top down . . . dictatorship can be imposed from top down, but not democracy, which can only survive with the cooperation and the belief of the people. India is also helped by the fact that it is large enough for the parts to protect the whole. When, for example, democracy in India was threatened by the Emergency, some sections of India supported the Emergency. But enough of India fought against it to defeat it. And that is really the strength of the democratic idea that plurality is always right.

RJ: Well, from the very beginning of independence, there was a tension between the modernizing aspirations of the Indian state and its commitment to democracy. This tension, not to say contradiction, was sought to be managed on the terrain of political society. But the post-Gandhian political society constituted a space that lacked the ethical transparency and clarity of a moral language. And this is a problem that we have till today, which we did not have with people like Gandhi . . .

MJA: I don't know whether we have had a problem of moral language. Because I don't think anything called a Gandhian state could have existed, it was too utopian. You could have a Gandhian movement based on non-violence, but no state has yet been devised which is based on non-violence. The first challenge before Gandhi after freedom was that within six weeks of freedom, we witnessed the invasion of Kashmir. When India responded militarily, Gandhi was asked what happened to non-violence. He just shrugged and claimed a little speciously that he could not tell the government of India what to do. Maulana Azad and many other leaders explained that non-violence was a part of our freedom struggle but was not a part of our national struggle for survival. Similarly, I wonder if Gandhian ideas can be applicable to nation building. Gandhian ideology should not be confused with theology. Gandhi was a leader but Gandhi was no god. And we might have had a very bizarre kind of society if everyone had to live according to Gandhi ... there was a lot of moral dictatorship in Gandhi's view of how his disciples should live. He gave India a successful democracy but his personal life was full of dictatorship.

RJ: But don't you believe that from the very beginning this idea of modernization was confronted with the idea of democratization?

MJA: No, Jawaharlal Nehru was very clear, both went together. In fact, how old is democracy as an idea? People think of America as the world's youngest country, actually in some senses America is the world's oldest country. Because, democracy as the theme of the polity, first appears in America and democracy is now the preferred structure of a modern polity. India is in that sense the oldest country of the emerging world because it was the first country to adopt democracy in its postcolonial phase.

RJ: But do you really believe that India still has heroes like Nehru ... who became moral heroes?

MJA: A nation needs heroes occasionally. No nation needs heroes permanently. And it's a great failure of nation-building if only heroes can build a nation. Heroes really come in moments of crisis. They don't come in normal times. Maybe, environment also creates heroes. But I think the great success of India lies in the fact that its normal phases of history are run by normal leaders and it is done very successfully. Nobody has the courage to disturb the structure the heroes left behind. Of course there is corruption, and there is exploitation and so on and so forth ...

RJ: So who would you say is the last political hero of India, J.P. Narayan or Jawaharlal Nehru?

MJA: There is no comparison between J.P. Narayan and Jawaharlal Nehru. J.P. Narayan was a moralist. I myself was very impressed with him when I was young and followed his movement and so on and so forth. But, Jawaharlal Nehru had a far more difficult task ... He built a nation. You know, it is much easier to stand outside and criticize than it is to get inside and remain true to certain ideals and certain basic philosophical underpinnings. It is a sign of Nehru's stature and value that things like corruption never touched him or affected his reputation, although they did come close to some of his friends. If he had failures, then they were political failures, misjudgements. He did not understand the need for strong defence, did not understand the need for the evolution of defence as a basic reality of a modern state. He was perhaps surprised and defeated by time. His conviction that equality and shared space between potentially conflicting identities like Hindus and Muslims is the essence of the modern nation-state. This has been borne out. Today, the one thing that Indian Muslims do not want, and you can take any poll in this matter, is another partition. Irrespective of the problems that they might have, they know that unity is far preferable to disunity.

RJ: Do you think that politicians in India have failed in living upto the expectations of the people, leading to a gradual erosion of the institutional fabric?

MJA: I have a paradoxical view. I think problems actually strengthen the country. When the cloth is put to wear and tear, then only do you find out how strong it is. And if all the time it is going to be silk which you keep in the cupboard and only bring it out for the weddings then you never really know how strong the fabric might be.

RJ: I read one of your editorials in which you say that one of the problems of the Indian democracy is the institution itself. What do you mean by it? Of course, you were referring to the political problems and problems of communalism, terrorism ...

MJA: What I meant was institutions like the police and I was talking of the jam of justice in courts or bureaucracy, not of the democratic culture. A society and a nation will be judged by its ability to correct it. It will require reinventing itself without losing its basic core principles. I mean, I would not agree with anyone who would want to reinvent India as a dictatorship.

Competing Identities

RJ: Yes, of course ... but from the very beginning I would say that there was a conflict between different conceptions of nationalism in India. Conception of Hindu nationalism, a conception of Dalit nationalism, people like Ambedkar and others ...

MJA: Let's be very clear. Dalit nationalism basically constituted a liberation movement. It was a movement based on anger. It did not quite envisage in a realistic way a Dalit nation. It was using the dialectics of its time, many ideas were floated on Hindu nationalism, Muslim nationalism. The greater challenge to India came from united Muslim nationalism. But sixty years down the line you can see for yourself that those forces that sought to create a rift within the subcontinent have actually weakened. You must remember that India is secular not because only Muslims wanted it to be secular. India is secular because a majority of the Hindus also want it to be secular.

RJ: I understand that. But I don't know how much you agree with me that a process of Dalitization has not always accompanied the process of democratization in India if you can call it this.

MJA: Well, positive discrimination as a concept was first institutionalized in India. And it is something that the Americans learnt only after 1965 with the African Americans. We had it from 1947 or even earlier with Gandhi's Pune Pact with Ambedkar. I think we can see the significant change in the situation of Dalits now. I am not saying they are totally happy, but they are far better off.

RJ: For me, as a non-Indian, what has always been interesting is that this equality has been instituted at the level of the law but not at the level of the mentality of the people.

MJA: I agree, I often feel we need a new mindset on the understanding of basic issues. I often ask my brother Indian Muslims: when did you become a minority? It's a rhetorical question. Muslims have always been a demographic minority but then I ask were Muslims a minority under Mughal rule? And the answer has to be no. Minoritism is not a function of numbers, it is a function of empowerment. When I feel empowered, I do not see myself as a minority. So, in that sense, Dalits perhaps are the only minorities, as they have never been empowered before democracy. And the story even a hundred years ago was pathetic, appalling, and disgraceful. Nothing is as cruel as the treatment, which was meted out to the Dalits. It is a big stigma and a stain on Indian society. But the evolution is heartening. After all we are a nation, which is committed to peaceful change, we are not committed to violent change. And that is the great strength of democracy. I have always said that the difference between a dictatorship and a democracy is that in a dictatorship the government is stable but the society is unstable. In a democracy, the government is unstable but society is stable.

RJ: Well, you know, this reminds me of what Clement Attlee used to say ... he defined democracy as the government by discussion and certainly I believe, as somebody who loves India, that in India you have this discussion. But at some point I don't understand ...

especially at the level of communalism, which is a very important issue, this dialogue stops and violence takes its place, and for the past sixty years India has not been able to solve its communal problems. You know the Hindu-Muslim unity that Gandhi was talking about, as state as an ideal, has not been realized. When you have the Gujarat carnage, when you see the Varanasi bombing blasts …

MJA: Wait … the Varanasi blasts are not a result of Hindu-Muslim problems. They are the work of mischief-makers and terrorists. I know, I suffered Gujarat and I know the pain of Gujarat, but you must realize the number of times a Gujarat has not happened in our country despite provocations. The people have refused to be provoked. Even in Varanasi people have refused to be provoked. Gujarat also happened because the government was mischievous and the government was involved. I think the great strength of India lies in its ability to manage contradictions, slowly and over time, but I think, successfully.

RJ: Do you really think that India has achieved its security goals or terrorism remains one of its weaknesses?

MJA: Terrorism remains one of our weaknesses. No doubt about it. And as I said, it is easy to blame people outside. We have to also look at ourselves. Where we have gone wrong …

RJ: Is this related to corruption in politics?

MJA: There is a problem in the system. Yes … must be …

RJ: : So how is it possible to go beyond it?

MJA: Oh, very easily. Just because you have a few warts in your body, it does not make you a dead man. India has warts, problems; and India has ailments, but nation-building is a long process. We will find the strength within us to heal these problems. In the end real success will come with prosperity. Nothing sorts outs primal passions like a prosperous economic society.

RJ: My last question is related to your own work as a journalist. You have been one of the leading journalists in this country and have been fighting for civil liberties through your journalistic work. What role do you think has journalism played in the past sixty years in empowering the people of India or in confronting the evil of the dictatorship of the Indian state when it might have appeared like in the American state?

MJA: Oh, a very important one. Because, actually, journalism, that is media, is not just the weapon of last resource in our country. Sometimes, it is a weapon of the first resource in a democracy. The media's ability to keep a check on the political class and business class, makes the media loved and trusted by the people. I am quite sure that without free media Indian democracy would find it impossible to survive.

His Holiness, The Dalai Lama

Buddhism and India

RAMIN JAHANBEGLOO (RJ): Your Holiness, you turned seventy on 6 July 2005. Today, your fame and influence transcend far beyond some six million Tibetans. You have become a global conscience keeper. No previous Dalai Lama travelled as much as you did and found himself responsible for so many worldwide issues. May I ask Your Holiness, what is the secret of your vitality and how do you manage to take care of so many issues at the same time?

HIS HOLINESS, THE DALAI LAMA (HHDL): I think it has to do with my practice. You know, I think all major religions talk about the practice of love, forgiveness, tolerance, and such other things. So also in Buddhism, compassion becomes the foundation. Within Buddhism, you may have heard of the Pali tradition and Sanskrit tradition. In the Sanskrit tradition, the compassion is not just the feeling of the other, but there is some kind of pledge to dedicate oneself to the others. So a part of that practice is my whole being and it's not only just me but all our practitioners, whose existence is dedicated to the benefit of others not only in this life but also in the next life. That kind of determination and pledge is required in Tibetan Buddhism. Take the example of a Tibetan monk who is eighty-five years old. After 1959, he spent eighteen years in a Chinese *gulag* (prison). In the early 1980s, he came to Dharamsala because the

Chinese gave permission to some Tibetans to leave Tibet. In my talks with him, he told me that during the eighteen years in the Chinese gulag, he faced many dangers. I asked him about these dangers. He said that the worst of all dangers was the danger of losing compassion towards the Chinese. So that's why I think compassion is so important and if that compassion is damaged, mankind will be in danger. I may not be at the level of this Tibetan monk. I may be a person who loses his temper. But in whatever capacity and whatever level I am, I can and I must be of some benefit to others. I feel this is an opportunity for me as a Buddhist and as a Dalai Lama . . . Because I have the name of Dalai Lama and compared to these monks, I have a better opportunity to help others. So I utilize this opportunity. Once you have that kind of attitude in life, you get no feeling of tiredness. So that's the secret of my vitality.

RJ: It must be almost impossible for Your Holiness to pursue some of your interests and hobbies, such as manual work.

HHDL: I do not have enough time for these kinds of things. I also do not have much interest in manual work. Reading is my favourite hobby these days. Whenever I have time I read some of my classical books and also some new books. These are books which are mainly written in Tibetan.

Buddhism in the Contemporary World

RJ: How do you explain the increase in the popularity of Buddhism in the West and the East? Can we say that there is a revival of Buddhist thought in the world?

HHDL: I don't know if there really is what you call a 'revival' of Buddhism. I think with more information available now, more books available, and also because of an increase in tourism, information has become much easier to reach to all places and people also have access. But what is certain is that different individuals have different dispositions. So, to some people, Buddhism or ancient Indian thought is something new. Actually, sometimes out of curiosity and sometimes out of logic and common sense, the Buddhist way of approach to life appears to some as more suitable. I think that's why in different places, different people who traditionally had no connection with Buddhism, are now showing an interest in Buddhism because of the circumstances and the information available. And in the meantime, among the Tibetans, such as in the Buddhist community, because of more information, some are more critical about Buddhism now. Buddhism was at one point totally banned in communist China. But now, because there is more availability of information, there is more interest and more excitement for Tibetan Buddhism.

RJ: It seems to me that the teachings and sayings of your Holiness on non-violence and compassion have been very effective because most of them emphasize a peaceful dimension of religious thinking.

HHDL: I consider myself to be a follower or student of Mahatma Gandhi and an admirer of Mother Teresa. But there are a lot of differences between Mahatma Gandhi and myself. Mahatma Gandhi was a saint. I am a humble man. But, my approach on non-violence does not rely on teachings and relies on common sense. When I give some sort of talk about non-violence I never take a quotation from Buddha or from any other religious tradition, but just talk about common experiences. Violence means hurt. Peace means not just the mere absence of pain, but also a way to save and protect happiness. The goal is to protecting oneself from suffering and to promote a source of inner happiness. That's peace, either by using scientific findings or common experience. I am not talking about life after death or about God. In fact, Buddhists have no clear idea about God. From the viewpoint of a Christian or a Jew, I am a non-believer. But, communists consider me to be a believer. So I don't know, maybe I am somewhere in between. So that is why I sometimes describe Buddhism as a bridge. Buddhism also sometimes accepts higher values of meditation and prayers. And we are also connected with the believers. Although we have no concept of God, yet we have a concept of a higher being to whom we can pray and seek blessings. And to the radicals some people describe Buddhism as not a religion but as a science of mind. So Buddhism has also some connection with science …

RJ: So your Holiness, if you say that non-violence is common sense and if we agree that our world is a violent world, it means that our world has lost its common sense?

HHDL: Oh yes, I believe that our world has lost its common sense. Losing common sense is at two levels. At one level, you lose your common sense and then you go mad. But at the other level, for twenty hours a day, one acts like a very normal person, but only for few hours you feel hatred and during that time, that person's way of thinking is not using common sense. Because common sense is based on rational thinking, then when our mind is dominated by hatred, it cannot function properly. So during that period of time, that person becomes a mad person. This sort of madness is worse than normal madness. So here you compare the two mentalities. In one case, the person is going to become insane but he is not going to get involved in adverse things. But in the other case, when the person, due to the domination of hatred looses normal thinking, that is worse as he can create so many disasters. It's like a person who is always telling lies, then his or her lies are not dangerous as everyone knows that he is always telling lies. Nobody trusts him. Usually, if a very reliable and truthful person lies, then that lie is very dangerous. Similarly, a man who is mad twenty-four hours per day is not very dangerous. Usually, a very normal and very fit person who occasionally becomes mad, like some of our political leaders in the world today, are dangerous people.

RJ: How do you think that different religions could work together for the advancement of world peace?

HHDL: First, we need personal contact, which is very essential. We need to sit together and to know each other and exchange individual experiences. Then we can find similarities. For example, in my childhood in Lhasa in Tibet, some Muslims were living there, a small community of Muslims from India who lived there for at least four centuries. These Muslims had almost no record of quarrel and were very peaceful, and very gentle. So when we reflect on those Muslims, the Muslims now in India and also the Muslims in Ladakh, we can say that they are very gentle people. This is why, as a result of my personal contacts, I have some Muslim friends in India. Indian Muslims are more familiar with me, especially Ladakhi Muslims. Last year, for the first time, I had the opportunity to visit Jordan. I met some Muslim leaders, Muslim scholars, and Muslim students. They were very friendly. For me, as far as Muslim and Buddhist practices are concerned, the values of compassion, prayer, and devotion are all the same. Even among Christians, Muslims, and Jews, there is one God. Similarly, within Christians, there are Catholics and Protestants, as there are small differences among Muslims, like the Shia and Sunni. Similarly, among the Buddhists also there are differences. Among Tibetan Buddhists also there is the difference of at least different colour of hats. This is not an important element. But for ignorant and uneducated people, the colour of hats are very important. Similarly, the differences become important among Muslims, Christians, and Hindus. That's the source of trouble. And for Western media and some Western scholars, to their minds, a Muslim looks like a terrorist. So sometimes, the Western man gets the impression that there is a clash between Western civilization and the Muslim world. But in reality, there is no clash! I think when you say Western civilization, you mean more a modern civilization. More modernity means more technology. A modern society is also an industrialized society. Thus, another pattern of human society emerges. But Muslim countries have also gone that way, India also has gone that way. A Buddhist country like Thailand has also chosen the way of modernism. It is a lifestyle and not the basis on which you can make the distinction between the West and the non-West. But in today's world, where there is a different way of life, there is a different way of thinking. The distinction is between the modern and the non-modern, not between the Western civilization and the Muslim world. As far as religion is concerned, I think Islam is one of the major religions of the world, as are Christianity and Judaism. I always make that clear. Now, the concept of one truth and one religion at the individual level is very important. For example, I am a Buddhist, so Buddhism is the only religion, only truth and Buddhism is the best for me. But to my Christian friend I cannot say that Buddhism is the only truth or only religion. For my Christian friend, Christianity is the best and is the only truth and the only religion. But then, together, we have to accept two truths and two religions. At the community level, several truths and several religion must be accepted. If Muslims say to themselves that there is only one god, Allah, then it is all right, but if you say to the whole world that there is only one god called Allah, then the trouble starts. If I say to the whole world that Buddhism is the best, then the trouble starts. So that is unrealistic. Even Buddha never attempted to convert the whole world to Buddhism. Some Muslim leaders try to convert the whole world and some Christians also did that but they failed. So again here common sense is required. Even Jesus Christ said that my teachings should go as far as possible and that means he tried to convert the whole world to Christianity. But during the period when Jesus Christ was living, his world was limited to a small area. He appeared as realistic about his goals. Now, in today's world, that statement is unrealistic. So we have to use common sense. So there is no contradiction if we say that there are several truths and several religions instead of only one truth and one religion. I usually give the example of medicine. You cannot say one medicine is the best for all problems. A particular medicine is good or bad according to your illness. For headache, this medicine is best ... for joint pain, this medicine is best. So according to each patient and each disease you need a suitable medicine.

RJ: You often refer to yourself as a practitioner of the Nalanda school (the world-renowned Buddhist education centre of India, established around 200 BC), which is a tradition of wisdom. When you read and meditate on the Hinayana and the Mahayana traditions, do you feel a connection with a living tradition or with something that belongs to a past history?

HHDL. I think these traditions are very alive. All these Buddhist precepts are part of the same tradition that we call Hinayana. For example, when I go to Sri Lanka, or Thailand, or Burma, I see that the Buddhist practices are all the same, as far as monastic rules are concerned. There might be some minor differences, but the traditions are the same. For us Tibetans, the Hinayana teaching is also very important. This is what links us to our traditions. But one has also to speak of Buddhist Tantriyana practices that are well preserved among Tibetans. So when we talk about the Buddhist tradition, we are referring to something that does not belong to the past, but is very alive. I think this concerns not only the Tibetans but also Buddhism in China, Mongolia, Japan, Korea, and many other places. As a Tibetan Buddhist, I carry a life of monk. Therefore, I practice the Hinayana tradition and the Tantriyana, meaning the way of yogic methods. My main practice is what we call 'infinite altruism', which is the basis of peace and happiness. If you want altruism, you must control hate and you must practice patience. There is also the practice of compassion, which is a necessity, not a luxury. As I always say: ' If you want others to be happy, practise compassion. If you want to be happy, practice compassion.' These are part of my daily practice. As you see the Hinayana tradition is very much alive.

RJ: How do you define the word 'tradition' in all this? Do you consider that 'tradition' is something that has been handed down to us by previous generations?

HHDL: Certainly. I think tradition is something that has been handed to us by previous generations. It was in the seventh century AD that Buddhism began to flourish in Tibet. When Trison Detsan, son of Tride Zhotsan, came to power, he relied on Buddhism to fight ministers who rallied behind the Bon religion. As part of the effort, he invited the famous Indian monks Zhibatsho and

Padmasambhava to build the Samye Monastery in AD 799. Seven noble children were later tonsured in the monastery which became the first monastery in Tibetan Buddhist history to tonsure monks. The event was the beginning of the system of Tibetan Buddhism. Then, the eighth century onwards, great thinkers and philosophers came to Tibet from Nalanda University, which was a flourishing residential university with over 10,000 monks and 1,500 teachers. The great philosopher Shantarakshita travelled to Tibet at that time. However, many powerful people at the Tibetan court were opposed to Buddhism and they put pressure on the king to expel Shantarakshita. The king discussed the matter with Shantarakshita and they decided that it was better for him to go to Nepal for the time being. Meanwhile, Shantarakshita suggested to the king that Padmasambhava, a famous master of meditation should be invited from India. Padmasambhava was able to remove all opposition to Buddhism in Tibet. Shantarakshita continued to teach in Tibet until his death. From this date onwards, many Indian spiritual masters visited Tibet. The eleventh century saw a great increase in contact between Tibet and India and a corresponding growth in Buddhist activity in Tibet. The great Tibetan meditator and poet, Milarepa, belongs to the eleventh century. Buddhism continued to flourish in Tibet from the fourteenth century right through to the present century, but there was a decline of Buddhism in India in the fourteenth and fifteenth centuries. From the fifteenth century onwards, Tibetan Buddhists received no more teachings from Indians. They developed their own spiritual masters. There were more than 5000 monks in each of the monastic universities around Lhasa, Ganden, Drepung, and Sera, while there were at least 500 in each Tantriyana college. So, as you see, all my knowledge and all my practices come directly from my past teachers and masters.

RJ: Lord Buddha tells us: 'Do not believe in anything simply because you have heard it. Do not believe in anything simply because it is spoken and rumoured by many. Do not believe in anything simply because it is found written in your religious books. Do not believe in anything merely on the authority of your teachers and elders. Do not believe in traditions because they have been handed down for many generations. But after observation and analysis, when you find that anything agrees with reason and is conducive to the good and benefit of one and all, then accept it and live up to it.'

Could one say that Buddhism is a tradition which renews and revitalizes itself in each generation?

HHDL: Yes, but Lord Buddha also said: 'Just as a goldsmith would test his gold by burning, cutting, and rubbing it, so you must examine my words and accept them, but not merely out of reverence for me.' So what the Lord is teaching us is to analyse and investigate the concepts. This is the essence. But since every person reads and interprets Lord Buddha, there must be some element of renewing. This is necessary. But we need an essence, an ultimate element for renewal in every tradition. One must be clear and should not create confusion between the essence and its renewal, between the gold and the work of the goldsmith. I think, Lord Buddha made it very clear that his followers should follow his teachings relying on their own experiments. A Buddhist should not follow the precepts with blind faith. That does not mean that besides the teachings of Buddha the followers should not investigate and find new things. That is to say, I think Buddhism has three parts. First part is the Buddhist science which deals with what is called 'Reality'. Second part is the Buddhist philosophy which includes the possibility of salvation and Buddhahood. It deals with one's salvation on the basis of this Reality. There is a possibility if you change your mind and your way of life. Buddhism shows us that it is possible to change our mind and our emotion if we make an effort. The third part is spirituality and practices that it includes. These are the bases of Buddhist philosophy which cannot be renewed. The Buddha himself created a basic concept that we do not need to reinterpret. But the most important among all concerns are our emotions and our state of mind. I think our mind works today in the same way as it worked for Indians 2,500 years ago. Nothing has changed. Our human emotions are exactly the same.

So I think in the next 7,000 years, our emotions will probably remain the same way. Maybe our emotions will change after one million years. That I do not know. If our whole brain structure changes, maybe our emotions will also change. So even at this level, there is no need for reinterpretation or renewal of customs and approaches.

RJ: Do you see any common ground between Buddhism and modern science?

HHDL: I think quantum physics reconfirms the Buddhist explanation about Reality, but we cannot say the same thing about modern geography. Some of the Buddhist texts which had an erroneous vision of world's geography have been rejected and have been replaced by a new geographical approach.

RJ: If a Buddhist wants to understand the modern world, would you advice him to do it through reason and logic or through faith?

HHDL: Of course, through reason. But let me add here that I think Buddhism like any other religion is concerned with our mental attitude. It is concerned with spirituality. Of course, some Buddhist scriptures talk about science, but they don't talk about the technique of building a house or a factory. We have to rely for that on the science of our time.

RJ: Buddhism is becoming popular in Western countries today. Is it because unlike many other religious traditions, Buddhism can easily enter a dialogue with the modern world, while following the line of its own tradition?

HHDL: I have always respected different religious traditions because they served millions of people in the past and they continue to do so in the present. These religions provide hope to millions of people around the world. They provide them spirituality and a meaning of life. Of course, to understand these religions you need to carry their teachings properly. So for me it is not a question of whether a religious philosophy is right or wrong. Buddha himself knew that his followers were very different and they had different dispositions. So he deliberately presented them with different philosophies that were contradictory. I often tell people that Buddha produced contradictions not because he was confused and not because he wanted to create confusion among his followers. His main motivation was that different philosophies were more suitable for different people. It is a fact that among human beings there are different mental dispositions, different cultures, and different climates. Therefore, there are differences among human beings. Take for example the case of India, where in a period of 3,000 years there were so many different teachers with new teachings. I think the local condition was different at each of these periods. The same thing happened in the Middle East where you had three different religions, Judaism, Christianity, and Islam, with three different holy texts—the Old Testament, the New Testament, and the Koran. They all happened in the same region of the world but in different times. So new teachings are necessary because local conditions are different. To some people, new teachings are more useful than the old ones. I appreciate, respect, and admire all different teachings. But I also have some reservations concerning theistic religions. It is a little embarrassing for me to say this to a Muslim. But I think for theistic religions, the main question is the Creator or what we call God. For this way of thinking, there is a system in the universe, which has been planned very carefully. So there should have been some force to plan it. Therefore, one needs to believe that there must be a Creator who planned all this. This is what the three theistic religions say and we have no right to question it. At this level, a great deal of faith without reason is involved. In the Buddhist case, we can say that Buddha himself started something remarkable, although in the eyes of those who argued with him, he was a simple human being like any other person. But at the same time, we have stories on Buddha's miracles. But I think that Buddha was a charismatic person more than anything else. Saying this, I think that the faith could evolve. When a master speaks, the disciples follow, but after several generations, more reasoning is needed, because we cannot survive with only faith. Let us take the example of Nagarjuna who came 400 years after Buddha and he is often referred to as 'the second Buddha' by East Asian Mahayana traditions of Buddhism. Nagarjuna put a lot of emphasis on reasoning. I think that it was through Nagarjuna's philosophical efforts that Buddha's teaching were proved by way of reason. Once you use reason in religious thinking then you can talk of logic and epistemology. It was after Nagarjuna that the use of reason in Buddhist philosophy became more popular.

RJ: Many people say that Buddhism is not only a religious tradition but also modern thinking. Can Buddhism be a mediator between the world of traditions and the world of modernity?

HHDL: Now generally speaking, a modern person is a person who investigates and experiments and is not satisfied with the spiritual message of theistic religions. Let me give you the example of a scientist whom I met in the US. In the beginning of our meetings she told me that she refused to see any common grounds between Buddhism and modern science. She had a very negative attitude. Then our discussion started and we didn't talk about God or soul. We talked about particles and emotions. As we were progressing in the dialogue the American scientist was becoming more and more enthusiastic. At the end of our discussion she accepted that there could be a common ground between Buddhism and modern science. Maybe it had to do with the fact that Buddhism does not have the concept of soul and God as in the theistic religions. That is to say, some modern people who believe in reason want also to rely on faith. This includes some modern scientists who get some benefit from the Buddhist explanations about the mind or about the emotions. More and more scientists begin to realize that emotions are very important for our health. When Buddhism talks about emotions, it is not considered with salvation and life after death, but with having a better health, a happier family, and a happier society. Nowadays, Westerners show interest in Buddhist explanations of life not only because they are said by Buddhists, but because they are scientific. Of course, I think there are two types of westerners who are interested in Buddhism. The first category are people who are not serious and who follow the fashion. Today they are interested with Buddhism; tomorrow they are interested with Hinduism and the day after, they become Sufis. The second category concerns people, who are more critical and more cautious in the beginning, but they study Buddhism more deeply and they find some substance in their experience of Buddhism. These people show a genuine interest in Buddhism. I think the interest comes also from the fact that Buddhism is an open-minded religion because it does not believe in the concept of a central authority. Even Jainism believes in the concept of *atma* (soul), though Jains have no concept of a God as a Creator.

I just like to add that I think all religions without exception talk about love, compassion, and self-discipline. So you find a lot of similarities among religions. But since there have been many wars in human history in the name of religion, some people think that religion and compassion are two different things. Because of the religious wars in history, many people have told me that it is better to have one universal religion instead of having many different religions. I think such an opinion is due to a lack of knowledge concerning different traditions of thought and positive values like tolerance and compassion that they have perpetrated. I have a Muslim friend who believes in Allah and who says that because he believes in God, he loves not only other human beings, but also other creatures because God created them all. The Buddhist concept of love is the same. You find the same concept in Christianity and in Judaism. What makes problem in the minds of modern people is the memory of religious wars and violence that happened in the West. But fortunately, Buddhism was quite far from the West.

RJ: Maybe this is why Buddhism has become a non-violent alternative to the violent world of the West?

HHDL: It is because technology, capitalism, and imperialism were all produced in the West. When you look at the nineteenth and twentieth centuries, you see that all the European imperialistic powers like England, Germany, or France considered themselves as the centre of the world. The Chinese believed the same and continue to believe that they are the centre of the world. Maybe the Persians believe the same thing? Tibet had a chance of being far from the world. But anyhow, the West considered itself, for a long time, to be the centre of the world and as I said previously, there were many wars in the West in the name of religion. Buddhism escaped from these religious wars. So today, Buddha and Buddhism have become symbols of non-violence and peace.

RJ: As you said, Buddhism is very tolerant and not concerned with religious violence, that is why there have never been any wars fought in the name of Buddhism. Does this mean that Buddhism can never be a fundamentalist religion?

HHDL: Even among Buddhists you can find fundamentalists. But the world didn't notice these fundamentalists. I think we can say that in AD seventh century, some kind of violence in the name of religion happened among the Buddhists. But the outside world doesn't know about it. Of course, if we look comparatively, Buddhists have been more tolerant than other faiths. Let me give you an example. In the last 400 years, Muslims have come to Lhasa and settled there. They always had very good relations with the local people. The fifth Dalai Lama gave them land to build their mosque. So, generally speaking, the Buddhist community, in comparison to other religious communities, accepts foreigners more easily. Few years ago I heard that a Tibetan monk had settled in Kazakhstan and had organized a small community of Buddhists. But more recently, I heard that the Kazakh authorities closed the temple. So maybe one can say that the Buddhists have been more open towards other religions. This is also true about Hindus who are generally more open to other religions. I think, when you compare the Hindus and the Christians in history, you can say that

Hindus have been more open to other religions, although in the past, Hindus destroyed and killed Buddhists.

RJ: You have consistently espoused and preached non-violence and dialogue as a constructive alternative to violence in our world. However, the power of hatred and greed seems to have grown stronger in the twenty-first century. Is the renunciation of violence and harmony among religions, what Gandhi believed in, sustainable in the face of the radical terrorist challenge that we see in the world today?

HHDL: Oh yes. I think there are two types of terrorists. The first category concerns non-religious terrorists. These are politically-oriented terrorists. Even if there is good harmony among religious traditions, these terrorists will continue killing people for political reasons. The second category concerns those who kill innocent people in the name of religion. Take the example of Iraq. In the beginning, you had political violence that created too much emotion, which is now turning into religious terrorism among the Shias and the Sunnis. This second category of terrorism is due to fundamentalism and narrow-mindedness. This category can certainly be changed and stopped by the harmony and dialogue among religions.

RJ: Should we look for new ethical foundations for political power in our world?

HHDL: I truly believe that we need a new ethical foundation for our world. That is why I have been putting a great deal of effort in introducing the concept of 'secular ethics' which embrace the principles we share as human beings: compassion, tolerance, consideration of others, the responsible use of knowledge and power. These principles transcend the barriers between religious believers and non-believers; they belong not to one faith, but to all faiths. Compassion and affection are human values independent of religion. There is no relationship between these concepts and any particular religion. Even without religion, even as non-believers, we have the capacity to promote these things. Secular ethics is based on our common sense and our common experience. This is why I call it 'secular', because it is the promotion of ethical values through a non-religious way. I think that this is what our world really needs today.

RJ: Therefore, our world needs more compassion to become a better place?

HHDL: Undoubtedly. We need to practice compassion through awareness. In this reality, the two concepts of 'we' and 'they' no longer exist. The whole world is just we. So therefore, the destruction of another person is essentially the destruction of oneself. This is why the concept of war is now questionable.

Peter de Souza

Christians in India

RAMIN JAHANBEGLOO (RJ): Christianity is India's third largest religion, following Hinduism and Islam. It is believed that there have been Christians in India for almost as long as the religion has existed. Christians in India find their origin/roots back in Kerala when St Thomas landed in Malabar in AD 52. The Christian church uses the St Thomas legend to claim a first century origin for Christianity in India. It also claims St Thomas to be a martyr at the hands of a wicked Hindu priest and king. Better still, Christianity becomes the 'original' Indian religion, as it would be older than many of the sectarian Hindu cults practised in the country today. But the establishment of the Christian church in India was an intrinsic part of the European colonial enterprise. Some historians believe that the story of St Thomas, an apostle of Christ, coming to India and establishing an Indian church is a convenient fiction because the story gave Christians a caste status that was important in integrating them into Hindu society.

PETER de SOUZA (PdS): To understand Christianity in India you have to understand it historically in terms of waves. The early Christianity that came to Kerala—there may be some controversy regarding the exact century in which they came—got integrated into Kerala society and became a constitutive element of the society.

It developed a cultural form and evolved along with the evolution of other cultural groups of Kerala. It had a similar evolutionary path, as I suppose, of Hinduism or Islam in Kerala. In that sense it is very organic and rooted in the long centuries of Kerala history. The second wave then comes with the colonial period, particularly with the arrival of the Portuguese, the early phase of colonialism. We are talking about the sixteenth century here when Europe itself was undergoing convulsions in religion. This was a Europe that had not seen the Industrial Revolution or the French Revolution, and so the great ideas of Europe, the democratic revolution of 1648, the French Revolution, and the right of man had not taken place. What were taking place in Europe were convulsions and these convulsions had to do with the Inquisition that took place in Europe and that took place in India too. So I think the second phase of Christianity is very much linked to the colonial enterprise and the inter-linkage of the church with the colonial state. In this enterprise India was an important staging post in Asia for the spread of Christianity. The third wave starts with the arrival of the many evangelical churches with many denominations and sects and all these together make up Christianity in India. Christianity's presence in India is linked to different historical periods during which it has become an important and progressive force in India.

RJ: The Indian debate on religious conversion has been an ongoing one for a few centuries now. However, the mutual understanding between the advocates and the adversaries of conversion has not advanced much. Religious conversion has become the subject of passionate debate in contemporary India. One of the early twentieth century debates on conversion took place when *The Hindu* interviewed Mahatma Gandhi in 1931 about the role of foreign missionaries in independent India of the future. He said he would ask them to withdraw if they engaged in proselytizing by means of medical aid and education. His arguments were clear: 'Every nation's religion is as good as any other. Certainly India's religions are adequate for her people. We need no converting spiritually.' Where does Indian society stand today in relation to Christian missionaries?

PDS: The conversion debate puzzles me. If there is a large opposition to conversions in India, and in the public domain most people, by and large, are opposed to conversion, it puzzles me at many levels. At one level, one finds a very fascinating debate in the Constituent Assembly on the freedom of religion where the words 'profess' and 'propagate' are deliberately chosen to safeguard this freedom. In fact, on the word 'propagate', the debates were clear that propagation is a part of practice. So at one level you see a liberal concession to the forms of religion, which require the believer to propagate. This is a great protection of the Constitution. The other thing that puzzles me is that I can't see what does 'propagate' entail? Does it represent a stage before conversion or does it necessarily lead to conversion. If one can change one's belief about everything else, then why should one be so obsessed with the changing of beliefs in the domain of religion? Indian society is very open to the change of beliefs in the field of economy, fashion, politics, and everything else. They are happy to borrow thought frameworks and everything else from music to the economic policy, but in the realm of religion, they create a wall. I don't see why people should not be encouraged to become atheists or whatever they want to become. Why should the state enact laws to decide whether the acts of conversion are free or coerced? Laws against conversion should be enough instead of having anti-conversion laws.

RJ: From the study of the Christian minority in India over the past sixty years, one can discern two trends. On the one hand, a section of Indian Christians had striven successfully to identify their community with the nationalist cause. On the other hand, confronted with the social and political changes that followed independence, the Indian Christians extended and intensified their efforts to establish an indigenous basis for the Christian church, both in organization and in cultural expression.

PDS: Indian Christianity is very diverse, within which there are many churches. Some churches have worked really hard to develop symbolic forms, which can be recognized as part of the Indian civilizational domain. I don't know if we can talk about it, since I don't know the indigenous form in India. I would be a bit uncomfortable with such language of indigenity since in India names, habits, dress, and rituals are so varied that anything becomes very fast indigenous to India. So, to refer to some authentic indigenity I find very unacceptable. The Christian community in India is both more cosmopolitan and equally indigenous.

RJ: How is it that the Indian Christians were the first minority in India from whose ranks emerged the earliest political leadership of the depressed classes? Was it a way for the Indian Christians to follow the task undertaken by Christian missionaries?

Pds: I think the Christian church, by which I mean the Catholic churches, whom I know best, has always had this internal tension, and in recent times, between liberation theology and conservative theology. Service has been an important part of the school's activities in India, especially in the realm of health and education. In both of these areas, the church has introduced the best institutions right across the country. You must remember that these are areas of considerable neglect in this country. So these institutions, over the last hundred years, have gained a sort of respectability. You can see this in the idea of 'convent education' that in the popular language is short form for a good education. Having established these good institutions, I think the traditional churches have always had to take a stand on internal tensions, such as the fact that since we have good institutions and these good institutions draw the élite, is our mandate to serve the élite or the subaltern? The Dalits and the adivasis are seen as the main subalterns. I think it is similar to the debates in medieval Italy between the Franciscans and the Papacy. Which is the true work of the church?

RJ: The Christian church in India is still an eighteenth century colonial church financed from abroad. Some of the other Christian churches have a sophisticated international support system in place and this is especially true of the newer American evangelical churches. Has this process created communal problems among the Christians and the Hindus?

PdS: I think here again one need to segregate between the older and the newer churches. The older churches did receive some funding from abroad but they have fairly established institutions in the country also which are self-sufficient. Of course they receive money from abroad but so do other religious groups. I think the question buys into the terms of the communal discourse and is, in a sense, somewhat slanted.

RJ: In the recent past, Christians have made much headway in converting large numbers of Hindus. Is it because India is the only major country where missionaries can freely practice their evangelism? Or is it also because missionaries wish to use India as their foothold and home base to expand elsewhere in Asia?

PdS: The way you have framed the question, I think, determines the answer. I think many of the people who are working among the poor, particularly among the Dalits and the adivasis, do it in the spirit of service and not to convert. In a sense, they are doing things, which the state should be doing and the civil society in India should be doing and they don't, particularly looking after the marginal groups of the society who at least are getting some solace from the missionaries and the charities. The state doesn't come in the picture at all and so I have great respect for those working in extremely difficult situations. Whether this is a part of the larger strategy to get a foothold in Asia or not, I think is a bogus question. Statistically, the Christian population has not increased tremendously over the years, in fact, it has decreased. We need to get our statistics right. I think that there is so much service work that still needs to be done. I don't think that conversion is really a serious issue.

RJ: If conversion is not the question, then why is it that violence against the Christians is based around conversion? I have been reading and found so many isolated cases of violent responses from local communities to the Christians. The veracity of the tales of Christian persecution in India have become a cause of dispute among different Christian churches in India. There has been resistance in several parts of India against the aggressive conversion drive of evangelical groups and the Catholic Church. There are also isolated cases of violent response from local communities against the Christian groups. According to some reports, 136 people in Orissa re-joined Hinduism in what nationalist Hindu groups describe as a 'home-coming' ceremony. In Rajasthan, Christians were beaten because of their faith in Christ. Are Christians still persecuted by the Hindu community in India?

PdS: I think that the episode you are talking about opens a debate about a certain understanding of religious mobilization that is used by particular groups. I don't think we can talk of Hindus as if they are undifferentiated socio-demographic group. There are certain sections among Hindus, only sections, who have used this politics of mobilization. The politics of mobilization requires you to accept the other and the other must be portrayed as an enemy. I think that the Rajasthan episode that you talked about was about groups of Christians who were worshipping and a rumour was spread that they were converting and that is why their place of worship was vandalized. Take the case of this Australian missionary who was working with leprosy patients. He and his two sons were burnt in a jeep. It is the hate that this politics of mobilization produces that is what we should be concerned about. Most Indians and most Hindus abhor this politics of hate. On religion, India is a more accommodating country then either the Islamic world or the Christian world.

RJ: It is difficult to obtain an accurate estimate of the total number of Christians in all of India today. Government, church, and the media estimates that we have seen vary from 1.8 per cent to a high of 4 per cent. The total number of Christians in India according to the 2001 census was 24.08 million or 2.3 per cent of the population. Catholic Church leaders are alarmed and practically resigned to what they see as the inevitable near disappearance of their congregation in India as a result of this demographic trend. It is a fact that the percentage of Christians in India's population has actually come down since independence. If this trend continues, fifty years from now, the percentage of Christians in India's population will be under 3 per cent. What are the main reasons of this decrease?

PdS: I think the decrease is mainly because of economic prosperity. By and large, the Christian communities have access to education and because of that, it has access to all the things that education provides and one of it is small families and so in a sense, it is following a demographic trajectory of other regions of the world where there are people who get education and get into the work force and marry late and have small families. Second, there is out migration. Large numbers of Christians from India have resettled in different places right across the world. I think we also have to see what happens when people enter the middle class and become professionals, they seek their future lives elsewhere. The consequence of this demographic decline is the fact that many of these good institutions will not have people to run them and I think that would be a loss. Institutions were set up in remote regions such as in areas of rural Bihar, Madhya Pradesh, and Jharkhand. Who is going to run these schools? Also the strength of India lies in its multicultural dynamics and in that sense a robust Christian presence in India is good and the greatness about India is that communities have lived fairly comfortably here together. By and large, the religious groups have found mobility, acceptance, and a space for diversity. Sometimes, when one reads the history of Europe one is very disturbed by the slave trade on which the entire European development was based and now forgotten. We have oppressed groups in India but religious minorities have not faced that kind of thing.

RJ: For the most part, Muslims and Christians form the same vote bank in the left of centre arena of politics, typically at odds with

Hindus. However, in troubled areas of India, Muslims and Christians have come into conflict with each other. What are the main reasons of such a conflict between the Muslims and the Christians? Is this political, or religious, or ideological? Have you heard about any such case?

PDS: I think the disturbances occur in areas where the Christians are in large populations, like Kerala, parts of Tamil Nadu, and so I think it has to do with demography. Where there are large Muslim or Christian groups, the tensions might arise. It won't arise in northern India where the Christian population is so small that there is no conflict. The other thing is that there is no inter-faith mechanism of communication and that is something, which is not developed in this country.

RJ: Vivekananda entertained a vision of India having a Vedantic brain, an Islamic body, and a Christian heart. Do you think India today has a Christian heart?

PDS: I think that if there is something like Christian heart then we would like to have it. I think the idea of fraternity, brotherhood, and sisterhood is there in Christianity. The world is moving away from these sensibilities and that's the cause for some degree of gloom actually. I think that globalization in a sense is making us uni-dimensional. Its quite alarming that we are worshipping the material so much that the qualities of the heart need to be restored.

RJ: Could we say that the Christian minorities in India, because of their Christian religion, faith and background had this aspiration for globalization and democracy?

PDS: I think intuitively you are right because Christianity in terms of treatment is more egalitarian (an egalitarianism of persons and not of results). So I think that people do not necessarily distinguish on the basis of birth. I am not saying that caste is not there on the Indian scene but I think that it is less so. This is a connection between urban Christianity, particularly metropolitan Christianity like in Mumbai, Kolkata, and Delhi. I think that because it is more egalitarian, it is also more emancipatory for oppressed castes of India. That is why you are seeing a lot of militancy within the Christian community in southern India. They are in a sense challenging decades of oppression. A lot of human rights groups have a strong Christian presence. I would like to add that if one is looking at sixty years of Indian independence, independent India must acknowledge its multiple, colonial experiences. I think this is important for us to see this not just as a painful part of our history but also as a potential resource for our history because I think that multiple postcolonial pathways give us resources which can strengthen our plurality and make us a more dynamic and outward-looking society. The region I come from, Goa, has that potentiality. It should not be seen as some small exotic aberration on the cultural face of India, an aberration on the cultural map, but as one of the positive attributes of the cultural map. If India can make this transition I think that will be great. That's the challenge for contemporary India.

T.R. Andhyarujina

Role of Parsis in Modern India

RAMIN JAHANBEGLOO (RJ): If we were to name one minority community that has enriched India educationally, industrially, economically, and culturally, it is the Parsi community or Zoroastrians. Through hard work and social commitment, they founded business empires, colleges, hospitals, and research institutes, and in the process, a very vibrant business culture in Mumbai. Parsis also established the first cotton mills in India, the first newspaper, and the first Indian-owned bank. Parsis have not only produced entrepreneurs and businessmen, but also artists. This small but talented community has produced composers like Zubin Mehta, novelists like Rohiton Mistry, and the late rock star, Freddie Mercury, the former front man of the band Queen. How do you explain the multiple successes of such a small community inside and outside India?

T.R. ANDHYARUJINA (TRA): Well, you have taken the names of certain eminent personalities from the community and because the community is small, it appears that the community is very talented. I am sure that there are talented people in other communities as well. However, the tiniest community, which would otherwise be regarded as of no consequence, has still maintained its eminence for over two centuries partly because they have been leaders in certain fields that might be a matter of historical accidents and it is to be seen how much of that prominence is still maintained in the future. One thing is that the initiative of the Parsi community is not equalled by the initiative of other communities. Also the diminishing number is in itself a problem. The example of Tatas is the one that shows how Parsis have come to eminence. Jamshedji Tata conceived the first cotton mill in India and then he conceived the first hydrocarbon project, which is unique throughout the world. He established the steel and iron mill which defied every doubt of the Britishers and has still maintained the tradition of a high degree of integrity.

Since Parsis had the advantage of education and the English language, they were found in liberal professions as doctors, lawyers, and engineers, etc. Most importantly, the attitude of the community towards the rest of the Indians was very adaptive. There is a famous story that when the Parsis first landed in Gujarat, the ruler of Gujarat asked what guarantee the Zoroastrians could give of their behaviour and the leader of the Parsis brought a cup of milk and added sugar into it and said that as the sugar has mixed into the milk, so will they assimilate and sweeten the Indian community. So also they adapted to the British and then to the Indian ethos after independence, and that way they are a very remarkable community. Sometimes people compare the Parsis with the Jews but I think that is a very wrong comparison. The Jews are known for their parsimony, Parsis are known for their benevolence and the institutions of charity that they have established throughout India. One of the remarkable aspects of the Parsis was that they always spoke the truth and that is considered to be one of the greatest tenets of the Zoroastrian community even today. Next to speaking truth is the principle of not borrowing money. It seems to be a matter of history rather than any myth and these qualities have endeared themselves to the rest of the Indian community. Parsis are not very obtrusive. They are perhaps known more by their idiosyncrasies today than by their talents. They are known for their humour, as they are able to laugh at their own foibles and accept criticism, which other people have made and in that sense this community is very prominent in India.

RJ: Parsis had deep ties with the colonial rulers and they fell under the sway of European manners and morals. They were actually the first Indians to be knighted by the British crown, and it was a Parsi, Dadabhoy Naoroji, who was the first Indian to serve as a member of the British Parliament. Have the Parsis been criticized in the past for their close relations with the British rulers?

TRA: They have not been criticized in any derogatory sense. Naoroji was the first Indian to give the call for *swaraj*. He was the president of Indian National Congress a couple of times. There were other leaders from the Parsi community like Mr Mehta who was called the lion of Bombay and Dinshah Badshah. Besides the first lady to unfurl the Indian flag abroad was a Parsi lady, Bhikaji Cama. So there has been a very remarkable nationalistic streak among the Parsis and so apart from the fact that they took advantage of the British rule as they had adapted themselves to the British rule, it was never to the degree of being anti-national or being totally subservient to the British.

RJ: Is there also a self-criticism among the Parsis for their colonial complicity? How do Parsis seek to cope with their declining cultural authority, taking responsibility of their own demise?

TRA: I think that 'colonial complicity' is a wrong expression to be used. There was never a colonial complicity to the extent of the betrayal of Indian interests to British interests as I have already mentioned that there were several freedom fighters from the community. There was a tendency among certain Parsi families to be a bit imitative of British ways and a bit phony about the British monarchy and perhaps that gave the impression that the community identified with the British people and their ways but that was never the case and no body ever said that the Parsis were betraying Indian national interests. On the contrary, prominent industrialists like Jamshedji Tata were true nationalists. So the word 'complicity' is wrong to be used and it should be 'ideological tendencies', which were never very strong.

RJ: In her book, *The Good Parsi*, Tanya Luhrmann traces shifts in Parsi identity—from self-confidence to self-denigration that mark the community's transition from the colonial to the postcolonial era. Luhrmann argues that Parsi self-criticism is less a reflection of actual community decline than the discursive inversion of symbols associated with a more glorious past. According to her, Mumbai Parsis obscure the reality of a changing national landscape with fantasies of community decline because they are unable to alter the fact of a postcolonial India in which the Parsi community is little more than a cultural anachronism.

TRA: There is a certain amount of despondency among a small section of the community but it is never to the extent of denigrating the community. One can't expect the community as a whole to do as well as it did centuries ago. I don't think that the author is justified in saying that there is lack of confidence among the community. Sometimes there is a feeling that the community is wasting too much of time in trifles such as the orthodoxy proposing inter-marriage or the orthodoxy opposed to any changes in the religious practices such as the disposal of dead and concentration on such matters seems to be totally unproductive. At the same time, the small community still hold its eminence in industries, professions and services. There are Supreme Court judges who are Parsis. The most prominent doctors in Mumbai are still from this community. The community has done a lot of introspection and the community also denigrates itself in the sense of emphasizing eccentrics, but that is not something that could be considered as a reflection on the community.

RJ: Sixty years after independence, Parsis have nothing to fear but themselves. They are the only community in fertile India that has a diminishing birthrate. Indian Census data for 2001 records 69,601 Parsis in India, with a concentration in and around the city of Mumbai. A recent demographic study predicts that by 2021, when the population of India will be 1.2 billion, the number of Parsis will drop from their current level of 69,601 to just 21,000.

This means that the Parsi community is facing the threat of extinction—for reasons that are linked to the belief structure of their clergy. For most communities, the prospect of extinction would unite members, but it has divided the Parsis. In Mumbai, the gulf between those who refuse to question orthodox Zoroastrianism and those clamouring for reform is breaking apart a once close-knit community. Do you think the Parsis would accept to change their traditions in order to survive demographically?

TRA: This will happen and Parsis will change their orthodoxy but it will not come from any community leadership. The forces of demography and necessity would inevitably make the community change. The community, in fact, is adapting itself. There is a large number of inter-community marriages and there is a strong movement to bring into the fold children from the marriages of Zoroastrians with non-Zoroastrians. There are far more liberal views on these matters outside Mumbai. One may not get any centralized leadership for this, as the orthodoxy is strong but among the young people, the liberal attitude is perforce brought in to bring in changes.

RJ: Many analysts of the Parsi community in India accept that the new Parsi orthodoxy is the result of the inherent instability of a diasporic community. It is interesting to see that the new Parsi orthodoxy does not promise salvation, redemption, and return to the past. Nor does it imitate the religious fundamentalism of Christianity and Islam. The goals of the Parsi orthodoxy are the direct result of the risk of diaspora. That is why the aim of orthodox Parsis is mainly to persuade Parsis to marry within the community. What are the main factors which have contributed to the rise of a new orthodoxy among the Parsi community in India?

TRA: The Parsis tend to exaggerate the forces of orthodoxy in two ways. One is that there is a controlling body for fund and property control of the Parsis called the Parsi Panchayat and the trustees are in charge of that. The trustees being invisible leaders tend to be conservative as they are elected from the mass of the preponderant orthodox section and thus seem to be giving directions for anti-change, whereas the rest of the community prefers to be quite inert. It is not uncommon for any community to have fundamentalists but it is not the same degree of fundamentalism, which you expect from other countries. The Zoroastrians, when they migrate to other countries, tend to keep their ethnicity but inevitably, the second generation finds it difficult to keep themselves within the strict tenets of Zoroastrianism. The liberal tendencies are more visible in the Zoroastrian communities residing abroad. The Zoroastrians in Iran are far more liberal than the orthodoxy in Mumbai. They don't believe in ritualism, which the conservative Parsis in India do and are far more tolerant towards the non-Zoroastrians. Their places of worship are in a very skilful way open to the non-Zoroastrians also. By abroad, I not only mean people who have migrated to other countries but also those who are outside Mumbai as the control of Parsi Panchayat is not that strong out there.

RJ: Since independence in 1947, many younger Parsis have emigrated from India, thus strengthening the sense of crisis in the Parsi community. In recent years, many Zoroastrians have emigrated to the US, Canada, Britain, Australia, and other countries. What are the links between the Parsi community in India and the Parsi diaspora?

TRA: The communities who have settled abroad in Australia, Canada, Britain, and the US somehow look back to their roots, particularly the first generation. These people try to make the point that the Zoroastrian religion is very liberal and at the same time try to maintain their link with the motherland. They have representative associations in the US, Canada, Britain, and Australia which tend to look back to the mother country and even in small places they tend to congregate on important days. There are occasional contributions from the Parsi community abroad to Indian institutions.

RJ: In most Bollywood movies Parsis are shown as absent-minded, lost people who speak Hindi with an accent and provide entertainment to the audiences. Parsis are also shown riding a vintage car with their sizeable family; the vehicle breaks down in the middle of the road, leading to verbal duels with other commuters and the films end up depicting all Parsis as an odd and peculiar community. Do you think Indians in general have a correct perception of the Parsi community or do they lack knowledge about the cultural particularities of the Parsis?

TRA: There is a popular conception in the movies where Parsis are depicted as long nosed individuals wearing funny caps and at times talking nonsense. This is something that people will also say of another minority such as the Sikhs. Nobody takes that as a serious representation of the community and whosoever does that is also aware of the tremendous contributions of the Parsi community, and the fact that despite their small numbers, the community has produced eminent personalities.

Mushirul Hasan

Challenges to Islam in India

RAMIN JAHANBEGLOO (RJ): The history of Islam in India is well over a thousand years old today. It has blended beautifully into the background of its adopted land and contributed immensely to the formation of a composite Indian culture and the building of the Indian nation. But this Islam and its practitioners are not a homogeneous entity as is widely believed. In fact, there is a great deal of diversity in the manner in which Islam is practised and perceived throughout India. Muslims in India have responded well to the challenges of living as a minority in a religiously plural society. But this process of assimilation into the Indian society has not been an easy one and the challenges that Muslims of India face today continue to exist with the constantly shifting national and international state of affairs.

MUSHIRUL HASAN (MH): I think the second part of the question is more important. Despite the partition of the country and the problems it gave rise to, it was a testing time for the forty to forty-five million Muslims who stayed back in India and it is quite right that they responded quite bravely and resolutely to that challenge. Yet it must be said that there were problems then and there are problems now. The Muslim population, which now stands at about 140 million, close to about 13–14 per cent of the population, the second largest population, has not yet acquired the religious, social, and economic profile. The community still survives on the margins of mainstream Indian life. And so there is all the talk going on about the poor representation of Muslims in the governments, poor representation of Muslims in the professions, and so on.

RJ: Muslims constitute today nearly 10 per cent of the population of India. They are spread all over the country, forming significant minorities in all states except Kashmir, where they are in a majority and Punjab, from where they were expelled after the partition. However, Muslims across India are economically and educationally backward, compared to other sections of the community and they are severely under-represented in government employment. There is no state in India where the representation of Muslims matches their population share. Muslims, in the words of one analyst, 'suffer double discrimination, by virtue of being Muslim and poor'. What are the historical and political reasons of such discriminations in India?

MH: The experience of discrimination is there and there is no question about that so that if you look back at the past sixty years after independence, you can see that the process of exclusion and discrimination has been at work and this has created a major problem, I believe. We may not realize it but the fact of the matter is that if you leave out 140 million Muslims from the nation-building project, you will come out with a very major and serious problem. At one level, the Indian state has failed in so far as it has not created the opportunities for the Muslim communities to be properly integrated into the development process. But at another level, as far as the process of assimilation is concerned, apart from UP and Bihar, which are considered the Hindu heartland or the cow belt, the Muslims of other places are fully assimilated into the local culture. They are very much a part of the local culture and the Islamic orthodoxy has not penetrated into their lives until now, what might happen in future and that is difficult to say. The little tradition still continues to be important and in that sense, assimilation and integration are not just antiverts but they carry meaning to large sections of the Muslim community living in semi-urban and rural India. There are historical reasons for that discrimination but that doesn't provide any justification for its continuance, as it is suicidal for the Indian state to let this continue. It is not a healthy sign and you will find discrimination not only in central and state government employments, but in day to day lives, for example, it is very difficult for a Muslim to find a room in a place like Delhi despite the fact that it is a metropolitan city and these are the things that are to be set right because these are not stories but reality.

RJ: The BJP-led government consolidated what had begun earlier, but had not been institutionalized: the complete marginalization of Indian Muslims. One Gujarat was more effective than scores of little communal riots and make Muslims all around India feel insecure and helpless. As a result, Muslims were pushed further into their ghettos. Is India still gripped by a Muslimophobia?

MH: What is true is that the Indian state is secular. There is a consensus among all the political parties except BJP that India could progress only by professing a secular doctrine. The political process is secular in this country. The media is by and large secular but the society isn't by and large secular, so there are these autonomous entities. The extent to which these entities impinge on the lives of ordinary Indian citizens is difficult to ascertain and as far as Muslims are concerned, there are legacies of the past which have not been taken into consideration because we assumed that the Indian state was secular, the Constitution was secular so everything else will be set right in a secular manner. But the fact of the matter is that this is not the case and there was this report in *Outlook* magazine that there is not a single Muslim in the Indian intelligence agency, Research and Analysis Wing. In the security system of important people, Muslims and Sikhs are systematically excluded. And this is very bad if it happens in Gujarat and this is bad too if it happens in a dispensation, which, claims to be secular. A clear distinction that is to be drawn is the one between a BJP-run state and a non BJP-run state. I don't know how to draw that distinction because in terms of performance, there is not much difference.

RJ: Many Indians believe that the overwhelming majority of Indian Muslims are loyal and law-abiding citizens because they have not allowed their anger against the Indian government or the Hindus for any reason to drive them into the arms of terrorist organizations. But it is estimated that at least a hundred people participated in the execution of the 11 July 2006 Mumbai blasts. Without committed local Muslim support such a despicable act would not have been possible. Intelligence experts say that at least twenty-five Muslim organizations are working on Indian soil to breed alienation among the Indian Muslim youths and to suck them into the global whirl of jihad. What has been the response of the Muslim masses to these organizations? Has it been of complete apathy and indifference?

MH: I don't know whether Muslims are concerned with jehadization or not. Until we have sufficient documents, these things are difficult to ascertain. I think after what happened in Iraq, one has to be very careful of what the intelligence report suggests and how people are dubbed as terrorists and who kills whom and for what reasons, who is connected with what. These are issues that need to be looked in a very, very different manner. I suspect that we have to be very careful in the way the media plays up an incident because you get up next morning and find that this is not true, but by the time the truth comes out, it has done the damage because you have already sensitized many of your readers of the fact that Muslims are terrorists and jehadis.

RJ: The other sore point in the subcontinent is the issue of Kashmir, a predominantly Muslim land that was never allowed to decide its fate at the time of partition and was taken control of by India. As many as 750,000 Indian troops are stationed in Kashmir in order to quell the aspirations of the people for merging with Pakistan, which provides moral support and has fought three wars with India, in 1948, 1965, and 1971. Do you think one day there would be a solution to the problem in Kashmir?

MH: As far as the Kashmir issue is concerned, I don't think it concerns Indian Muslims outside Kashmir. The Indian state and Sheikh Abdullah have deliberately kept it largely away from the Indian Muslims outside the valley. So it has remained a Kashmiri movement both in its orientation and its origin and it has distanced itself from the problems of Indian Muslims and so the Indian Muslims are also not concerned about what is happening in the valley. There is a strange disjuncture. I would have thought that it should have built bridges with the Kashmiri people and with the Kashmiri movement, not as members of the same community, but as members of a group that shares many common problems in the field of education, social, and economic and these are the areas that could have provided the platform for the Muslims to act in unison. But this has not happened. Both the Indian and the Kashmiri leadership has very systematically created this wedge and even in the case of civil rights violations, it is the NGOs outside the valley that take up the case much more vigourously than the Indian Muslim organizations or groups, which I think is not a good sign and I think we should share some of the aspirations with the Muslims in the valley and identify areas where we can work together and in harmony.

RJ: As the Vice Chancellor of the Jamia Milia University in Delhi, do you take a pride in being a liberal Muslim living in a secular India? What does it mean exactly to be a liberal Muslim in India today?

MH: I don't label myself as a liberal Muslim but I do have a world view which is greatly influenced by the Nehruvian vision of society because at the heart of the Nehruvian vision is a type of modernity that people like Ashis Nandy reject, which is forward looking, enlightened and in so many respects, very inclusive. And if you place Nehru in the context of what happened in 1947—the violence, the riots, the bloodshed, and the distrust that existed in the Muslim communities and the differences he encountered not only from the opposition parties but also from within the party—then you realize how great this man was, in the sense that he was able to transcend the immediacy of his context and work towards the creation of a polity, and a society, which would be modern, forward looking, and enlightened, and which would be recognized in the spirit of the European enlightenment, equality of opportunity, rule of justice, and social justice. So I think that we tend to ignore his contribution, but his contribution is immense and it is in that sense that there is a certain pride in being an Indian and an inheritor of a legacy that I think is worth preserving and worth pursuing and spreading far and wide.

Sudhir Kakar

The Indian Psyche

RAMIN JAHANBEGLOO (RJ): Let me start with the first question regarding what Jawaharlal Nehru said about India. Jawaharlal Nehru described India as 'an ancient palimpsest on which layer upon layer of thought and reverie had been inscribed and yet no succeeding layer had completely hidden or erased what had been written previously'. For you, as an Indian psychoanalyst, what is the peculiar spirit of the Indian psyche, which continues to keep alive the notion of the sacred in the twenty-first century? Especially, when we consider that any non-Indian looking at India today considers the place to be the last reservoir of spirituality in the world.

SUDHIR KAKAR (SK): I would say that India still has the romantic vision of reality that has disappeared in most of the Western world. The romantic vision does not deny that life is tragic and full of tribulations. But it says there is more to life than tragedy. If you persist on the spiritual path, you will be rewarded with an exaltation beyond normal human experience. Here, there is no ironic acceptance of life's underlying tragedy as in much of contemporary Western philosophy. One could also say that in the romantic view, the world is pervaded by a numinosum, even magic if you will, which is only waiting to be let in your humdrum life. I don't think the sacred, the romantic, and the magical are very different. They are all alike and very much alive in India.

RJ: How do you explain the fact that despite the rapid changes in visible areas like politics and economics in India, religion continues to provide a psychotherapeutic safety net for Indians? Apparently, the religious world and the metaphysical world still work as a psychotherapeutic net.

SK: Yes, because the sacred world is so vast and has solutions to most human dilemmas, recommendations are tailored to suit different kinds of personalities. For someone who believes his emotional difficulties come from outside—from the actions of malignant spirits or the evil eye—you have the rituals of the exorcist. For the more sophisticated who believe mental disturbances have their origin inside the person, in his mind, you have the highly philosophical ministrations of the guru. All of these and others co-exist in the Indian sacred space and have a definite healing effect. Indian religious space is like a tool box from which you can select the desired tool that you need to enhance your psychological well-being.

RJ: I am under the impression that after sixty years caste has been out of the Indian Constitution, there is equality regarding the laws; but caste is still in the minds of the Indian people. They practically live with it as one can see in the marriages for example. Do you think it is very difficult to get rid of the caste system and the caste mindset?

SK: The cruelties and inequalities of the caste system may be easier to get rid of than the caste mindset which is related to the Hindu horror of dirt. For the upper caste child, the untouchable is a member of a group that is permanently and irrevocably dirty. The child's knowledge is not anthropological or religious-textual but a *knowledge-feeling* that is preverbal and, so to speak, has entered the child's very bones. Many a time while growing up, the child has sensed the sudden kinesthetic tension in the body of his mother, father, aunt, or uncle when a Dalit has approached too near. He has registered their expressions of disgust, unconsciously mimicking them in his own face and body at any threatened contact with an untouchable. Given the child's propensity to place himself at the centre of all experience, he effortlessly links the family's disapproval and revulsion towards the untouchable to those times when he has been an 'untouchable' himself, that is, when he has been unruly, animal-like and, above all ... dirty. What the caste system does is to keep much of the aggression toward other, 'dirty' groups within Hindu society. Of course, the 'dirt fantasy' I am talking about is common to other societies who have dealt with it in other ways—religious, racial, etc.—than through a caste system.

RJ: What are the political and social distortions of religious thinking in India today? Have there been any distortions at the social and political level of religious thinking in India. When I say distortion, I mean that Hindu fundamentalism is a distortion of religious thinking. So you might agree with me that in India today, what we had in Babri Masjid and the carnage in Gujarat could be considered a political distortion of religious thinking. Are there other examples of that? Do you think we continue at the same level going on with these distortions?

SK: I don't think I can comment on the political distortions. That is something which everyone knows about. I think these distortions are two sides of the sacred. On the one side, the sacred gives you therapeutic assistance in the journey of your own life, while on the other side, it can be used for destroying the lives of others. The question is whether the sacred comes as a package or whether one can choose some of its aspects while rejecting others. I don't think you can only have 'pure' sacred without distortions since the sacred mobilizes some of the strongest human emotions. And emotions are always susceptible to distortion. Passion can lead to great exaltation but also to great cruelty and violence. I don't believe that most people can have religion—in the sense of strong religious feelings—without passion, and thus without distortion.

RJ: There might be a rise of religiosity among the Indians, but I have a feeling that rituals are all getting homogenized. I think that cultural and religious diversities are being lost in India. Do you agree with me?

SK: Yes, that is very much so because of the great increase in migration from the villages to the cities and also because of changes in family structure. Nowadays, you don't learn rituals, and the tales and legends associated with them from your grandmother. You learn them from a mass-produced cassette or a book, which only give you a single version of the ritual and its associated tale. Grandmothers, on the other hand, were not homogenous. The loss of diversity is as inevitable as it is tragic.

RJ: You know that the new and younger generation read more of Mahabharata or see it as a TV series than it being recited to them?

SK: They do not have recitals anymore. They do not have the time to sit through the night listening to the Mahabharata being recited by a wandering bard. And of course our relationship to a recital and to oral transmission of knowledge in general has changed. What you see on the television screen is more credible than what you hear. The prestige of the aural, as compared to the visual, has plummeted in the last decades.

RJ: Being a psychoanalyst, you keep meeting people. Do you think this results in a change in the psyche in not having older traditions anymore and having an individualistic approach to religiosity?

SK: Yes. I find it a narrowing of your perspective and world view if you have only one version and not many, as was the case in traditional Hindu religiosity. And I also think there is less tolerance when other versions begin to disappear.

RJ: I read in an interview that according to you the Indian has always been context sensitive. In other words, the Indian has no absolute ethics. He never says this is bad and this is good. He rather says that it depends on the context. This was a very interesting point for me. Could you explain a little bit more on that? Why are there no absolute ethics?

SK: The main feature of Hindu ethical sensibility, in which it diverges from its Judeo-Christian and Islamic counterparts, is a pronounced ethical relativism which has become entrenched in the Hindu way of thinking. For how does any individual *know* what is right action, that he is acting in accordance with moral law and in 'conformity with the truth of things'?

The traditional answer has been that he cannot since right action depends on the culture of his country (*desa*), the historical era in which he lives (*kala*), on the efforts required of him at his particular stage of life (*srama*), and, lastly, on the innate character (*guna*) that he has inherited from a previous life. An individual can never know the configuration of all these factors in an absolute sense, nor even significantly influence them. Nor is there a book, or its authoritative interpreters such as the church, which can help out by removing doubts on how the individual must act in each conceivable situation. 'Right' and 'wrong', then, are relative; depending on its particular context, every action can be right ... or wrong.

In lessening the burden of individual responsibility for action, the cultural view of right action alleviates the guilt suffered in some societies by those whose actions transgress rigid 'thou-shalt' and 'thou-shalt-not' axioms. Instead, an Indian's actions are governed by a more permissive and gentle, but more ambiguous, 'thou-canst-but-try' ethos. On the one hand, this basic uncertainty makes possible the taking of unconventional and risky actions; on the other hand, actions are accompanied by a pervasive doubt as to the wisdom of individual initiative, making independent voluntary action unthinkable for many who look for psychological security by acting as one's ancestors did in the past and as one's social group—primarily, caste—does at present. This relativism supports tradition *and* modernity, innovation *and* conformity.

Since there is no notion of a *universal* human nature in Indian culture, we cannot deduce ethical rules like 'Man shall not kill' or 'Man shall not tell an untruth'. Truth telling, for instance, is not an unconditional imperative. 'An untruth spoken by people under the influence of anger, excessive joy, fear, pain, or grief, by infants, by very old men, by persons labouring under a delusion being under the influence of drink, does not cause the speaker to fall (i.e., it is not a sin),' says an authoritative ancient law book.

Another example: The Christian injunction against coveting 'thy neighbour's wife' is shared by Hindu law books, which proclaim that '[For] in this world there is nothing as detrimental to long life as criminal conversation with another man's wife'. In fact, Hindus are even stricter in defining adultery; talking to a woman alone in the forest, 'or at the confluence of rivers', offering her presents, touching her ornaments and dress, sitting with her on a bed, are all adulterous acts. The nature of punishment, of course, depends on the respective castes of the adulterous couple and there are also exceptions, such as the one which condones adultery with 'the wives of actors and singers'. In spite of a chapter with the title 'Other Men's Wives' in the *Kamasutra*, the celebrated text shares the Hindu disapproval of adultery. But it, too, lists exceptions to the rule, for example, when your unrequited passion makes you fall sick, and the text proceeds to outline the various ways to seduce other men's wives. Its position seems to be, 'You shouldn't do it. But if you must, then these are the ways to proceed. But, of course, you shouldn't have done it in the first place.'

RJ: This is very interesting and I was thinking of adding another question to it while you were talking. If there is no absolute ethics because of diversity then how is it that you have violence and communal riots? On what basis do people go and kill others if there are no absolute values?

SK: Killing in a communal riot becomes sanctioned precisely because the context of a riot is different from normal times. If one asks about the morality of killing one might get an answer like this: 'It was wrong (killing) when times were different but is not wrong now'. Similarly, space is also involved in moral judgements. Hindus often say that actions such as beating up of a Muslim or arson or looting of Muslim shops during a riot are wrong if you live in a Muslim majority area but all right if you are living in a Hindu majority neighbourhood. As a consequence of this contextual stance, wrong actions by the members of the community during a riot evoke far less emotion and righteousness in the community.

RJ: But do you think there is a shift in focus vis-à-vis ethics and ethical problems in their role in today's India?

SK: Yes, I think there is a shift towards ethical absolutism among the middle classes and in the so-called modern India. Yet they too fall back on context-dependent ways of thinking wherever their own or their family's interests are threatened. You wax eloquent against corruption but are happy to give and accept bribes. Context-independence is demanded from other groups, not one's own.

RJ: When you say that India is a culture of *shame* rather than *guilt*, do you mean that sexual acts of whatever kind are okay, provided you are not humiliated socially? In other words, do you think that in India morality and sexuality are fused together?

SK: Sexual morality in India also depends on the context. Forbidden sexual acts are alright as long as my family and friends don't know about it. It is a matter of great personal shame if they become aware of them. Guilt is more personal and independent of the context, or rather the context lies far, far back in our early childhood.

RJ: For example, in today's India, is homosexuality accepted as a very balanced thing or not?

SK: It is accepted as long as you don't talk about it. In Indian homosexuality, the problem is not really about the sexual act, as it is in Christianity or Judaism, where homosexuality is loaded with images of sodomy. Here the problem with the homosexual is that he refuses to marry and produce children. I remember a well-known homosexual activist, Ashok Row Kavi saying that when he was getting older, his aunts used to keep coming up to him and asking why was he not getting married. One day Kavi got completely fed up and said, 'Listen I cannot get married because I fuck men'. And the aunt said, 'I don't care if you fuck elephants or crocodiles, but why can't you get married!' In a different way, this attitude toward homosexuality was reinforced by the Islamic period of Indian history, where in the upper classes, you could have sex with boys as long as the men also fulfilled their husbandly duties towards the wife.

RJ: How is a treatise like *Kamasutra* read by Indians? For the West, it is known as a book of sexual positions' that is all. But I think for the Indians it does not have to be read as a sexual or immoral book, but has to have other significance.

SK: Well, I don't think they read it anymore; they only look at the illustrations of the sexual positions. What the *Kamasutra* is *really* about is the art of living—about finding a partner, maintaining power in a marriage, committing adultery, living as or with a courtesan, using drugs—and also about positions in sexual intercourse. It has attained its classical status as the world's first comprehensive guide to erotic love because it is at the bottom about essential, unchangeable human attributes—lust, love, shyness, rejection, seduction, manipulation, that are also a part of human sexuality.

RJ: Do you mean by that *Kamasutra* is mostly bought by tourists?

SK: Yes. I think so.

RJ: Do we still find nowadays in India a conflict between the ideals of asceticism and eroticism?

SK: Yes, although if you look at television programmes, lifestyle magazines and surveys of sexual attitudes in the English language media, eroticism seems to be on a definite upswing among the upper class élite and the emerging middle classes. But the conflict between the two is a fundamental part of Indian cultural history. The ascetic ideal, too, is quintessentially Indian, perennially in competition with the erotic one for the possession of the Indian soul. It is very unlikely if ancient Indians could be or were ever as unswerving in their pursuit of pleasure as, for instance, the ancient Romans. Although today there are again signs of a change, a tentative re-emergence of the erotic, the strain of asceticism, the road to spirituality through celibacy, held aloft through centuries by the Hindu version of William Blake's 'priests in black gowns ... binding with briars my joys and desires,' has dominated Indian sexual discourse for the last few centuries and will not be easily overthrown.

RJ: Are sexual attitudes still very conservative in India or are they accompanied by more freedom of the psyche and body?

SK: There *are* changes taking place in urban India. Young girls are developing a greater acceptance of their bodies. They have begun to place importance on clothes that accentuate body contours and are eager to inform themselves on the care and ornamentation of the body through television programmes and women's magazines. Yet, this increasing body consciousness stops with deeply internalized feelings of shame around the genitals—one's own and those of the male. Many girls and young women from higher castes do not even have a name for their genitals. At the most, genitals are referred to obliquely—for instance as 'the place of peeing,' though even this euphemism carries a strong emotional charge.

It is undeniable that in urban India, young girls move more freely in public spaces than was the case with the generation of their mothers. But it is also indisputable that public space remains a domain of men and there are few signs that this will change in the near future.

RJ: Personally speaking, you see a lot of presidents and prime ministers of other countries with their wives. In India, the prime ministers and presidents are generally not women and even if they are, their spouses are always invisible. Not too many people know about Feroze Gandhi or the wife of Manmohan Singh or Narasimha Rao. This aspect is always invisible. Has it to do with what we were discussing?

SK: It very well might be that to give an impression of possessing spiritual ascetic power, to which Indians are very susceptible, a leader needs to exile his wife from his public presence. One wonders whether the aura and charisma of our last prime minister, Atal Bihari Vajpayee, was not also fuelled by his being a bachelor.

RJ: The portrait that one gets by watching the Indian cable TV is that women are experiencing a change in urban India, but I read that 90 per cent in rural India have their first sexual experience after marriage. I think there is a gap between what you watch on cable TV and what happens in rural India.

SK: Yes I think that gap is very much there, and not only in rural India. Cable TV is a world of fantasy. Your actual role models still come from the family, a parent, an uncle, an aunt. Otherwise you will not be able to understand statistical surveys, which show that arranged marriages are overwhelmingly preferred by young people, including the college-educated. The consensus in favour of arranged marriage through the centuries is truly astonishing; in fact, the only ancient Hindu text that considers love marriage as the highest form of marriage is the revolutionary *Kamasutra*. What, then, of Bollywood movies and cable TV where love marriage reigns and is depicted as the only road to happiness? Here we should remember that Bollywood movies are not a guide to Indian marriage but a doorway into the universal dream of love. In a society that is deeply hierarchical, with caste and class barriers that are not easy to cross even by the god of love, the dream is of love unimpeded by the shackles of family obligations and duties towards the old and all the other keepers of society's traditions. What Bollywood offers is not role models for the young but romantic nostalgia for the freshness of love's vision to men and women, of all ages

RJ: I have a feeling that when I go through Bollywood movies that there has been a change. I remember when I was a kid I used to watch *Sangam*, which is one of the most famous Raj Kapoor movies. I do not want to use adjectives, but it was deeply conservative. It was a very mild lovable story with lots of boundaries. I think these boundaries are no more there.

SK: Perhaps the boundaries are more porous, but they are still there. The loss of love, because of unsurpassable barriers, used to be a prime theme of earlier movies. Now the pleasure is increasingly in love's fulfiment. But you still have enormously successful movies like *Devdas* 'celebrating' the enjoyment of love's suffering and the loss of the beloved.

RJ: When we talk of India we have the Hindu India and the Muslim India. Do sexuality and the social role of the women divide the Hindu and the Muslim India?

SK: I know little of Muslim India. In thirty years of psychotherapeutic practice, I have only had five Muslim clients, most of them upper class women. Muslim India is said to be much more conservative. Yet, it too is surrounded by changes taking place in the rest of society, to which it cannot remain impervious. I believe the changes here are much less visible than in Hindu India. In Hindu India, social change in the last three decades has been largely spearheaded by women. There are two reasons for this: one, the change in traditional views on the education of a daughter, which now encourages higher education for girls and thus makes their participation in socially-respectable work possible, and two, the growing financial needs of middle class families, partly due to their higher consumption aspirations, which welcomes the woman's contribution to the family income. These two factors will increasingly apply to Muslim India and I think the pressure for change will come from Muslim women.

RJ: I think what has been happening in Muslim India regarding Babri Masjid, etc., has brought Muslims closer to their religious community. Has it?

SK: Yes it has. And the valourization of the religious community may act as a brake in the way of change. I also fear that the strengthening of the feeling of community among Muslims might produce a counter closing together of the Hindus. After ten years of peace, I think we may be again headed for some religious violence.

RJ: At the end of your book *The Colours of Violence*, you describe yourself as an optimistic realist who believes that 'we are moving towards an era of the recognition of Hindu-Muslim differences rather than pursuing their chimerical commonalities.' Do you really think that no more clouds of violence loom over the future of Hindu-Muslim relations in India?

SK: As I said, I think the clouds are gathering again but I hope the thunderstorms will be brief.

RJ: When describing India today, how does somebody like you can help India to move towards less violent, more pragmatic and optimistic living. How does your daily encounter with psychoanalyses help writing on India?

SK: Psychoanalytic encounters cannot change society. All I can do is to write about what we have just talked about for a larger audience. Write about the cultures and peoples of India without ideological blinkers, hold up a mirror that is neither dark nor distorts.

Nivedita Menon

The Woman Question

RAMIN JAHANBEGLOO (RJ): It was in the context of the nationalist movement that the Indian Women's Association and the All India Women's Conference were established. But they both lacked a mass base and did not attempt to mobilize rural women.

NIVEDITA MENON (NM): There was a way in which nationalism subsumed the particular interests of women. It took the women's movement and feminist thought a long time to get out of the shadow of nationalist hegemony. During the national movement there was the mobilization of women by the Congress, and women were active among revolutionaries, but the primacy was given to nationalism. The question of women's rights emerged gradually.

The question of 'social reform' is very complex for feminists because the social reform debates were conducted, in a sense, between Indian men and British men. The question that was being debated had less to with women and was more about the fitness of Indian men to be independent, women were simply the terrain on which these debates were conducted. This is why the social reforms of the late nineteenth-early twentieth century are not traced by feminist scholars as the beginning of the women's movement. Questions that had to do with women, their access to power and resources and so on, were raised very much later, after independence, from about the 1970s. For example, women's suffrage was not an irresolvably contentious issue, but not because the nationalist élite recognized women as autonomous political actors, but rather because numbers counted where elections were concerned. The nature of British colonialism was such that the élites since the late nineteenth century, had been incorporated into governing through limited suffrage, and every vote counted.

RJ: Do you agree with Partha Chatterjee's claim that within the nationalist struggle the 'woman question' was resolved through the separation of the outside material sphere from the internal spiritual sphere. It means that as long as women occupied only the inner sphere, they were shielded from the influences of modernity.

NM: This is precisely the point. By the nineteenth century the woman question is settled for the male nationalist élite—they would move into nation-building and women would perform their duty by bringing up future citizens. However, there are complexities produced in different kinds of contexts. Take for example, the abolition of the *devadasi pratha*, the temple courtesans, which was a caste-based occupation. Exploitative though it was in many ways, nevertheless, you will find that it was a system in which women had the right to property. It was a matrilineal system as far as property and descent was concerned. With the coming of modernity and the abolition of the system in the name of social reform, basically patriarchy got reinforced as the norm. So modernity and development and progress actually ended some spaces that women had.

If you look at the debates here, the 'inner-outer' argument doesn't work exactly in the same way. For the nationalist male to accept in these kind of contexts, where traditionally there is some degree of female autonomy, that 'we' are 'different' in the inner realm—is to accept the continuation of this female autonomy. So, it's a sort of cruel dilemma for the male nationalist élite under matrilineal circumstances (whether with the *devadasi pratha* or say, Nair matriliny in Kerala), because to be properly nationalist, they must accept the difference—that is, the superiority of women in that particular context. While to be properly male, they must institute male dominance and patriarchy, but in the process, erase the 'difference' in the inner realm. So when you translate the narratives in different cultural contexts, you can see the fissures and the breaks, but overall, Partha's [Chatterjee] frame has been very insightful.

RJ: What were the challenges before the women's movement during the Nehru years? How do you analyse the link between the growth of Indian middle class women and the evolution of women's rights in those years?

NM: If you look at the women's movement after independence there is a decline in militancy because the assumption is that we have found independence and we can leave it to the state to bring about development and so on. So during the Nehru years there is not much feminist activity as such. There are, of course, women who are politically active in different kinds of movements but I am making a distinction between women who raised questions of gender inequality and women who were generally politically active. Generally, when we categorize the women's movement in India, we categorize it like this: the first wave was the nationalist and the second wave was in the post-Emergency period. So up to mid-1970s there is a kind of lull and then there is again a rise of militancy.

No, there were no particular measures for women in the Nehru era and in fact, it was exactly the opposite because if you look at women who were becoming adults after independence like Vina Mazumdar she talks about being part of 'the daughters of independence' and being very certain that women needed no affirmative action. The suggestion of reservations for women in representative institutions was in fact rejected by the women's movement representatives themselves, from the Constituent Assembly to the Status of Women in India Report of 1974. The different five-year plans do take into account the female citizen, but more as a productive figure.

It is only in the 1990s that the recognition emerges within the women's movement that the 'citizen' imagined by the state was always male.

RJ: We witnessed a resurgence of political activity by women, especially in the Indian Left, in the late 1960s. Is this a new political phenomena which is more or less influenced by the counter culture movements in America and in Europe?

NM: Are you referring to the far Left?

RJ: Not entirely, but also the Communist Party of India.

NM: I will then say that yes, there were international influences but I would see the internal dynamics as determining the nature of political struggles here. The Naxalite movement radicalized a large number of young people. So I think it is possibly a combination of what '1968' meant in the world, but more of the fact that there was a radical left movement in India around the question of land. But the questions raised by the left too often ignored the question of gender. In fact, many women left the Left parties in the 1980s as they offered no space for the articulation of gender inequities.

RJ: Did the crisis of the Indian state in the 1970s and especially the Emergency mark a significant shift in the analysis and understanding of women's issues and in redefining feminist politics?

NM: Yes it does because by the 1970s, the faith in the Indian state is shaken and by the mid-1970s, it was becoming clear that the state was a class state, a state of the ruling élites. Political mobilizing around the Emergency marks a shift in the understanding of women's issues.

RJ: With the changing political discourse of the women's movement in the mid-1980s the issue of gender and political participation came to the forefront of women's movements. How did the search for an alternative paradigm that gives expression to the plurality and diversity of women's experiences take shape in those years?

NM: The 80s is the decade of the 'third wave' where you find in metropolitan cities and small towns, small militant groups of women who were able to make their voice heard in the media and to articulate their demands. They were autonomous organizations. Most of them had a very leftist edge because they came out of left movements. They started raising questions about the sexual division of labour, sexuality, and sexual violence. So the 1980s is a period of very active and militant activities. There was also a very visible presence of the women's movement on the streets in demonstrations against dowry deaths, domestic violence, and so on.

RJ: In the 1990s, the women's movement was more focused on the issues of ecology, health, education, and employment. Is this a fourth wave? What were the elements which created this move beyond the traditional concerns with legislation and social welfare to issues of civil society?

NM: I don't think of a fourth wave like that although there is a fourth wave. Eco-feminism, I think, is still a part of the third wave. It foregrounded the question of gender as a critique of dominant development paradigms. What I think of as the fourth wave in the 1990s, is that you see the beginning of funding, so what happens is that although there are several autonomous women's groups, they are ultimately autonomous of political parties but not of funding. By the 1990s they are all funded, and there are only one or two that stay resolutely non-funded. Most women's groups are really NGOs by the end of the 90s, getting funds from both external and internal sources.

So there is a way in which international rights and the language of 'civil society' and rights comes in with funding, and I would say it has blunted the radical edge of feminist politics at one level. Because there is a way in which 'gender' becomes a vastly fundable category and that is what I see as the fourth wave. Of course, every development has subversive possibilities too, so I am not simply saying that funding is bad but surely, by the twenty-first century, there is a strong feeling among many activists that a clear distinction needs to be made between political activities that are funded—NGOs—and those that are not—political struggles or movements. Whereas I find in discourse in the West, a complete collapse of the two, so that NGOs are taken to be the same as political movements.

Gender and Sexuality in Contemporary India

RJ: When was homosexuality accepted or became visible in the Indian society because there is no such thing in the Constitution.

NM: No, there is not, and in fact, there is a law that can be interpreted, and is routinely interpreted, as making homosexual practices illegal. This is Section 377 of the Indian Penal Code. This law was introduced by the colonial government. There are lots of scholars who show that in the pre-colonial period, there was greater comfort with the idea of non-normative sexual practices. This kind of scholarship emerges in the 1990s—homosexuality becomes 'speakable' in a sense, in the 1990s because of awareness about AIDS. Earlier, one talked about sex in the context of family planning but AIDS, paradoxically made it possible to talk about sex as a subject of pleasure. There was a landmark public protest against Hindu right-wing attacks on the film *Fire* as it depicted a lesbian relationship. This protest brought together a range of voices, from gay and lesbian groups to women's groups and democratic rights groups.

The relationship of the emerging movement of non-heteronormative sexualities (gay, lesbian, bi-sexual, transgendered, *hijras*) with the mainstream leadership of women's movement is more complicated. There have been a series of conversations over the 1990s in different cities and so there is a gradual coming to terms with this movement. So there have clearly been transformations on the terms of discussion and sexuality is definitely on the agenda. The sex workers' movement has emerged as very militant, and there are sex workers' trade unions in West Bengal, Maharashtra, and Kerala.

RJ: What were the reactions of the women's movement in India to the rise of the BJP in the late 1990s and the relation that the political right established between women's bodies and Indian culture, as if women's bodies became the trope of 'Mother India' who had to be protected against the contaminations of globalization?

NM: One of the serious realizations that women's movement in India faced was that the Hindu right was able to use traditions very creatively to mobilize women. If you look at the campaign before the demolition of the Babri Masjid, you will find for example, that women were to prepare food-packets for the *kar sevaks* who were going to demolish the Babri Masjid—these were to be distributed by the women themselves along the route of the processions. BJP definitely has more women representatives in the parliament ... more than any left party. So there are things that have to be looked at. At one level, they defend 'Mother India' and at the other, they give space to women and so they are mobilizing women at twin levels. If you look at the Gujarat riots, you will see that women were as active as men.

The women's movement has become very aware of the fact that women can be mobilized by any political tendency (that is, as Hindu or as upper castes), and not only as 'women'. An earlier imagination had assumed that once women were politically mobilized, they would act in the interests of women necessarily. This is clearly not the case.

RJ: Has the process of globalization contributed to the evolution of new strategies in India's women's organizations?

NM: By and large the left has been very critical of something that they call 'globalization'. The left tends to have a uni-dimensional idea of globalization as entirely negative. However, one must also recognize the spaces that globalization provides, especially at the level of culture—there has been work done on this aspect by feminist scholars, especially those who are working on sexuality and the media.

RJ: Most Indian feminists characterize Indian society as a patriarchal society. Yet, in comparison with other Muslim countries, Indian society has produced many top-level women in all fields. Could one say that India is a paradoxical country that is divided between two dominant paradigms: on the one hand, the 'masculine' character of Victorian ideology present in the Indian state's administration, and on the other hand, the 'feminine' character, which is more evident in the Indian traditions of non-violence and dialogue?

NM: I wouldn't characterize the bureaucracy as 'masculine' as so much as a product of colonial modernity. I also don't think there is an 'Indian' tradition of non-violence. Gandhian non-violence is a very modern political strategy. What is the 'Indian' tradition of non-violence, after all? That is an absolute myth. Hinduism is fundamentally based on the violence of caste-based oppression and violence against women, and lower orders are ritually sanctioned.

As for women at the top-level, then this is true for other countries of South Asia as well. Even my understanding of Iran is that while women have to be veiled, there are as many women in public places, holding positions of responsibility as there are say, in the US. In India, there is the Constitution that gives equality, but formal equality is not the question. For example, the government fails to recognize the idea that child-care should not be the responsibility of the individual women, it is a social responsibility, it should be the responsibility of the state to organize safe and affordable child-care options. Until that is recognized, women will continue to bear the brunt of the sexual division of labour, and their participation in the public realm will continue to be limited. So those are the levels at which patriarchy operates.

RJ: So do you think that it is general in the subcontinent that men accept the idea of women being in high places in politics, which is not to be found in America?

NM: There are different ways in which patriarchy operates in different cultures. So it does seem to be the case that women can be accepted as heads of state and government in parts of Asia while the question can still be debated so sharply in the US. In fact, Gloria Steinem, who visited India recently, said that despite racism in America, the chances of an African-American man becoming president are greater than that of a white woman becoming one. There are ways in which in India women are accepted in places of authority but that is not true for all women at all levels of politics. It is too simplistic to see this as 'men accepting women' in positions of power—most women in authority come from politically powerful families for example. Of course, even that does not seem to help Hillary Clinton in the US!

Vandana Shiva

Fighting Indiscriminate Globalization

RAMIN JAHANBEGLOO (RJ): How do you evaluate sixty years of political, economic, and social development in India? What have been the harmful effects of modernization in India?

VANDANA SHIVA (VS): I think there are three aspects of sixty years of India's independence. One is that, overall, there was a commitment to the larger public good—made of course, by the persons who were interested in their own vested interests and the last person was not totally excluded. Even where the negative aspects were concerned, there were attempts to do things in the national interest, for example, the so called Green Revolution meant to increase food production through chemicals was totally misconceived in that chemicals produced more foods but the production was focused on growing rice and wheat, and meeting food security. We are seeing today that the concept of public good is totally out and now we have modernization in a very brutal form and I call this as modernization taking the leftovers of Western society's evolution as India's tomorrow. Take an example, take a look at Delhi, the historical city and what has happened to it. Today's Delhi raises the slogan in all the advertisements—'from a walled city to a world city'. This means a city that is contained, a city with limits, a city with community, a city with dynamism internal to it, has now turned into a world city which means huge carbon footprints, grab all the farmers' land around, and an urban sprawl on a highly unimaginative scale of a highly populated country . . . adopting urban sprawl when everyone in the West is saying that urban sprawl is a wrong way to use land. Cities need to be spacious for living and not a concrete spread to drive longer and longer distances. So when I say that we had two steps of modernization, it means one that was Nehruvian modernization, which in my view was not as good as Gandhi's vision of this country, but at least better than the Reliance and Ambani model of modernization and I would distinguish between these two. I would say that for the first phase at least public good was in mind but for now, only the interest and greed of the corporates is significant.

RJ: So what would you say has been left of the dreams of the forefathers of the Indian nation?

VS: I think that the dreams of the forefathers of the Indian nation-state lives in resistance. They don't live in the dominant structure and the dominant structure is basically those who rule today. No element of those who worked for our freedom remains today. In fact, the opposite seems to persist. For everything that Gandhi stood for and everything that Madan Mohan Malviya stood for, the opposite stands now and that is the current trend. Not only because throwing national sovereignty and freedom to the winds is a part of the globalization project, but also because there seems to be this sense that being able to trample on the next person is a legitimate human activity and has been given the name of 'competitiveness'. Competitiveness in terms of strangling others was considered anti-social behaviour and those indulging in it were social outcastes. Today, these social outcastes are on the top of the social and political ladder! So if you look at the awards that the government and the industries give, you will find that it is constantly for the worst losers of society, for those who have violated the law the most, for those who have avoided the highest taxes but who are made out to be the role models of modern India. There is also this perversion of values that is taking place not just in India but everywhere else. Those in India who are adopting those perverse values seriously think that these are the next steps of evolution and don't realize that the system that they are creating is so fragile that something else will have to come in its place because this can't last and it can't provide for society as whole. The dreams of what freedom would be all about continue to inspire those who defend the rights of tribals, farmers, and women. All of my work is deeply inspired by the freedom movement and I see a lot of my work as the defense of our freedom. Today, after sixty years, freedom has been taken for granted because those who enjoy it didn't have to fight for this freedom against the British and because those were the freedoms that not even the British could take away. Yet, under the current regime, in globalized India with partnerships between global corporates and the élites, the élites think that they can take wealth away from their own brothers and sisters. At one level, I think that there are values that are alive in society, but they are not among the decision-makers.

RJ: Very often in your interviews you mention Gandhi and his ideals and principles. I would like to know which principles of Gandhi do you use and think are relevant for your own work.

VS: Two aspects of Gandhi's thought have been very powerful in allowing me to imagine possibilities where, otherwise, there would seem to be a total closure. One aspect of Gandhi's thought has deeply inspired the very work I do right now through Navdanya, the movement I started to save seeds and promote organic farming. It came out basically from a meeting where the corporates laid out how they would get help from the World Trade Organisation (WTO), get patents on life, unleash genetically engineered organisms, and control world health and food care. They said that nothing would stop them and they would have all the laws they needed to prevent any alternative. I kept on thinking that if every seed is patented by a handful of companies, if every aspect of food we eat is controlled by them, if every medicine we use is a patented medicine, then we are not living in a democracy but in a dictatorship of a kind where our very life is dictated and is only affordable to those who have adequate resources. I kept thinking very hard how to beat a system where law is used to deny you your rights. The very form of law becomes the base for taking away human rights and freedom. The only place where I could find an option was in Gandhi's *satyagraha*, that when laws abuse human freedom, then you have the duty to exercise non-cooperation and civil disobedience. I was then attending a meeting in Geneva where all this stuff about patenting was going on and then I came back and the first thing that I did was to translate these laws into various languages and tell people about it. But simultaneously, I also told them that do remember that Gandhi walked on the beach in Dandi and picked up a handful salt and told the British we don't have to obey and we will not obey. We have to do the same thing for the patent laws and since 1991 we have been doing satyagraha. Last year, we prevented a new seed law from being implemented that could have prevented farmers from having their own seeds. It is not a matter of seed but even saving was inspired by the idea of satyagraha. We have exercised satyagraha to prevent a bad law from being implemented and I think that we need satyagraha everywhere.

At present we are working in communities whose farmlands are being taken. This is happening across the length and breadth of this country, like in Singur, Gurgaon, Maharashtra, in Dadri near Ghaziabad, and at the end of it, you sit with the farmers and sit in the panchayat (I have been running in and out because I am organizing a meeting of the farmers with the parliamentarians tomorrow), you really think what you could do when a special economic zone (SEZ) is planned and it assumes that millions should be uprooted. I found only one option left there ... that I will not let my land be appropriated. It's a land satyagraha like Gandhi's salt satyagraha. For me, it's the ultimate defense of freedom in times of the ultimate destruction of freedom. It gives you the final tool to say that I don't need to participate in the destruction. I will bear the consequences of not participating as the consequences of participating are anyway worse than the consequences of not participating.

The second concept that has inspired me a lot in Gandhi's work is the very deep notion of freedom that he embodies in swaraj, self rule, not as a political rule of non-alien rulers, but self-rule in terms of the freedom of all within society, including the last person. Quite clearly, to build those structures of self-governance, you need strong motivation in society. Running a society on elected representatives who turn their back on you and abuse you for the next five years and remember you again when the next election is due is very different. This deeper sense of exercising freedom totally changes how you think of freedom because someone who holds power over you has based the whole rights discussion on your exercising rights. Swaraj means you exercise power but you cannot exercise power without first taking responsibility and that means that rights flow out of responsibility and that there are no short cuts to rights. When you put duties first you create spaces very different from the Western liberal view of freedom, which is supposed to be attained by giving up all duties and responsibilities and expecting someone else to provide you with freedom. Unfortunately, so much of the Western women's movement is based on that and the Western environmental movement is based on a dominant other as a provider of rights rather than the human as a shaper of rights, as a sovereign agent, and as a sovereign free person, free within the dominion of the bounds of duties.

RJ: How many villages have you visited and how many reports on the ecological and human costs of globalization have you published in the last fifteen years?

VS: I have visited more than two to three thousand villages in the last fifteen years because there are two levels at which the work involves me in travel to the villages. First, the work for resistance, the work we do to fight the WTO, unfair patent rights, and the growth of genetically-engineered seeds. The way in which we deal with it is by taking out *yatra*s and that means covering huge distances. Last summer, I took yatras against farmers' suicides and I started in Nagpur in Sevagram, in fact, in Gandhi's ashram on 10 May and went all the way to Bangalore and it went on for a month and the team visited and stopped in two hundred and fifty villages and I visited many more and the team held meetings in two hundred and twenty villages. We have been doing this since 1998 when I started building Navdanya. In 1991, when the first framework of General Agreement on Tariffs and Trade (GATT) started to come in, we started mobilizing. The second aspect of the work that takes me to the villages is the work we do on seed saving and organic farming. I don't go to every village where we work. We work probably at this point in more than 3,000 villages, which means that you are there for the farmers all the time. But I have visited many of these villages. Just a week ago, I was in Rajasthan and I covered the entire stretch from Jaisalmer to Jaipur and during the whole trip everywhere there was a meeting with the village communities in the areas that were becoming aware of the harm of organic farming and the harm of losing their seed sovereignty. In terms of pamphlets and papers, we must have brought out hundreds of thousands, in terms of reports, about a hundred.

RJ: How are you funded, nationally or internationally?

VS: It's a combination. The Government of India will fund me to start a lab and we accept that money to set up a soil lab. The National Commission of Women will fund me to organize public meetings on the impact of globalization on women. There are two aspects of our funding. One aspect is where I keep the institution totally free and I go, slog and teach in some universities and bring some money back and put it in our work and the second is from friendly institutions and friends who think alike.

RJ: Its interesting that Government of India will fund you and yet you are very critical of the Government of India and the politicians and I have read somewhere where you said that they are still in their Cold War mindset.

VS: This has happened to me so often. In the morning I will be in the Ministry of Environment as part of an expert group and in the afternoon I will be in the Supreme Court fighting the same Ministry of Environment. Three days ago, I was part of the delegation of the Government of India at an organic fair and they were using my photograph in the invitations for the seminar. Yet, we have a Ministry of Commerce and Ministry of Agriculture being contested in court on the import of wheat that we don't need. Fortunately, I am the same person and I have the same thoughts and my position doesn't change whether I am sitting as a delegate, or as an expert committee member, or whether I am sitting across the table as a contestant against the litigation, it's the government that is split. A part of them realize that it is better to be organic and I don't think one of them will dominate and I don't think India will hand over to Monsanto, but India will fight. I don't think that the Government of India will become so benign to the farmers that they will suddenly throw Monsanto out, that will not happen either. So this scheme of easing tension will remain and the healing will come from outside the establishment, it will come from how much we are able to get from the environment that compels policy to change and so I would say that our work is partly to help the official system to overcome its schizophrenia. We are a kind of psychotherapist.

RJ: Living democracy is a paradigm you present as an alternative to corporate globalization.

VS: Its an organic process that has grown both in terms of concepts and the institutional processes on the ground that we have been able to build and it is fuelled by two factors. The first is the fact that in India we have always been able to talk about *vasudev kutumbakam* (the human beings, the tree and the animals, all being part of this larger entity called earth) and as corporate globalization unfolds, it reduces the whole world to a global supermarket. The water of the Ganga is no more the water of the sacred divine river, she is now water to be sold by the world's biggest water company.

Our grain is no more Lakshmi but is now a commodity of Cargill or patented by some other company. So the wheat lying here on my table is to be tested to prove its patent rights belonging to the farmers of India from ancient times. So every thing such as Ganga water, grain, land, and soil are in the supermarkets and quite clearly that is a system that must by necessity destroy our humanity, appropriate the resources of the poorest, and dehumanize all of us and make it us impossible to inhabit this earth as beings who need to relate to food and water in a different way with a higher level of respect and reverence. So there was this idea of vasudev kutumbakam and we are an earth democracy and we should practise life as an earth democracy. But there is another side in which under the pressure of corporate globalization, increasingly, representative democracy is becoming dead democracy. Dead because it is totally useless for people today to exercise their priorities. It is as if the will of the people is locked in that ballot box and does not ever come out except for the count. It does not matter who rules, it could be the BJP, Congress, or any set of parties anywhere in the world, but it is like a revolving musical chair of total inconsequence as far as the protection of people's rights are concerned and when democracy is no more for the people, by the people, and of the people, and has been reduced to a system by the corporates, of the corporates, and for the corporates, quite clearly, democracy is dead and something else has taken its place. It has mutated into corporate dictatorship and this farce of democracy pretending to deliver obviously needs to be challenged with an alternative. The traditional alternatives are posed in terms of capitalism versus communism and that doesn't hold good today because capitalism has now become communism and communism has become capitalism in terms of total state control over everything on behalf of corporations and we see this in China where the communist party implements corporate rule with a vengeance and we in India are trying to catch up. So you need to give life to dead democracy and how do you give life to a dead democracy? You need to move beyond the market and you need to give space to a centralized state and move beyond the partnership of the state, the market, and the corporations into some system where people can retrieve their freedoms and democracies even while the systems that take those freedoms away are the ruling systems and that is living democracy.

RJ: How can India and Indians contribute to this idea of earth democracy as a 'shared planet'?

VS: There are two levels at which India must contribute. The first is that we need to start practising earth democracy once more within India and that means precisely that Reliance can't own all the land of this country, the Tatas can't reduce the country to a market place for their automobiles. As an earth democracy we in India need to guarantee the democracy of mobility, you see the bullock cart, the cyclists, and the motorists, and now we privilege the car, the highway, the airplane, taking away the possibilities of less destruction in terms of our daily lives. This privileging has to be changed and many of the movements I am involved in aim at reducing the carbon footprints of Indian élites that are squashing 80 per cent of India. The second thing that we need to do is that even when the Reliances, the Tatas, and the Monsanto trample on India, we need to understand that India is the largest sustainable ecological resource. So even though the Government of India is busy bringing in Walmart, one of the biggest threats to organized retail. I celebrate the *thelawala* who comes and stands in front of your house and asks which vegetables do you want for that day and knows exactly who needs which vegetable down the street and loads his cart according to the specific needs of the people. What could be more efficient than this house to house delivery that also provides employment to forty million people in this country.

RJ: Are you hopeful about the future of India? Do you think Indians will become disenchanted with the glamour of globalization?

VS: The upper class, the consuming class is enamoured but those forty million hawkers who are going to lose out when all vegetables are going to be sold by Reliance and Walmart, they are not enamoured by those malls. Similarly, the farmer who is losing his land is not enamoured. So there is a consuming class and there is a sacrificing class and the sacrificing class knows what is being sacrificed and I think that what is special about India is that here, the protection of the earth and the protection of the poor are the same project and because of that we can actually evolve an earth democracy which is about human dignity and social justice also and not just about ecological, viable sustainability. So while I was saying that there are not many middle class families who would think like me, I would also say that the majority of India does agree with me because that majority of India will have no life if they give up their lands, rivers, and forests as they have nothing outside of that.

Ruchira Gupta

Role of NGOs in People-oriented Development

RAMIN JAHANBEGLOO (RJ): NGOs in modern India have traditions that can be traced to the ideologies of the Ramakrishna Mission, Mahatma Gandhi, Sarvodaya, Jesuit missions, and even Marxism. Many NGO establishments in modern India have the aura of the traditional Hindu ashram. The accent is on austere community life in isolated project campuses and total dedication to the poor and deprived people in the area.

RUCHIRA GUPTA (RG): The word non-governmental organization is a post-independence phenomenon. Historically, traditions of civic participation in public life can be traced back to charitable acts by benevolent kings, merchants, and courtiers counselled by sages and scholars. Hindu, Buddhist, and Muslim statecraft defined charity as one of the necessary deeds of a ruler. The dispensation of charity helped forge direct alliances between kings and temples, kings and merchants, and kings and marginalized communities. Merchants and temple priests under the gaze of benevolent kings organized the distribution of food to the poor during famines, digging of wells, planting of trees, making of roads, and organizing of debates on issues connected with public life. Brahmanical priests/sages introduced the notion of *paap* (sin), which could be redeemed through charitable acts. This notion filtered down to the village level where the redemption of sin in this life could be done through charitable acts. Hindu priests began to take advantage of the belief of sin and its redemption by forcing individuals not to contribute to the public good but to the coffers of the arbitrator priests.

Buddhism—a reform movement against the oppression and greed of the Brahmanical priests—shifted the nature and ownership of charitable acts. The concept of paap and redemption in the next life moved to acts free of greed and attachment for public good in this life. Buddhist *sanghas*, as centres of learning and reform, were supported not just by rulers but by mercantile guilds. Gardens, universities, campaigns against violence and wars, and campaigns against the caste system were launched by monks and merchants who did not belong to priestly or ruling classes.

Meandering sufis who followed the Turkish conquerors into India continued the Buddhist onslaught on the hierarchy—especially the caste system by promoting the oneness of the spirit. They impacted on traditions of public service through Guru Nanak, who led the Sikh movement and promoted *kar sewa* and the system of *langar* for communities.

Various Muslim dynasties, including the Mughals, introduced notions of *zakat* (charity), including pensions for widows, homes for orphans, distribution of food and clothes to the poor, free medical treatment, and the establishment of public gardens, wells, granaries, road, and baths.

Under the British Raj, Hindu and Muslim kings and zamindars, impoverished by high taxation, stopped patronizing civil works in rural and urban life. Jesuit priests and missionaries tried to fill this gap but did not get adequate support from the British rulers, who were only interested in tax levies that they collected from colonized India.

Indian citizens had to look to their own resources to provide for certain public services, which now the colonizing state did not provide. This happened at a time when young educated reform-minded Indians were in touch with new concepts of modernity being debated in Europe, West Asia, and the Americas. Many of these young Indians had organized under the Indian National Congress and were part of the Quit India movement led by Mahatma Gandhi. Some were reading Tolstoy or Thoreau, others were reading Karl Marx, Lenin, and Trotsky, while some read Rousseau and Robespierre.

The British, as argued by James Fitzjames Stephen, justified the Raj as an absolute government, which was the requirement of the Indian civilization. They said only by such a government could any real benefit accrue to Indians. If sati, other human sacrifices, infanticide, disability to marry on account of widowhood or change of religion were to be abolished, as indeed they were to be, only an absolute imperial government could do it.

The Brahmo Samajis led by Raja Rammohan Roy and scholars like Ishwar Chandra Vidyasagar challenged the British justification and launched Indian-led enlightenment movements (Bengal Renaissance) for the abolition of sati, for widow remarriage, and for education of women.

Gandhiji took these ideals even further by linking public participation in civil life to dharma. He freed the notion of dharma for modern Indians from a hierarchical system of duties and obligations, and the preservation of status to democratic citizenship through notions of equality, liberty, fraternity, and mutual assistance. In *Hind Swaraj* he presents a vision of civic humanism—one contained in the Gita in potential but never practised. *Hind Swaraj* defines what Gandhi's concept of modern India should be and how politics may be made into the highest form of active life. Sarvodaya, or the uplift of the absolute poor through acts by both civilians and the state was an integral part of *Hind Swaraj*.

Sarvodaya was also an integral part of the freedom struggle. Dr Rajendra Prasad led the sarvodayis in Bihar in earthquake relief as did the Marxists in Bengal during the famine. In the postcolonial modern Indian era, Gandhi's influence inspired Vinoba Bhave's land-gift (*Bhoodan*) movement and J.P. Narayan's resistance movement against Indira Gandhi's authoritarian regime of 1975–7.

The British sought either to take credit for such activities or depoliticize them by insisting on all reform activities being registered under the Charitable Trust and Societies Act. They deliberately put family trusts, temple trusts, reformist societies, and extremely political voluntary agencies under the same Act. They hoped in this way, they could co-opt some of the young reform minded Indian intellectuals in the service of the British empire. Thus anti-establishment groups and pro-establishment groups came under the same umbrella.

After independence, no attempt was made to amend the Charitable Trust and Societies Act. The British model prevailed and the act continued to be the only law whereby legal entities could be created for social work, charitable acts, and alternative economic nation building. So public service-minded Indians who wanted to contribute in the building of the new modern independent India had to take recourse to only this one Act to set up girls' schools, establish electric crematoriums, or continue reform movements. Baba Amte's ashram for lepers, Radha Ben's ashram for girls' education, ashrams established by Gandhiji or Gandhians offering an alternative way of life based on Gram Swaraj to promote khadi and village enterprise and schools, and hospitals set up by the Tatas, the Birlas, and the Bajajs, came under the brush of the same act. All these came to be known as the voluntary agency movement.

This continued into the late 1960s. The focus of the work was on development of village enterprise through the promotion of khadi in all its forms, tribal development, and campaigns to end untouchablity and promote girls' education.

In the pre-Emergency 1970s, the voluntary agency movement, which later was the basis for the Indian NGO network was co-opted into official development plans and received government funds. The emphasis of these groups was on rural development, community development, employment generation, slum improvement, and betterment of living conditions.

Two sectors, the formal and non-formal sectors were created. In the 1960s, the non-formal sector was utilized for relief, rehabilitation, and charity-oriented projects. In the early 1970s, grassroots work among, (a) poor, agricultural labour and harijans,

(b) tribals, (c) urban poor-slum dwellers and unorganized labour, and (d) women was prioritized.

This work was often sabotaged by socio-economic structures of feudalism of caste and land ownership. A passive rural poor was not motivated to take advantage of these schemes. Therefore, different consciousness raising and organization struggles among the oppressed and the disempowered began to be advocated and put into practice. In 1975–6, all major donor agencies listed in their funding programmes the object of not only assisting developmental activities but also steps to organize and educate the 'absolute poor'.

Many voluntary agencies began to be called 'action groups' at this stage. Rajni Kothari, D.L. Sheth, and Dunu Roy led the vanguard of these groups. They coined the term non-party political formations. These groups worked directly with the people, took up concrete issues of oppression and exploitation, and moved beyond the conventional politics of transformation. They supported J.P. Narayan's movement against the Emergency, thus moving far away from charity based trusts and societies, which had only direct services as their main activity.

The 1980s opened the floodgates to foreign funds as well as higher allocation of government funds for development projects implemented by non-government organizations. Actions groups became implementing agencies or nodal agencies. The philosophical roots of many voluntary agencies, based on *Hind Swaraj*, were shaken. Gandhiji's statement that, 'Real Swaraj consists in restraint. He alone is capable of this who leads a moral life, does not cheat anyone, does not forsake truth and does his duty,' required a restrained austerity in the process of implementation as well as goals based on Gram Swaraj, which did not necessarily match the requirements of the Indian state or foreign donors.

The 1990s saw the word 'development agency' added to the lexicon of non-government agencies. The government has now begun outsourcing projects and services to NGOs. The new millennium now has NGOs working like contractors, taking up a project and working on behalf of the state to implement them. There is a growing nexus between the voluntary sector and the government sector with many government officers choosing to resign from government jobs and starting or joining development agencies.

Areas of NGO Activity

RJ: NGO initiatives in India are also related to the political evolution in contemporary India. The growing disillusionment and the resultant discontent with party politics among the masses gave birth to a number of NGOs in the 1960s in India. I believe what we can call the new social movements came from the spark from Naxalbari in 1967, followed by the anti-establishment protests across university campuses in Nav-nirman Andolan in Gujarat and the Total Revolution by J.P. Narayan after Indira Gandhi announced the suspension of democratic rights on 25 June 1975. How do you see the evolution of NGOs in India in relation with the democratization process in this country?

RG: It is important to remember and recognize that the J.P. movement was a purely political movement led by the socialists and supported by Gandhians and the CPI(M). It was never led by NGOs. Some prominent NGO leaders like Rajni Kothari and organizations like Gandhi Peace Foundation, and Peoples Union for Civil Liberties supported the movement but the majority of NGOs stayed out of the movement. Due to the contribution of a few of these NGOs, the NGO movement once again got validity and was perceived as leading social change. It was actually the socialist and left leaders, who were in and out of jail and campaigning for the restoration of rights, who led the movement against the Emergency.

When Indira Gandhi was re-elected after the Emergency, these NGOs had to pay a price. In 1980, the Kudal Commission was set up to enquire into the affairs of Gandhi Peace Foundation and allied institutions. The Commission submitted five interim reports. Many Janata Dal MPs opposed the Commission and finally it was wound up under Rajiv Gandhi in 1986–7. In an interview to *Indian Express* on 7 October 1986, Rajiv Gandhi spoke about the 'harassment' of voluntary organizations by the government saying, 'I know, the problem is that the Home Ministry is a bit paranoid about all this, not only about voluntary agencies, but also about foreigners and missionaries.'

At this stage, some sarvodayis and socialists who were disillusioned with the Janata Party government joined bodies like Lokayan and Gandhi Peace Foundation sponsored projects or set up their own NGOs.

Also, many Naxalites, after the disintegration of the Naxalite movement and the resultant theoretical disarray in the early 1970s gravitated towards voluntary agencies as it allowed them to continue working among the poor and provided them with a livelihood. The Rana-Nandy faction was not opposed to foreign funding compared to the S.N. Singh faction and this caused a split in the Naxalite group.

Religious fundamentalists of all hues began to use the NGO sector to set up front organizations to mobilize students, Dalits, tribals, women, and the elderly at the grassroots. While disillusioned sarvodayis, socialists, and Naxals joined the NGO sector as an outlet to work among the poor, members of organizations like the RSS took advantage of the legitimacy that the NGO movement had acquired and set up front organizations to work in the service of a planned Hindu fundamentalist state. Their demand for a Hindu state is slipped in along with many genuine issues such as restoration of land and forest rights to tribals, or educational courses for Dalit children in slums, or medical care for the elderly. Thus, these organizations were able to mobilize tribals in Gujarat to massacre Muslims in 2001.

The democratization process of India has always been led by its multi-party and federal system. The NGO sector has neither responded to it nor used it to its own advantage.

RJ: Has there been a significant shift of the focus of NGOs in the past twenty years from developmental and tribal issues to the question of individual rights, mainly of women and children?

RG: Developmental issues encompass the rights of all individuals left behind in the process of development, such as women and children, or Dalits, or tribals. Economist Amartya Sen has termed this as the right to development.

So the rights of all minorities such as women, children, tribals, Dalits, the rural poor, artisans, craftsmen, the disabled, ecologically-displaced, agricultural workers, migrant workers, and the rural poor are interconnected and if any one group is the victim of lop-sided development, all groups are affected.

The focus of NGOs is still very much on all the groups mentioned above. However, the approach or method of dealing with them has shifted. For example, on women's issues the focus in pre-independence India was on widow remarriage and ban on sati, in the 1970s it shifted to girls' education, delayed marriage, dowry, and family planning. Now the focus is on the woman's body and her right to control it in terms of reproduction and sexual activity. It is less focused on her struggles within the patriarchy of class, caste, and gender. The debate is more biological than structural.

One of the reasons for this is the changes in sources of funding. A combination has emerged of foreign funding agencies, top bureaucrats and big business houses coordinating their resources and efforts to effect a change from above. Some of the big houses which finance ventures in the voluntary sector are Hindustan Lever, the Tatas, ITC, the Modis, the Thapars, Reliance, and the DCM group. Apart from corporate social responsibility, they also use NGOs to funnel funds out for tax purposes. Multinational corporations like Pepsi use NGOs to legitimize their brand name or counter bad publicity launched through grassroots movements.

This has, in fact, made the voluntary sector less radical and made them creatures of 'safe' change and vehicles of sanitized reform. So while the talk may seem to emphasize individual rights, it actually shifts the focus away from structural rights. For example on the issue of women's rights, the focus of NGO work is on domestic violence, lesbian rights, delayed marriage, sexual harassment in the work place, and inheritance rights. The focus has moved away from organizing women to struggle for equal access to education and jobs as these require structural remedies.

Today, many NGOs are no longer agents of change at the grassroots. They are simply implementing agencies for the government, the World Bank, or other big donors who set the agenda in Davos or Washington DC. They work as project factories. The bulk of foreign funding is given bilaterally to the Government of India and then via them to NGOs.

Some voluntary agencies participate, assist, and monitor plan projects and development schemes. They work in collaboration with the government and sometimes decide priority areas where they want to invest. This collaboration can often be enriching for development and sometimes ends up preserving a not-so-desirable status quo.

Problems in the Non-governmental Sector

RJ: Does the work of the NGOs truly and sincerely translate the demands of the underprivileged in India? What is the guarantee that they are not working against the interests of the underprivileged?

RG: Sometimes they do represent the interests of the underprivileged and sometimes they do not. There is no one answer to this. Like any other sector in democratic India, they represent a variety of interests, some of which may overlap, some of which may be cross-cutting, and others which may cancel each other out. NGOs are only one sector in India, among a variety of sectors. There are no laws insisting that they work for the underprivileged. They can perform a wide variety of functions. This is both good and bad.

It is good because voluntary agency workers were able to support anti-colonial struggles, and later on, the movement to restore civil liberties during the Emergency do this. Indira Gandhi did establish the Kudal Commission to look into the working of NGOs, but her son Rajiv Gandhi suspended the commission after a public outcry that the commission was a witch hunt against those who had opposed the Emergency.

It is bad because NGOs, who are simply project factories implementing privatized government services related to health and education against a profit margin, are treated with the same respect and provided the same benefits as the low-cost voluntary agencies run by Gandhians, socialists, and leftists. They get tax rebates, they are allotted government land, and they take corporate salaries and yet don't have to give back to the state as any other government contractor would. Today, they will work on environment, tomorrow they might work on health and sanitation, and next week on disaster management.

It is also bad because even the agendas of well-meaning NGOs can be manipulated, subverted, or hijacked without any checks or balances.

Sometimes NGOs are used by corporate interests to legitimize or create the climate for certain corporate activities. An example of this is the work that NGOs are doing to re-settle and rehabilitate victims of rural displacement in Maharashtra, Gujarat, and Haryana on behalf of the Ambanis and Tatas who are setting up huge economic processing zones, ports, or housing projects.

I will give you another example. I have an NGO called Apne Aap Women Worldwide working to end sex trafficking. We have organized women in prostitution in the red light areas and slums of Maharashtra, Bengal, Bihar, and New Delhi. Cut off from their families and society, deprived of education and inflicted with multiple diseases like AIDS, tuberculosis, jaundice, psycho-social trauma, sexually transmitted diseases, malnourishment, and insomnia, the prostituted women are ideal guinea pigs for multinational and national pharmaceutical companies.

We have come across widespread free drugs trials and product testing of pharmaceutical products on these women by NGOs and their affiliates. The women don't even ask what drugs are being given to them, what information is being gathered from them or what focus group discussion are being conducted to test which product. They trust the NGOs and the doctors brought in by the

NGOs who conduct these trials. Three years ago, at the International AIDS Conference in Bangkok, Thailand, women in prostitution from Cambodia said they should be compensated for the drug trials being conducted on them by NGOs in partnership with foundations set up by pharmaceutical companies.

The women of Sonagacchi and Kamatipura cannot even ask for compensation since they do not know that the trials are being conducted on them. They don't know if they have consented or not. There is nobody to ask any questions should they die in the process since these women anyway die early at the age of thirty or thirty-five and are cut off from their families and ostracized by society as prostituted women.

I have seen NGOs conduct endless rounds of focus group discussions on the female condom—did it fit them well, did it hurt them, etc. These women are daily wage earners who don't have disposable time but because they trust and respect the NGOs who work with them, they agree to come to one hour or two hour-long discussions without getting any compensation and information as to what is going on.

Huge procurements of condoms, voluntary counselling, testing kits, and anti-retro-viral (ARV) drugs are made from pharmaceutical companies by the health ministry on 'behalf' of the NGOs who claim to represent the women in prostitution.

The word 'agency' (choice, autonomy, desire, voice) is turned on its head when the health ministry, in collaboration with these organizations, says the poor, disempowered prostituted woman in the brothel wants the condoms, kits, and ARVs. This justifies the purchase and marketing of the products (condoms, kits, and ARVs) with their inherent commissions for all interested parties, never mind that the average prostituted woman/ child can hardly say no to unwanted or unprotected sex and therefore cannot use the products. I have visited brothel after brothel where condoms are simply lying around and children use them to make balloons.

The interested parties with their inherent commissions and salaries develop a vested interest in the continuation of brothels to be able to distribute these drugs easily. They promote a merchandise model of development where they say that they have distributed so many condoms in so many brothels and that the average women is raped nine times at night, so she must be having nine buyers, and so even if half of them use condoms, then the spread of HIV/AIDS has been reduced by X amount.

In the whole story, the objective of ending the rape of the woman or her captivity in the brothel is not even considered. All that is considered is how to protect the male buyer of prostituted sex from HIV and AIDS.

So yes, sometimes NGOs end up not representing the interest of the underprivileged woman but of either the patriarchal state or the corporate sector.

RJ: It is said that though NGOs fight for the transparency of the government, they do not believe in practising transparency when it comes to their organization. Up to what point would you say that the work of the NGOs is transparent?

RG: There are three main mechanisms to monitor or hold NGOs accountable—the Charitable Trust and Societies Act, the Foreign Contributions Regulations Act (FRCA), and the Income Tax Exemption Act. Through these acts, the government can study annual reports, tax returns, and audited reports to see that the expense statement matches the stated objective of the NGO.

However, the government cannot and should not provide internal oversight of the daily running of the NGOs. This would destroy the independent nature of NGO work. Even now, NGOs who mobilize the underprivileged at the grassroots come under greater scrutiny by various arms of the government than NGOs performing simple charitable services. Sometimes NGOs are victimized for having leaders who contradict certain positions of the party in power.

On the other hand, there are NGOs that exist only on paper, have bank accounts, raise funds, but never operationalize their projects. There are also NGOs who have no internal oversight. Recently, a staff member of an NGO running a shelter home for street children in Delhi was found selling some of the children for begging. None of the trustees of this NGO were held accountable and they continue to get both government and foreign funds.

NGO accountability and transparency is a very delicate balance. Perhaps, a self-regulatory board for NGOs, which is very much like the one we have for journalists in which there is a press information bureau and the journalists are given identity cards to practice, after their bona fides are checked by senior credible journalists, may be the answer.

Also, caution should be exercised to discern genuine social work and charitable organizations. The Societies Act needs to be amended to differentiate between, (a) trusts and societies which perform social welfare activities such as health care, running schools, hospitals, etc., (b) voluntary organizations which speak of organizing or mobilizing sections of the people for their rights, (c) think-tanks and policy research organizations, (d) government project implementing and monitoring agencies, (e) religious trusts and societies, and (f) cultural organizations. They should also be categorized on the basis of how they raise and spend their money, (a) foreign funding, government funding, or contribution of individual citizens, or (b) what is their profit margin and savings from their projects.

A re-categorization of NGOs and a reappraisal of their benefits and rights based on the categorization would be fairer and more just.

RJ: Don't you think that there is a lack of coordination among the NGOs in India?

RG: There is coordination among NGOs as and when required—either thematically or geographically. The Right to Information campaign was successful due to the coordination among NGOs.

The daily lack of coordination is healthy as NGOs should not speak with one voice at all times. India is a democracy and needs a variety of opinions and stands.

The big donors have already divided which issues they will work on and also marked out geographical territory. They fund networks and nodal training and monitoring agencies which coordinate the work of NGOs they fund. They organize conferences, meetings, and encourage exchange of information through the setting up of documentation centres, databases, and websites.

The problem is lack of transparency and accountability. Ill-equipped charity commissioners cannot monitor the financial or the programmatic workings of the NGOs. Any scrutiny results in a public outcry against government interference. As I mentioned elsewhere, some children were sold for begging from a home for children rescued from the streets by a staff member. This shows a complete lack of oversight of the home, by either the government, or board members of the trust, or society. While the staff member may be held guilty in court, the trustees will not be held accountable for this lack of oversight. Similar situations have come up on issues related to diversification of funds. The NGO is neither blacklisted nor are the trustees suspended and new trustees appointed as would have happened in the public sector.

Gandhi's Influence

RJ: How do you reassess the real relevance of Gandhi's ideals in the work of the NGOs in India?

RG: It is more relevant today than when Gandhi formulated these ideas. Every NGO should understand the concept of *antodaya* and work for the betterment of the poorest of the poor. They should also read closely Gandhiji's notion of trusteeship and understand that they are simply custodians of public wealth and cannot waste or misuse the resources in any way. Ideas of austerity and sacrifice related to public service are also important in NGO management as these form the vary foundations of the philosophy of voluntary agencies in India.

Our own NGO, which works to end sex-trafficking and organizes women in prostitution in the red-light areas and slums of Bihar, Bengal, Delhi, and Maharashtra has based its work on the twin Gandhian principles of ahimsa and *antodaya*.

We believe that prostitution is a form of violence against women. We feel that the demand for prostituted sex will end if men internalize the principle of non-violence. The buyer of prostituted sex first violates something within himself before he violates the prostituted woman. This leads to internal unrest and makes him physically violent with the woman during the sexual act. If man internalizes the principle of non-violence he will want a relationship based on equity and dignity where neither does he indulge in self-violation nor in violation to the other.

If the prostituted woman internalizes the principle of non-violence, her self-hatred built over months and years of constant abuse will disappear and she will find the inner resources to resist the violence against her.

We believe that the prostituted woman is the last woman—the absolute poor—and it is her uplift that we work for. Hence the concept of antodaya.

To some extent, our method of addressing gender discrimination is Gandhian. We try to transcend gender by looking at the feminine and masculine unity in each human being as Gandhi did. Gandhiji, dressed and spoke in a non-aggressive feminine way and said that this depicted the poorest in our country. This sends two important messages, one is that the poor in our country are genderized into a feminine body language and secondly that even the feminine can be strong and powerful without being aggressive and macho. Gandhiji also speaks of understanding the moral pressure of non-violent satyagraha from his mother, who would not speak to his father when she wanted her way and his father would respond more easily than to fiery or loud arguments.

The justification of prostitution as a service to incessant urgent male sexual need—especially in the absence of or in excess of marital or 'legitimate' sex often justifies the trafficking of women for prostitution by legitimizing the demand for prostituted sex. Gandhiji's bold experiment with sex where he slept naked with two naked women friends and did not have sex debunks the myth of unbridled male sexual desire publicly. Gandhiji tries to conquer his sex urges and says that he needs to learn more from women who are taught from birth to control it. This radical experiment shows that men and women are both capable of controlling sexual desire and choosing an appropriate place and time for sex. The demand for prostituted sex is constructed by the sex industry.

Challenges

RJ: How has your organization progressed over the years?

RG: Apne Aap Women Worldwide began as a community-based organization four and a half years ago of twenty-two women in prostitution who helped me make an Emmy-winning documentary, *The Selling of Innocents*. Today, it has grown to a membership-based non-government organization of over a thousand women in prostitution in Bengal, Bihar, Delhi, and Maharashtra, with the aim to end sex-trafficking.

Members of Apne Aap have testified in Parliament on the Immoral Trafficking Prevention Act Amendment Bill, have spoken at the Indian Social Forum, have conducted study trips to communities of women in prostitution in Rajasthan and Jharkhand, and bring out a news monthly written for and by women in prostitution called *Red Light Despatch*. They have interviewed Nobel laureates like Shirin Ebadi and submitted petitions to district magistrates, local MLAs, and judges. They have participated in trainings of law-enforcement officers asking for the blame to be shifted to the perpetrator from the victim. They have prepared a play called *Apradhi Kaun* (Who is the Culprit) and have brought out a book called *The Place Where We Live is Called a Red-Light Area*. They represent the trafficked population of India. They represent SCs, STs, and OBCs.

They are no longer silent. They are willing to make visible their oppression and analyse the root causes for the violence against them. All this has happened in the space of four years.

The first challenge to my organization was the ostracization attached to prostitution and the notion of sex being a taboo subject. It was extremely difficult to get social support including the recruitment of committed staff to work in red-light areas.

The other challenge was the entrenched caste structures that entitled men to think that low-caste women were disposable creatures. We faced this at many levels when police authorities actually said that they did not want to protect young girls locked in the captivity of Mumbai's brothels because, (a) prostitution was a necessary evil and it protected girls from good families, (b) these girls were brought up to be exploited because of their caste.

The third challenge was from the organized criminal networks. Our offices have been ransacked and files have been stolen, a knife was pulled out on me, a staff member was propositioned, another was told she would be buried alive. Our members have been beaten up for listening to us and sometimes the police have also beaten them up.

The fourth challenge was from HIV and AIDS in two ways. One was its impact on the health of our members and the increasing death toll, leaving orphaned children who would be pulled into prostitution to replace their mothers. The other was the vested interest created by the harm-reduction models being promoted by the AIDS lobby in the perpetuations of brothels.

Hunger is the biggest problem. Women are malnourished and skipped meals. Space is another problem. Insomnia a third. Our women used to sleep on roads and were constantly interrupted, threatened, beaten, or robbed. They didn't even have toilets. They used to feel like criminals for wanting to use the toilet, sneaking around in the dark looking for a private space.

And finally, we have to contend with the loss of identity. Our members lose a sense of self, suffer from psycho-social trauma and self-hatred, low-self esteem, and have no understanding of citizenship.

We have managed to restore a sense of self to our members and the desire to fight for their rights as citizens of India. They not only look up now, but speak up. We have major milestones on other structural fronts as well.

We have international standards to combat the trafficking of women. The UN has a protocol to end the trafficking of people, especially women and children. India is a signatory to the protocol. I remember working with other women's organizations to get the protocol passed in 2001 in Vienna.

India is now working on changing its law on trafficking to meet the standards set out in the UN protocol. It is also working on the National Action Plan to combat trafficking. It has begun to allocate more resources to the anti-trafficking work. Our organization, Apne Aap, has again played a role in lobbying and suggesting changes in the Immoral Traffic Prevention Act (ITPA) as well as contributing inputs for the National Action Plan. We are in the Steering Committee of the Planning Commission for Women and Children as well as on the Working Group of the Department of Women and Child in the Ministry of Human Resources. We have been training police officials on shifting the blame from the victim to the perpetrator.

Internationally, I am on the advisory boards of the Ricky Martin Foundation, Asia Society, Coalition against Trafficking in Women, and Vital Voices, chaired by Hillary Clinton. We work in solidarity with international organizations to end sex-trafficking. I have also helped ten countries develop national plans to counter trafficking.

So we feel that the anti-trafficking movement has come of age and we need to push a little further to make a huge irreversible dent.

RJ: Do you see the future of the NGOs in India in an uncertain light?

RG: Not really. If I did not have faith in the NGO movement, I would not have set up an NGO. However, I would like to add that the future of NGOs is related to the health and strength of Indian democracy. NGOs will remain strong if Indian democracy remains strong.

Geeta Kapur

The Story of Modern Indian Art

RAMIN JAHANBEGLOO (RJ): Modern Indian painting can trace its roots to pre-independence India when Western influences started to make an impact on Indian art. A number of Indian painters drew inspiration from the Western schools and used Western principles and technique in their paintings. While the development of a new artistic language was for Western artists a means for going beyond the post-Renaissance tradition, for Indian artists, the assimilation of Western modernism was double-edged. On the one hand, it gave them a modern identity and on the other, it encouraged them to reconsider their own traditional antecedents. Raja Ravi Varma is a perfect example of such painters. In your book *When Was Modernism*, you present Varma as a painter who 'creates a re-vision of Indian civilization for his contemporaries'. In other words, Varma is part of a process of appropriation of identity through an Indian manifestation. The neo-classical style he adopts is conservative in the West, but it is new and non-traditional in the Indian context.

GEETA KAPUR (GK): I will start with the last part of your comment that the neo-classical style he adopts is conservative in the West, but it is new and non-traditional in the Indian context and answers the paradox you are referring to. Ravi Varma, appropriated the conventions of oil painting—which is not a traditional medium of painting in India—and he did this through copies of old masters and contemporary British and French 'salon' paintings circulating in nineteenth century colonial India. So he was at the far end of a derivative process and one would imagine that it would hardly count as a pioneering moment for modern Indian art. But the paradox turns precisely at this point. The fact that he adopts the 'new' medium of oil and easel painting—new in India—gives him access to a different kind of painterly materiality, to the sensuousness, graspability, even seduction, embedded in the medium and language. He also gains access to a certain kind *situatedness*-in-the-world developed in a Western materialist aesthetic through a pictorial proposition that is emphatically scaled, framed, and formatted; it leads further to a new and different relationship between a subjective and objective apprehension of the 'real'. So, when he paints a portrait, he is able to situate his sitter, often an aristocrat sitter, within the material world to which s/he belonged but more significantly, when he paints narrativized figures from the epics and Puranas: he stages a 'real' world through means that are designated in terms of the philosophy and aesthetic of 'realism'. Although his influences derive from oil paintings in the attenuated and even decadent neo-classical mode, he catches distant reverberations of realism and the best that is associated with that genre, which is a concretely historical concern for the material world whereby an immanent form of emancipation can be said to have been projected.

This argument and the process of derivation it defends has larger implications. When Dadasaheb Phalke became a filmmaker in the early twentieth century, his utmost desire was to materially envision for the Indian people, their beloved gods and goddesses, and to stage their narratives in realistic settings. He was passionate about the miraculous possibility in celluloid to materialize myriad figures from Indian mythology and to allow the viewers/believers to fulfill the experience of this surrogate encounter as though it were real and in what may be assumed to be a 'realist' manner.

This proposition is built into the colonial imagination: that you can adopt the means that the colonizers bring—culturally and, of course, economically and politically—in order to address your own personal, and even national needs and desires. In the case of artists and intellectuals, it means that you address your cultural peers and the populace (in the case of cinema) with unprecedented means that modernity (and its attendant technologies) offer. So, of course, there is a paradox built into Ravi Varma's, as in Phalke's, proposition. Through the paradox you can bring the advantages wrested from the colonizers to purposes other than what they were intended for, which is, in fact, how you transgress beyond the adopted means in order to be able to re-energize the imagination in new directions.

I would say, further, that through the twentieth century, this conscious and unconscious provocation—to use the means to subvert the privileged monopoly of means—is precisely what gives to extant traditions emancipatory nuances that resonate with modernity.

Foreign Influences and Traditional Approaches

RJ: The Bengal Renaissance and modern art, influenced by Europe, also made their mark. The doyen of Indian modern art, Abanindranath Tagore, used Japanese and Chinese techniques in his paintings and drawings. The Nobel laureate, Rabindranath Tagore, was an accomplished painter. His contemporaries, Nandalal Bose, Samarendranath Gupta laid the foundation of modern Indian painting. Modern Indian painting came into its own when artists began to fuse traditional approaches with the bold experimentation of the West. Would it be correct to say that Abanindranath and Nandalal were artists who thought of an Indian modernism that could bypass the West by varying degrees.

GK: I would like to make an important correction here. The Bengal school of painting was much more influenced by the Eastern aesthetic traditions than by Europe—and indeed they made an ideology of it. But more about this in a moment.

Early twentieth century Bengal artists were, of course aware, like all 'Victorian Indians', of English cultural and artistic traditions—for example, the conventions of watercolour painting and graphic techniques of etching woodcut, and lithography. Watercolour as a medium became popular in India among professional as well as amateur artists. That Indian artists were inducted (in addition to 'salon' style paintings) to a minor tradition of Western art yet again—and *not* the modernist avant-garde beginning at the turn of the twentieth century—has to be admitted. This minor tradition did however have a larger aesthetic ideology linked to William Morris and Ruskin whose anti-industrial, anti-capitalist stance was understandably attractive to thinkers and artists in India: from Ananda Coomarswamy to Rabindranath Tagore and Gandhi. The revival of arts and crafts, and a 'back to nature' call, in that it stood against a coercive/exploitative modernization, fed the anti-colonial struggle and integrated into what was called the Bengal Renaissance.

Consciously and ideologically, however, the Bengal artists looked Eastward. If the Bengal Renaissance was seen as reviving the great Indian civilization, it flowed into the emerging pan-Asianism of twentieth century Asia. Specifically, Abanindranath Tagore, a consummate watercolourist in the English tradition, began to look at Indian miniatures in the first decade of the twentieth century; he took his cue from Mughal miniatures with their more naturalistic approach, combined it with the 'wash' technique of far-eastern painting, and contextualized himself into a contemporary genre. On the other hand, Nandalal Bose, his student, paid his homage to the great Ajanta murals and made that heritage part of his artistic vocabulary—imparting this preference to the art movement as it developed further in the art school in Santiniketan, at Tagore's Viswabharati University.

This was also the path that linked itself naturally to Japan and China, to the Buddhist tradition, and to its diverse and subtle aesthetics. From Chinese murals to Sino-Japanese scrolls to Japanese woodcuts—these became a means by which several linguistic and pictorial structures could be envisaged.

RJ: Contemporary of Abinindranath and Nandalal is Amrita Sher-Gil, whom you compared with Frida Kahlo in your book. What is interesting with her as a modern Indian painter is a marked departure from the spiritualist image of Indian art advanced by earlier nationalist painters into a removed realist idiom infused with sensuality.

GK: Before going any further I would like to mention two major artists, at Shantiniketan: one is Binodebehari Mukherjee and the other is Ramkinkar Baij. Both of them were students of Nandalal Bose. Their ideological affiliation with the Eastern mode, particularly the Japanese tradition, is evident. Binodebehari travelled to Japan, Ramkinkar never went abroad, but both understood very well the importance of the choice and logic of the language forged in Santiniketan. Importantly, they also made their relationship with the West; they both tackled modernism outright—Binodebehari, the scholar-artist, with quiet care, and Ramkinkar with flamboyance.

Binodebehari moved from very small nature-based drawings—largely in the Eastern mode—to large scale frescos and, then, during his blind decades, to paper-cuts. Binodebehari knew the Buddhist paintings of Ajanta, he understood Giotto, he also relates to modern Western painting, including the post-impressionists and Cézanne, the expressionists, and finally Matisse. His 100-foot fresco of 1947, situated in the premises of Santiniketan, stands as an epitome of Indian painting. Here, in a truly great synthesis, Binodebehari elaborated on the theme of medieval Bhakti saints, drawing on Buddhist as also medieval Christian traditions of figural painting to celebrate the syncretism of the mediaval mystics (exemplified in the Hindu-Muslim identity of Kabir), heralding, as it were, the larger, civilizational, basis for independent India.

Ramkinkar made a direct relationship with the ruptured language that comes out of expressionism, cubism, and Picasso. He broke the taboo on oil painting, adopted the spontaneous style of a native-modern rebel, and was sympathetic to the Left. He worked on a monumental scale as a sculptor and produced public sculptures of tribals, peasants, and the proletariat in direct cement.

Now to Amrita Sher-Gil who was Indo-Hungarian—her mother was Hungarian, her father an Indian Sikh. She was brought up as a child in Hungary, went to Paris in 1929, and was trained at the École des Beaux-Arts. She returned to India in 1934 when she was twenty-one years old and painted only a few years before she died at the age of twenty-eight. In those seven years in India, she made a telescopic journey into the past, looking first at Indian classical sculpture and the Ajanta murals—on the basis of which she painted a set of major paintings (in oil and easel format) called the South Indian Trilogy—but soon felt that this was too grand a civilizational mission and that as a modern painter she must devise a more informal language. Turning to Indian miniatures, Mughal miniatures in particular, she was able to devise a genre by which she might speak for contemporary (rural) India. Even by the standard of her peers in Paris, she was an extraordinary painter and able, with her intelligence and painterly confidence, to get a grip on what she understandood to be 'Indian reality'. As compared to Binodebehari Mukherjee and Ramkinkar Baij she had very few years to induct herself into the social and cultural circumstances of India but she used the advantage of her youth to live and paint boldly, even arrogantly, and therefore signal the moment of modernity in Indian art.

When I make a comparison with Frida Kahlo, it is to emphasize Sher-Gil's persona, her experiments with her own body and with her own sexuality. I suggest that she, like Kahlo, makes herself into an icon, a female icon, which then gets inducted into a representational struggle at a national level—each becomes, expressly, a national icon. There is nothing gained by comparing their paintings, it is their position within cultural contexts hegemonized by male consciousness and the ideology of nationalism that is comparable. And what I will conclude with here is that they find a unique place for themselves in theatric terms even as they relentlessly seek a language which renders their subjective attitudes, their social orientations, with deep affect.

Art in Modern India

RJ: Modern Indian paintings use materials from around the world but they remain entrenched in expressing Indian culture and experiences. The ability to combine tradition with modernity has produced some amazing works of art. Modern Indian art can be called a phenomenon because although the artists are steeped in Western modernism, they also recount their cherished stories, or imbibe Hindu philosophy in their work.

GK: As we know too well, modernity came to various parts of the world by and large through colonialism. This encounter with modernity is based on the contradiction of outright exploitation as also emancipatory possibilities drawn from the Enlightenment, from a materialist historiography, from ideas of national sovereignty, and peoples' revolution. Artists around the world have tried for a century and more to make what has been called a 'derivative discourse' into an autonomous 'reality'; to re-appropriate to their advantage as willing agents of change—what they have been forced to encounter. So in my mind, it is not unique to Indian artists to have close acquaintance with the West, with Western art, and then to use those means to undermine what they are appropriating in order to valourize what they believe to be important in their context, socially and culturally.

To answer your question: I think I would qualify the extent to which Indian artists actually deal with Hindu philosophy. I would say that they deal with spirituality in a more general sense and if they use Hindu iconography, it is more by virtue of the fact that this mythology is so figuratively exuberant. This is a resource that is inevitably going to be seductive, sometimes generative. I am not very sure that this practice of cross-referencing the contemporary self with the (Hindu) myths has any kind of consistency. The transaction is far more eclectic than what is implied by your question. Eclectic because of the range of resources available to the modern Indian artists and it is also expedient in that these can be appropriated without necessitating any kind of ideological and religious affiliation except those which facilitate a contemporary narrative.

RJ: Are there any Muslim painters during the period of Bengal Renaissance as there are later on?

GK: The most well known of them is M.A.R. Chughtai who later became a major figure in Pakistan's art scene. The influence of the Bengal school was very widespread in the 1940s and the 1950s and so painters across the board, of different ethnicities and religions, used that idiom. What is more interestingly is that among the first self-declared modernist artists of the late 1940s, the major figures come from religious and ethnic minorities. Besides the flamboyant, Goan Catholic, Francis Newton Souza, there is Maqbool Fida Husain and Syed Haider Raza, both originally from central India, followed by Akbar Padamsee and Tyeb Mehta from Bombay. What immediately needs to be emphasized is that in this period, their identity as Christian or Muslim is no more important than that of a Hindu artist. We are witnessing an Indian modernity of a particular historical period at play, an emphatically secular modernity defined by Nehru and the liberal-left intelligentsia. Even today, hardly any Indian artist would like to be identified in terms of religion; they would either like to be identified as simply Indians, or, if they don't want to be identified nationally, they will identify themselves ethnically/regionally and link themselves to a regional language, regional culture, and regional literature.

However what they actually do with cultural resources is another and more important feature of modern Indian art. What a painter like Husain is able to do with iconography, Hindu iconography, or let us say mythological and epic iconography that still moves and affects the contours of Indian cultural life, or what Souza is able to do with the Christian God and the Catholic church—brought to Goa by the Portuguese—is a narrative of some power in the history of Indian art.

RJ: Shortly after independence, a group of young enthusiastic painters decided that they needed new ways to express independent India in the modern world. The founder members were six very important artists, namely—K.H. Ara, S.K. Bakre, H.A. Gade, M.F. Husain, S.H. Raza, and F.N. Souza. This group known as The Progressive Artists Group, founded in 1947, became the foremost amongst a number of collectives that came to represent the new art of post-independence India. This group didn't have a very long run (it was dissolved in 1956), but it left an indelible impact on modern Indian art. Though the group was dissolved in 1956, it was profoundly influential in changing the idiom of Indian art. Almost all India's major artists in the 1950s were associated with the group. Some of those who are well known today are Bal Chabda, V.S. Gaitonde, Krishen Khanna, Ram Kumar, Tyeb Mehta, and Akbar Padamsee.

GK: The Bombay Progressive Artists and their associates not only adopted the modernist language, they also imbibed and manifested the iconoclastic strain within modernity and made a direct affiliation to expressionism (German and Viennese expressionism, by and large, and to a lesser extent surrealism). Here I would, insert, parenthetically, that Ramkinkar Baij, was also attracted to expressionism and performed as a major iconoclast within the heart of Santiniketan—flaunting every rule of the haloed school. Yet he would not make a declaration of the kind that the painters of the late 1940s did: he would not claim that he is an outright modernist. It is significant that the circumstance and the need to make such a declaration came at the time of independence. The young rebels of Bombay wanted to shake off, in what may be called the 'last anti-colonial gesture', the burden of civilization imposed on Indian intellectuals and artists in the pre-independence phase of nationalism. That is to say, they saw themselves emancipated from a civilizational role, and also overt nationalism, and while they did also try to confront the hegemonic influence of the West, modernity as an existential condition became virtually irreversible. This is all the more interesting in that Husain came from a conservative Muslim family and Souza from a lower middle class Catholic family and Ara from an extremely poor, lower caste background—and that they ruptured the terms of the contract with their own background and formative ethos to become 'universal' modernists. Starting off in Bombay and then, going on in some cases, to England and Europe, they ruptured traditions, they broke ground with the early phase of modern Indian art, and when they returned to certain iconographic codes, they did so to break the protocol of conventions as they had inherited them.

RJ: The painters that influenced the Bombay Progressives were mainly from Germany and they used expressionism, a pessimistic, negative sense of nihilism that you will find in all expressionist works, be it cinema or painting. How is it that they are more influenced by that than by good impressionism?

GK: It is slightly accidental. There was an influx of a group of Europeans in the late 30s, in the period of the Second World War—and they were either trained artists or connoisseurs and collectors of European art. They brought with them a few actual works but largely reproductions and they made these available to young artists in Bombay. These groups of émigré art lovers happened to be central and east Europeans (Dutch, German, and Viennese) and partial to expressionism as they were to what I am calling the iconoclastic language of modernism. As for the young Bombay painters, it is not that they were not familiar with expressionism, cubism, and Piccaso, but this encounter convinced them that the English art school vocabulary had limited them, that they had been trained in the most conservative mode of art education possible in the twentieth century—and they immediately grasped the urgency of widening their range of references.

The persona of the artist in the twentieth century is that of a rebel and so no matter whether the vision is optimistic or pessimistic, this persona captivates everyone's imagination. I think that these artists were attracted not to the actual pessimism that came out of the European experience of war, their affiliations were based on their ability to find self-expression, to be able to manifest the self in opposition to the world and to be able to create an existential resource for becoming—'new'. So it's a different take on expressionism. In any case, I don't want to overdetermine their work with expressionism—it's a movement, which allowed them to mark a rupture. Later most of them were much more affiliated to the lyrical school of Paris. Raza and Padamsee, and Ram Kumar became part of that.

RJ: Raza settled in Paris where he was shortly joined by Ram Kumar, and Akbar Padamsee. M.F. Husain was the only important artist with the group who decided to remain in India until very recently. So for several decades the leading lights of the Indian contemporary art scene lived, worked, and exhibited abroad. But did they make a breakthrough on the international scene in the sense in which the avant-garde concept requires?

GK: Certainly M.F. Husain is the most important of this group of artists who didn't ever move out of India on a long-term basis—but the other artists too came and went all the time. And as they would return to exhibit here, they always remained a part of the Indian art scene. Ram Kumar was in Paris for about three years but was back for good in 1956; Akbar Padamsee stayed in Paris much longer but came back in 1965; Tyeb Mehta went for five years to London and came back in 1963. Raza and Souza were the two that continued to live abroad.

The second part of the answer is that, yes, they didn't make a breakthrough in the international art scene in the sense that the avant-garde principle requires. They were part of the school of Paris and they were recognized to be good painters but there were not quite among those very few non-European artists who were regarded as part of the vanguard—like Wifredo Lam from Cuba for instance. Paris was the congregation of the world's aspiring painters, the school of Paris was like a universal resource in which artists were nurtured and in which they produced significant works. The did not so often become the leading light. And this is true for a large number of painters from Japan, China, and even Latin

America, though the Latins had greater access to the vanguard ethos of Europe.

RJ: In the 1960s, the question of identity was once again in focus. The new quest for an Indian modernism, however, differed from the earlier nationalist efforts. As a result of this, a whole movement in neo-Tantric art grew and some of the important members of this group like G.R. Santosh and Biren Dey came to it through some forms of expressionist abstract painting. J. Swaminathan who in many ways belonged to this group took a distinct stand by calling into question the concepts of modernism and progress and emphasizing that Indian artists had uncritically embraced Western modernism and this had been inhibiting them from finding themselves.

GK: By the early 1960s, the next generation felt a certain discomfort with the way the school of Paris had absorbed the energies and talents of Indian artists. Indeed, everywhere in the post-war period, which is also the period of massive decolonization, there were dissentions developing vis-à-vis the West: against the dominance of its culture and political economy. In India this phenomenon was related to the fact that after ten years of independence, Indians saw themselves as no longer beholden—either to Western civilization or to Western modernism—the emancipatory force of which was now seen as well-imbibed and therefore needlessly hegemonic.

As the non-alignment movement and the concept of a 'third world' emerged, Indian artists looked at the non-Western cultural formations with a new focus. Let me take the case of Swaminathan who became a close friend of Octavio Paz. The artistic and intellectual movements in Latin America, especially Mexico, had explored what the indigenous can mean in terms of pre-Columbian civilization; Indian artists found themselves in a good dialogue with this non-tradionalist/contemporary phenomenon: that we can look at our own pasts, not via the conduit of modernity but via a critique of modernity, and in the process, be able to reinvent ourselves in terms other than what Western modernity allows. Swaminathan was an ex-communist, a writer, a critic, and an artist; he was able to wedge himself into the critique of modernity. Over the next decade, he launched a rhetoric whereby the contemporary, which is polyvocal, gained precedence over modernity, which is designated as teleological. And he actually brought about a philosophical and ideological rupture with the very teleology of modernism. In practical terms, he established, in Bhopal, a twin museum of contemporary Indian art—one of urban metropolitan and the other of contemporary tribal art—suggesting that they are continuities of form and languages which flout the rules of modernity, yet find an equation in the contemporary. My take on Swaminathan is that he was actually tapping a certain primitivist root of modernism and that there are enough resources in modernism itself which allow him to theorize the contemporary in the way he does. That is one part of his persona; the other part is that he sustained a fiercely egalitarian relationship with the people of India and, so, even when he had left the communist party, his ideas and mindset envisioned a liberatory space—not only for the élites but for the neglected and marginalized peoples in the countryside of this subcontinent.

RJ: It seems to me that Indian artists in the 1970s and 1980s gave up the idea of a monolithic Western modernism and began thinking beyond modernism of new modes for creativity in a plural world. The adventurous eclecticism of a painter like Subramanyan spells out this trend.

GK: Subramanyan is a very important marker. He was trained in Santiniketan, was a direct student of Binodbehari Mukerjee and also regarded Ramkinkar and Nandalal Bose as his gurus. He went in the mid-50s to the Slade School, London, returned to India and started teaching as part of the Fine Arts faculty of the MS University of Baroda. He devised an entire pedagogical system—through his writings and teachings—and indeed, his first major contribution to modern Indian art is in these terms: about what Indian modernism might be, linguistically, culturally. His contribution as an artist comes alive later when, from the 1970s onwards, he makes his terracotta reliefs followed by a series of glass paintings, tapping aspects of the folk and popular traditions. After his gurus in Santiniketan, he is a precursor to the Swaminathan position—in different ways they define the contemporary in terms of the still living indigenous and artisanal languages in India rather than in terms of high art. Subramanyan's first collection of essays is called the *The Living Tradition*.

RJ: Indian women artists like Arpita Singh, Nilima Sheikh, Sheela Gowda, and Nalini Malani mainly influenced Indian avant-garde painting in the 1990s. In which way have these women artists been able to create a whole new narrative about female identity in India and redefine the meaning of civil society?

GK: I would like to include the name of Nasreen Mohamedi, a pure abstractionist and, unlike the artists you have mentioned, a lone figure. Retrospectively we can see that she was not only unique, but also very advanced for the time—she died in 1990. She didn't identify herself in any categorical terms, not as a feminist either, because she was emphatically a modernist, defining herself only in terms of the language, or rather the grammar she used. After Nasreen, Arpita Singh; and then a next lot of women artists come up in the 1980s and 90s—Nalini Malani, Nilima Sheikh, and others. I would suggest that they break new ground in the way they examine the female body and thereby their own subjectivity, bringing a new understanding to what the subject-position of the artist is. Until now modern Indian art rests strongly on male subjectivity. Amrita Sher-Gil does provide a precedent, and many later artists are beholden to the fact that one of the icons of Indian modernity is a woman artist—they make references to Amrita all the time. But now these artists are able to speak more forthrightly about women's bodies and the ways in which women have to negotiate cultural codes within the social, thus placing themselves in relationship to actually existing civil society norms.

The second level of contribution follows, as for example with the work of Rummana Hussain and Navjot Altaf. Rightwing violence, encountered in India from 1992 onwards, fractures the very structure of available art languages, and it is not a coincidence that several women artists take as a thematic their identity as woman in relationship to an increasingly violent society. Thus now it is not just subjectivity as explored through the female body, but its subjectivity as explored through the social contract which lies broken—the national, social contract of what would have been called socialism or what was, at the least considered constitutional equality. Under threat from the 1990's and, specifically 1992 onwards, after the demolition of the mosque and its terrible aftermath, some very moving work by women artists comes forth. Further, with artists like Sheela Gowda and Pushpamala, and now several others, we have a discourse in art that not only complicates the question of the artist-subject, it inscribes itself within the social in a way that gives the social itself a form of interiority even as it makes their art practice step into what may be called an avant-garde.

RJ: The art scene in India is enriched today by artists like Bhupen Khakar, Gulam Sheikh, Vivan Sundaram, Nalini Malani, Jogen Chowdhury, Sudhir Patwardhan, and many others who look at the tradition not as it is practised but at tradition as it survives and as a result most of them focus expressly on life and issues around them. Do you see in the work of each of these artists a response to postmodernity or simply a new edge to the discourse of identity in Indian art?

GK: The artists you have referred to above—their exhibition in 1981 was called *Place for People*. It was an ideologically pitched exhibition that emphasized the politics of place, of location—in this case the urban location of the artist as subject and citizen. All of them were interested in exploring particularities of urban lives in modern India, and then moving back and forth between the metropolitan and the provincial: as say, between Bombay, Baroda,

Calcutta. These artists reintroduced the figurative narrative mode of representation. They also introduced local and specific class-based culture within the narratives. They were a very important influence on the next generation of artists that came out of Bombay and Baroda; in fact, they developed what came to be called the Baroda school of painting.

To the latter part of your question—these are decidedly postcolonial artists and if they may also be categorized as postmodern, it is a conjunctural fact seen to operate in many parts of the 'third world'. It is this historically notable equation between the postcolonial and the postmodern that is in some ways reflected in their work.

RJ: Also, in the past six to seven years there has been a new wave of Indian artists who have been very conscious about all the problems which have been happening in India and world and they have tried to express them either through visual art or paintings that have not been the continuation of what was in the 90s.

GK: Whereas the generations moved very slowly until the 90s (for example, the Progressives were mentors as well as a hegemonic force until the 80s), now the change is much faster. There are several generations at work—even since the 1990s you could count waves of younger artists pressing for place in the institutions and in the market, but also demanding and manifesting major changes in medium and language.

As for content and ideology, let me stake out a few markers. In comparison to M.F. Husain, for example, the middle generation addressed the national in critical terms. Vivan Sundaram, Nalini Malani, Rummana Hussain, Navjot Altaf, all make subtle and overt critique of the given nation from inside its paradigm. Artists younger to them, artists who first emerged on the art scene in the 1990s, critique the nation from outside the terms of the national, they do not accept the category. They say there is a faultline in the very category of the nation, and so it is not surprising that the nation fails. And they look at other categories, like that that of community. This could be an equivalent to the subaltern position, it would certainly be equivalent to the post-national position that has emerged all over the world as an aspiration as well as a ruse. These artists may see themselves as world citizens in a globalized world. If, on the other hand, some of these artists do not believe in the ideal, the normative possibility of a global civil society, they may admit to its opposite, to a form of global entropy within which not only the category of the national and the social but also of affirmation and dissent could be redundant. There a legions of artists are critical of globalism, but most are able to find a confluence of interests on a global scale in a common mediatic language, in a digital technology aesthetic. By one route or another, they become part of a global force that presumes something like world citizenship of peer-like producers (of artworks) who have the updated tools to negotiate both critique and contract with the production process.

Sonal Mansingh

Indian Classical Dance as a Genre

RAMIN JAHANBEGLOO (RJ): Why is Indian classical dance so different from any other genre, both of the West and the East?

SONAL MANSINGH (SM): The figurine of Mohenjodaro (approximately 6000–8000 BC) who is naked and full of jewellery stands in one of the four postures of the body in Indian dance—that is standing with one knee flexed. That posture is something that has always attracted my attention. I started with the physical because dance is something very physical. The Indian body frame is very different from either the Western or Southeast Asian body. Indian women are different in the way they make their hair, the way they hold the body, the way their arms usually flow, the graceful movements of the wrists and the postures that are inbuilt for activities like gossiping and walking. That posture, if you notice, is very different from the body language of the West or of Southeast Asia or anywhere else. Southeast Asian women have slim bodies. The Western body is very different and now more and more so with idea of unisex appearance. Even when classical ballet in Europe began in the sixteenth and seventeenth centuries, defiance of gravity was the central point and they went up on the toes. On the Indian subcontinent, on the contrary, the earth has been very central to life and respecting that earth and the forces of nature and gravity, the flow of energy, and the environment has been important. I think the understanding of these is very different from the West. Ballet has never taken into account the face as a pivotal element, whereas in India, even if you happen to see the daily life of an ordinary man, there are so many expressions involved in the face with eyebrows, nose, mouth, the hand gestures, each expressing and in action. I think perhaps it was because of abundance of the landscape, the mountains, the rivers, the flowers, and the colours. The abundance of nature translated into abundance of physical activities. Thus the Indian classical dancer works with each and every part of the body without neglecting even an individual finger of the hands or the placements of the feet on the ground. The Indian art of dance is like telling a story, like the ancient rock-paintings that deal with the story of day-to-day living, the celebrations, and the circular dance. Circularity is another very important feature of Indian classical dance. The *taal* (rhythm) system, the *raga* (melody) system, and the understanding of the circularity of nature, for example, the seasons, the rising and setting of the sun and the moon, and a visible circular order of natural elements and phenomena are significant to this ethos. The taal is built around this circularity. Later, acutely specific mathematical divisions arose from observations of the various constellations, stars and planets.

The core of Indian dance has remained unchanged. The very definition of the term 'tradition', which comes from the Sanskrit word *parampara* itself suggests constant movement—*param* and *aparam*, it's like moving one foot forward and then the other. Parampara is the opposite of '*Roodhi*' that nails down, call it orthodoxy, which compels one to go round and round in circles at the same point. But tradition is like flowing water. Therefore, the neo-classical dance forms that have drawn inspiration from various expressions of nature, of human lives around, the environment and the planetary systems and have changed according to time, are still alive after 5,000 years. They are not something out of reach so anyone can understand the import and flavour of the dance. Even the Indian folk dances occupied the space where the classical dance existed. They did not drop from the heavens but came from the roots. The occasion to celebrate life revolved around festivals, harvests, birth in the family, etc. In fact, anything was good enough to be celebrated. There is a fallacy being perpetrated regarding classical dance that it is only temple dance, but it began as a social occasion. Bharata and his compendium on theatre arts the *Natya Shastra* do not mention temples. '*Natya*' was a comprehensive term which included dance, music, and acting. It was a very beautiful system by which dance unfolded within the ambit of natya. There was also solo-dancing called '*ekal-nritya*'. The audience was called '*sabha*' and they elected the '*sabhapati*', that is the connoisseur who would preside over the proceedings. The man had to deserve the title by being knowledgeable, courteous, and a real connoisseur.

RJ: How is it that regardless of the features and peculiar characteristics of each of the seven forms, namely Bharatnatyam, Kathak, Odissi, Manipuri, Kuchipudi, Kathakali, and Mohiniattam, it is possible to say that all seven are parts of a single whole?

SM: The unity is in the ideas and in the physical elements. There are certain postures, gestures, and ways of locomotion on stage that are common, but then there are differences as well. For example, Manipuri is very different because of the Vaishnavite influence. The Lai Haraoba was typical to that until the fifteenth century when Vaishnavism took root in Manipur. Nature and ancestral worship among the Manipuri people is still prevalent. Therefore, the combined elements of both have given a particular form and flavour to Manipur dance. In Kathak, we have Islamic and pre-Islamic Hindu influences, but they are mingled together in a technique which is the same, only the textual songs become different, the way of expression remains the same, except that instead of namaste, they may do the salaam. The infusion of music drawn either from the north Indian Hindustani system or from Carnatic of South India accompanies all the dance forms. Legends and stories from Indian epics, mythology, and history are common to all forms, although formal and individual interpretations vary.

So an invisible golden thread binds the Indian dance forms together. They are unmistakably Indian.

RJ: What is more important, is it the spirituality or the ritual?

SM: I don't know why we make this difference. Spirituality is the way a particular individual feels about a particular activity at a particular moment. When you eat or cleanse, it's a ritual because you are concentrating on that particular activity at that particular moment and spirituality is when the spirit is also engaged. So, in dance, if the spirit is not there, then an important aspect is not communicated to the audience. Dance is a totality of what you are, that is, your body, your soul, your expressions, your moods, your feelings, experiences, perceptions, ideas, thoughts. When all these coalesce harmoniously and flow out as the essence or aroma, the audience experiences that intangible touch of an uplifting emotion that we call spirituality.

Classical Dance in Contemporary India

RJ: What is the difference between the traditional and modern Indian classical dance?

SM: When people use English words to explain Indian things, they always fall into this trap. Indian dance themes are usually conceived as metaphors and unfortunately, we have lost the ability of reading between the lines or inside the words and to comprehend the inner meaning. If you don't express the metaphor, like when a dancer shows Krishna but does not herself understand the resonances: the message is not conveyed. For example, the word 'devi' is a metaphor not for anybody, yet refers to everybody. 'Devi' comes from the root word 'DV', which means light or effulgence which is omnipresent. Ram is not only the king of Ayodhya fighting the demons but comprises of three letters—r, a, m—which are the three seed-letters standing for fire, sun, and moon.

You become spiritual when you understand your identity. Every human being has two eyes and one nose. But Krishna is blue. Why?

Because blue is the color of the sky, space, water, and it is the colour from which every other colour emerges, whether traditional or contemporary, there is an unmistakable stamp of Indian-ness on the creations.

RJ: Would you say that when you dance you make new interpretations of forms and gestures?

SM: The form of dance does change from time to time to accommodate socio-historical factors that translate into artistic changes, it is in the art of interpretational and emotive element where a dancer's creativity truly flowers.

The challenging part of the dance is *abhinaya*, which means communicating through your body, face, fingers, hands, and other limbs an entire theme or emotion and also bringing to the surface the underlying meanings. Otherwise, it remains neutral dance like say, a painting without texture or colour. There are differences between dances and performances. In dance, one finds some kind of reaction because it points to something new, some hidden meaning, some unknown value. The movement alone doesn't make dance.

RJ: Do you feel that cable television has changed the dance form in India?

SM: To an extent, definitely, the onslaught of multi-channelled cable television has affected the quality of time for culture but let us understand one thing that Indian classical dance was never really meant for the masses. They were performed for the cogniscenti. Besides they do not perform their responsibility towards society adequately. Classical dance is not being aired because it is said that there are no viewers for it and channels do not want to risk their money. If that remains the case, all the classical dancers will have to go on the streets with a begging bowl. It is very unfortunate that the electronic media, which is the most powerful today, has not at all paid its due to society by giving glimpses of the other side of culture. Even the government only pays lip-service. The

Doordarshan Bharati on which classical dances are shown has very little viewership because of the odd timing. One cannot expect dance lovers to switch the channel on after one-thirty at night to be able to see some classical dances, that too not always of best quality. This despite the fact that tourists travelling all over the country want to see this aspect of India. The demand from domestic viewership as well as from abroad is tremendous. People want to see dance and music because this is the way they connect with India. People cannot watch TV for hours whereas we, the classical dancers, lift the audiences from the mundane every day and transform everyday reality into the extraordinary.

RJ: So how does Indian classical dance survive despite the fact that people are more interested in television programmes? Are students still interested in learning the art?

SM: I don't know but I think that God is great and it has given me a mission in my life. I do not have any other explanation because successive governments have not given me accommodation like it has to hundreds of other artists. I have been blacklisted time and again for speaking out. Yet I have survived. Maybe because there is something called conscience and soul, and if one doesn't speak out, one merely remains a robot. There is interest among young students. I take a limited number of students and shape them into solo dancers. The huge group activity that goes on now in the name of dance is not something I adhere to but that is the trend because it is said that that is the demand of the international festivals and stage performances. I do not agree. Solo dancing remains the soul of Indian dance. This is why many students find it challenging and fulfilling.

RJ: The guru-*shishya* system of training in Indian dance with its long period of apprenticeship seems to have become increasingly anomalous in the contemporary Indian socio-economic and political situation? Do you agree to this view? Do you indulge in such practices? Is the life of the learner very strict and do they have to follow strict disciplines? Do you promote your students after they have learnt the art?

SM: It survives in pockets and with me also. Otherwise it is not possible to transmit the art. It cannot be done through computers and audio-visual mediums. Art has to be learnt at the feet of the master but if that is not possible, then at least one needs a guru. The younger ones who come at the age of six or seven are first taught exercises or what one calls yoga because yoga is the basis of dance. It builds the body. Then they learn various movements of their body, also working on the eyebrows, eyes, neck, the arms, and the legs. Slowly, they learn the art of balancing their legs and back because if one tries to sit like a dancer in Indian classical dance, one can fall if one has not learnt the art of balance. I used to teach ten to eleven year olds and then they could do their debut performances on stage. They have to follow strict discipline and if they don't, they will have to go somewhere else. I also promote my students and given them the contacts so that people can see them more and more in performance.

RJ: When you perform outside India, how do you connect with the Western audiences in comparison with your Indian audiences?

SM: Even in India, audiences are varied in different parts of the country. I love performing in Latin America. I have performed in fourteen countries of South America, including Cuba, Chile, Costa Rica, Columbia, Brazil, Venezuela, Mexico, Nicaragua, Panama, Paraguay, Argentina, and Peru. I find the audiences there wonderful because theatre-going audiences anywhere are wonderful. But I avoid dancing for the Indian diaspora, if I can, because generally they are more into the lighter kind of entertainment, and anyway they can see me here in India when they are visiting.

RJ: What do you think of the current dance scene in India?

SM: I think that it is very vibrant but there is a horizontal growth. Vertical growth has to come. Horizontal means that a lot more people are now dancing and that is why group performances are becoming very popular because at the same time there are lots of people performing on stage and they love that, even if it is only for five or ten minutes. They get money and exposure and the teachers get money too, but vertical growth is like growing into the core of dance. There is more opportunity but less of depth in dances now. A dancer needs to be alone, to do reading, research, thinking, creating and this takes courage, conviction, and commitment. When the roots have dried up, then it doesn't take the tree time to fall soon.

Raj Rewal

Evolving Architecture with an Indian Inspiration

RAMIN JAHANBEGLOO (RJ): Today after forty years of hard and permanent effort in emphasizing on 'Indian-ness' in your architectural works, do you think you and other members of your generation have succeeded in creating a meaning for what we can call 'a post-independent Indian architecture'?

RAJ REWAL (RR): I had started my professional pursuits in the mid-1960s and part of it was research in traditional Indian architecture with specific studies of urban values in Rajasthan's cities like Jaisalmer and architectural concerns embodied in Fatehpur Sikri. There were many lessons to be learnt from historic examples about modulating space and light. I had rejected sterile imitation of modernism, which in the 1960s and 1970s implied building blocks, with reference to the place-making culture of Indian urbanism. The Asian Games Village built in 1972 perhaps characterizes Indian-ness and solves contemporary problems of pedestrian and vehicular movement. I believe that there is a seminal outlook. It needs to be studied by the historians.

RJ: Would it be correct to say that in your architectural work, you have extended the traditional Indian concept of '*rasa*', which is mainly used in dance and music, to architectural spaces?

RR: The rasa or essential character of a building should be primarily based on its function or poetic symbols rather than the contemporary trends or fashion. In the Parliament Library, I have tried to evoke the idea of enlightenment based on light percolating from above. The vocabulary of design is based on new technologies of space structures, lifted above the columns to luminate the research and reading. The message is derived from ancient symbols perceived in a religious building. In the Lisbon Ismaili Cultural Centre, the forms and spaces allude to the Islamic themes of Charbagh and geometrical patterns. However, the lattice structural system built with a combination of granite and steel is a part of new technology. You will note that I make a difference between trends and technological breakthroughs. Take for example, deconstruction as a trend and its application to every building type and you have a recipe for architectural disasters.

RJ: How can tradition be perceived and revitalized in a constantly evolving and changing country like India, while this process has not been possible today in many Muslim countries?

RR: We have to confront tradition with honesty and truth and adopt values, which have meaning for our times. The lifestyle and workspaces are changing continuously and we have to evolve architecture to meet its demands. We are in the process of designing office buildings based on new IT requirements. I suppose architecture would go through metamorphosis under these circumstances. Let us face it. Tradition has no relevance when you are making a car factory. India has to change to meet the challenge of rapid urbanization and growth otherwise the whole country would degenerate into slums. Muslim countries with oil are luckier but they would have to move with the times as well. When I talk of evolution and change, I do not imply that we have to follow the Western idiom of a building. We have to find our own creative solutions.

RJ: One could say that your architectural pursuit has been centred mainly on the attempt to evolve a contemporary architecture rooted in Indian memory and heritage. By practising this type of architecture, do you manage to meet the practical needs of the modernization and urbanization process in India?

RR: Memory and heritage are significant values. Slavish adherence to tradition and sometimes superstition can be counterproductive. We have to evolve contemporary architecture and urbanism to meet practical realities. The past can be an inspiration but not a solution.

RJ: I suppose that the architects of your generation were faced with the difficult task of negotiating between the uncompromising universalism of the modernist position and a much more dialogical interface between the universal and the particular? This harmony is very much present in your last works.

RR: My generation of architects who had studied and worked abroad had to confront the Indian situation with a fresh eye. Modern architecture is based on several strands. It has been enriched by Scandinavian, Italian, and Japanese concerns. My aim has been to instinctively marry modernism with Indian roots. India is one of the few countries where the craft tradition persists with state-of-the-art technologies. We have the potential to use both the idioms and synchronize them in a new vocabulary.

RJ: The danger of a return to the past in architecture could be a montage of bits and pieces of the past, without a clear sense of the community.

RR: You cannot return to the past in historical styles in architecture. It would be an aberration. You cannot marry your grandmother. Reinterpretation of traditional architectural values certainly does not involve superficial montage of historical design elements with new building techniques. We have this ridiculous example of a Mumbai high-rise housing with Greek temples on its top floor.

RJ: Do you think that the man in the street could perceive clearly the references in your building to historical monuments like Fatehpur Sikri? How does your architecture provide a reinvigorated notion of a sense of community?

RR: Traditional typologies based on courtyards, public enclosures, merging of indoor and outdoor spaces have significant lessons for large-scale housing schemes and contemporary urban centres. I suppose the general public appreciates the cultural and climatic concerns. Sustainability has become a major issue, and passive energy control systems utilized in Fatehpur Sikri have important lessons for us.

RJ: Architectural critics in India and elsewhere seem to worry about the globalization of architecture and what they consider as a loss of a meaning in Indian architecture. Would you say that a truly Indian architecture now exists in India, which has achieved its independence of spirit while remaining a part of the global network?

RR: Globalization of architecture implies easy access to certain technologies, which should be welcomed. Excessive utilization of glass and air-conditioned workspaces are becoming a norm in the so-called shining India. We have to view all this modernisation from the point of view of sustainability. On the other hand, we should not forget that 30 per cent of our cities are urban slums and 70 per cent of our country still lives in poor villages. Low cost housing of one or two rooms with basic amenities should be considered part of the infrastructure like roads or bridges. Solving the basic problems of poor India would give incentive for a truly contemporary Indian architecture.

Mrinal Sen

Filming India

RAMIN JAHANBEGLOO (RJ): What were the circumstances that led you to become a filmmaker?

MRINAL SEN (MS): I am a filmmaker by accident.

RJ: Did you have any filmmaking experience at all when you started? Did you always want to become a director?

MS: No ... never.

Early Influences

RJ: Who are the filmmakers who have been of great importance in your life? What was the influence of modern and contemporary Bengali writings like Tagore, Samaresh, and Bhowmik on your filmmaking?

MS: I feel uncomfortable when I am asked to drop names. Instead of namedropping, I would love to talk about trends and trendsetters. Now, taking up the above questions, five in all, here is a summing-up—Just two years after the release of *Pather Panchali*, and that was in 1957, Satyajit Ray gently chronicled how he had realized that, 'all who set about making films need luck as much as they need the other things, talent, money, perseverance, and so on'. Ray did not have enough money of his own, nor any backer, but he had perseverance, talent, and the ability to organize. To be honest, I had none and had hardly had any interest in cinema. In my early days, I was not even a habitual filmgoer. Once, in the mid-1940s, when I used to read a lot, reading whichever book came my way in the city's largest library, called the Imperial Library, now National Library, I bumped into a book on cinema, on its aesthetics and on its sociology, written by Rudolf Arnheim—a gem of a written text. That was the beginning, an accidental beginning, and I fell in love with the aesthetics of cinema. In a few months, I read the entire stock available in the Imperial Library. Having read it all, I felt I had been adequately educated! That was the time when I started haunting the city theatres, but feeling uncertain if the stuff was all worth viewing. Gradually, with exposure to world cinema through various channels, through foreign consulates, and, later, through Calcutta Film Society, I became a whole time activist. Then I turned my hand to writing on the aesthetics of cinema, on its philosophy, the social relevance, and on the need to evolve a new language, New Cinema. While studying cinema and watching films, and relating the same with other arts, literature in particular, till then my first love, I developed a taste for Soviet cinema of the 1920s and early 1930s, neo-realism of post-war Italy, and for all that used to stand for New Cinema in new language, and all said and understood, for cinema that takes a moral position from which to look at the world. Instead of dropping names, I was head over heels in love with trends and trendsetters.

RJ: You are a difficult judge of your work. You always say that your first film, *Raat Bhor* made in 1956 was a disaster. But it started your learning process in filmmaking.

MS: Looking at what it was, I had no choice but to be a 'difficult judge' of my first film. It was a disaster. Having made such a lousy film, I had reckoned I had humiliated myself.

RJ: Two years later you made your second film *Nil Akasher Niche* about a Chinese hawker, the opium trade, and politics, which was banned by the government for two months, but it was greatly appreciated and even Nehru saw it and had a talk about it with you.

MS: I ask you to stand corrected if I say that the Chinese hawker in my film was not trading in opium, but was hawking his popular merchandise, *cheena* silk, though not real silk. In spite of my reservations on several counts, the film was, by and large, received with a certain grace. Even Nehru liked the film; quite possibly for its political content, which unequivocally espoused that our national struggle against colonial rule was inseparably linked with the democratic world's fight against fascism. The story and its setting dated back to the mid-1930s when militarist Japan attacked China. So much so that Yono Noguchi, the great national poet of Japan, took a strong stand in defence of aggression and wrote the same to Tagore. To which Tagore said: 'I wish your countrymen whom I love so much not success but remorse.' Nehru's tribute to Tagore then was: 'He has given to our nationalism the outlook of internationalism'. What a world we have left behind!

RJ: In those years, Satyajit Ray was making his *Pather Panchali* and *Aparijito*. Did Ray's cinema have any influence on you? Did you have a long friendship with him?

MS: Satyajit Ray was very special in Indian cinema. He made his first film and shook the world. Followed the second of the trilogy, a stupendous film, and then the third. He continued making films, a minimum of one film every year. Barring two titles, which I am happy with, the decade starting with 1955, the year of *Pather Panchali*, was, indeed, highly productive. For diverse reasons, I was deeply impressed, if not influenced. Living in the same city and meeting as often as we did, he and I had hardly any reason to be unfriendly.

RJ: Do you see a line of thought or a common structure in your first films? If so, where do you see the line of break? Is the line of break with *Akash Kusum* (1965) or with *Interview* (1970), the first of your Calcutta trilogy?

MS: I do not think it is a question for me. Ask yourself, if, however, you have studied my films critically. Allow me to quote a highly erudite critic and writer, Samik Banerjee [of the Seagull Arts and Media Resource Centre]: 'In a way, *Akash Kusum*—apart from the technical and stylistic elements which at that time had a certain shock effect—was resisted by many people. I personally welcomed it for being gimmicky, why not! This is one aspect of it. On the other hand, the trappings of realism in the film—the story, the relationships that unfold and develop, even clash against each other—breaks away from the structures of realism and moves towards more of an abstraction in terms of film language. There is a desire: a dream of success in life and career, and success in love—the two are almost linked to weave a fantasy, and then, trying to live that fantasy. The plot, predominant in realism, with its psychological relationships, slow developments, breakages, and cleavages—you break away from all of this and move daringly towards a level of abstraction in your film. This aspect appeared to me to be much more striking than the technical'.

This was one point of view, whereas, at another level, Ray's understanding is very different. So much so that he and I, and my writer had a very long debate that appeared in Kolkata's *The Statesman*. It went on for about two months, and about a hundred letters joined the fray. It was a wordy battle. Finally, it was nobody's gain, nobody's loss. But the edited version of the controversy involving just three of us, my writer and Ray, and I, appeared in a special edition at the at Cannes Film Festival.

I care not for the verdict or for the controversies, but since the film created a big noise, I would agree with what you say about the line of break. And, yes, *Interview* could also be another break. Given my own choice, *Ekdin Pratidin* (A Day like Any Other) could as well be the beginning of yet another line of thought and structure.

Calcutta in Sen's Films

RJ: To what extent has the city of Calcutta been present in your filmmaking? Would it be correct to consider you a Calcutta filmmaker like Martin Scorcese and Woody Allen are considered New York filmmakers?

MS: To a large extent, yes. No, I was not born here, but, true, I was made here. I must make it abundantly clear that I am not the person to ever treat my city as a sacred cow. But I find it buoyant, creative, erratic, even hopelessly disengaged where, at times, life gets paralysed, partially or totally caused by the excesses of monsoon or of political passion. Mercilessly maligned and dangerously loved, Calcutta has been the breeding ground of many of my films.

RJ: When you look back today at your Calcutta trilogy (*Interview, Calcutta 71*, and *Padatik*), do you consider it as a political statement and a critical analysis of the contradictions and paradoxes of Indian society?

MS: A friend of mine, Albert Johnson, tall and dark, who teaches cinema at the University of California, saw *Interview* and *Calcutta 71* and terribly enjoyed the continuous play with fact and fiction and fantasy because, so he said, he could freely relate all three to contemporary life and reality. 'That was a novel way of understanding the times and history,' he said, sounding like himself, an academician.

RJ: In one of your works, 'An Uncertain Journey' you say that: 'A highly conformist society like India is most likely to breed conformist viewers'. Does it come to you as a surprise that the contemporary Indian psyche is somehow ruled by Bollywood?

MS: Yes, I remember what I said about conformist society breeding more often than not, conformist viewers. But I do not understand how and why you relate my statement to Bollywood psyche. Isn't it the same everywhere? In varying degrees? More or less? What I meant to say, and I said it, was that conformist viewers were found to go in for what I termed 'stock responses'. The point would be to combat, to fight, to confront, and to see how the frontiers created and closely guarded by the conservatives could be broken. Don't you see that the non-conformists among the filmmakers are almost always popular failures? The equation such as you said wouldn't suit us.

RJ: I read somewhere that you contest the concept of 'national cinema' both in terms of subject matter and in terms of form. What does it mean to you to be an 'Indian' filmmaker?

MS: I do. In terms of subject matter, yes. More so in terms of form. By and large, an Indian filmmaker is one who, by nationality, is Indian. As simple as that, by definition. But an Indian filmmaker, whether or not the film is made in India or abroad, will have to have plenty of features to familiarize the audience with—outfits, food habits, local customs, regional rituals, modes of expression, and of course, the language spoken, the body language, and so on. Not so simple to familiarize with and fall in love with, until a kind of respect is developed for the circumstances in which the characters live, love, and grow, or perish.

RJ: *Bhuvan Shome* (1969) was your first Hindi film. Was making a satire on Indian bureaucracy in Hindi a way of addressing your message more directly to the Indian public?

MS: True, to a large extent *Bhuvan Shome* was a satire on bureaucracy. But the protagonist was an unhappy figure of ridicule, not a figure of fun. Yes, indeed, it was my first Hindi film, but honestly, it could as well be my ninth Bengali film. Be it in Hindi or Bengali, it would have made no difference to me.

Social Issues

RJ: After dealing with contemporary issues and social conflicts and problems like bureaucracy and corruption, you decided to make films like *Ek Din Pratidin* (1979), *Kharij* (1982), and *Ekdin Achanak* (1989), also considered to be three films with a common thread, where you depict the complexity of middle class urban life. I remember reading in one of the reviews that a member of audience wanted to hear from you that nothing 'wrong' could have happened to the middle class working girl in *Ek din Pratidin*. Do you usually get this kind of reactions from the Bengali middle class who feel disturbed by your social or political films?

MS: Since you've raised the point, I will tell you something funny about public reaction. *Ek din Pratidin* was released in one of the best theatres in Calcutta, Metro. The response was very positive and I loved to be mobbed. It was wonderful feeling to meet the friendly crowd at the foyer. A large number among them had a question for me. The same question every time: What happened to the working girl and where had she been? Interestingly, most of them were working women. They liked the film, they loved it, and yet they had the question. They were just curious, they said.

Just curious? Just that? I was not quite sure. Could it be that they wanted me to assure them that she did not do anything unacceptable to the society? That she did not violate social norms? A certificate from me testifying her character?

One evening, when I was mobbed by viewers, the large chunk being women, a man looking very respectable, should be of my age, presumably a thoroughbred Bengali, asked me in English, assuming a tone that was distinctly superior, 'Mr. Sen, it is important that we know what happened to the woman'.

Sounding much less than superior, I said in Bengali, 'My dear sir, I made this film for you. For you to watch and suffer. You'll suffer because you will not get the answer.' I added, 'If you ask me again, my answer will be: I do not know myself. I do not want to.'

Surprisingly, when, a decade later, a national daily, *The Indian Express*, carried excerpts from a letter—the letter from Satyajit Ray, written to his friend, reportedly, not for public consumption—in which he referred to me, and said, 'Never before has the maker (of the film) showed ignorance about characters authored by him. I suspect Mrinal does not know too why the professor disappeared in *Ekdin Achanak*'.

Honestly, Ray's suspicion was not untrue. But, equally true was my reaction when I read the excerpts of his letter. I read and instantly saw before me the gentleman in front of Metro cinema, who assuming a tone that was distinctly superior, reprimanding (!) me.

Incidentally, *Ekdin Pratidin* was a social film, made politically. For your information, the question was very common all over India but never in the West.

RJ: I think that your cinema is as provocative as Godard's used to be in France. Do you think that a film should disturb spectators in order to engage a dialogue with them?

MS: Absolutely!

RJ: In 1986, you made *Genesis*, which is a metaphorical story involving two men and a woman, set amidst ruins, away from civilization. *Genesis* is quite different from your previous films. Would it be correct to say that *Genesis* is a provocative examination of human interdependence, illustrating the irreconcilable dilemma between societal altruism and individual attraction?

MS: True, *Genesis* is quite different from my previous films. It was a multinational production, a parable, within the framework of an Indo-French protocol. Involving four characters, just four, language being Hindi, the story was planted in a no-man's land, frightfully desolate. Simple and clear, the concept could be read as a world built or gained is but the world lost, to be rebuilt or regained. Genesis, over again. The theme, as in a parable, could be read as the following: Wretched are the poor and the meek because they shall not inherit the Earth. Disinheriting the Earth, the defiant among them build a new world. The new world breeds virtues and vices. The exploiter comes back and the rest is history repeating, as always.

When made and released, the viewers saw the parable in many ways. Some liked and some did not. I find one of the interpretations of Jean-Claude Carriere to be highly fascinating. He said, 'One is also able to read behind the film a story that all Indian children know—that of two birds flying with a big worm picked up from the earth held in their beaks—a single worm for both of them. A hunter follows them, bow in hand, never drawing it. He stops when the birds stop, and starts again when they fly. Surprised, a man asks the hunter, 'Why don't you strike?' And the hunter replies, 'I am waiting for them to fight'.

Thus, within the limitations of a parable, simple and yet not quite so, we tried to present a story of the growth, development, and decay of a civilization, only to have it catch up with another. The press conference at Cannes elicited a few interesting questions including one regarding *The Origin of the Family, Private Property and the State* [Engels].

RJ: Your film *Antareen* is a cinematic adoption of Sadat Hassan Manto's story. The young writer strikes up a telephonic relationship with an anonymous female caller. These conversations provide the writer with material for his fiction. In the end, the two protagonists meet each other in a train compartment. This film reminded me of Antonioni's films. Do you feel close to the intimate cinema of Antonioni?

MS: Of course, Antonioni is a favorite of mine and I feel close to his intimate cinema. Here, while getting ready to write the script based on Manto's, I felt I needed a support, and that support came from Tagore's *Kshudito Pashan* (Hungry Stones). So, in the ultimate analysis, it was a mixture of Manto and Tagore, and if you feel it reminds you of Antonioni, I shall be happy.

RJ: You are absolutely right. And when you speak your lines, Dostoyevsky comes to my mind who, when condemned to four years of hard labour in Siberia, wrote a letter to his brother, and said, '... Human beings remain human everywhere' (*Notes from the Dead House*).

MS: Not to speak of completing fifty years in cinema, every time I see my own film, I wish it were a dress rehearsal, so that I could do it over again. Correcting my own conclusion! For myself.

Madhup Mudgal

Significance of Hindustani Classical Music

RAMIN JAHANBEGLOO (RJ): Music in India forms a vital part of the everyday life of people. Even the humblest Indian knows a song with which to cheer his long hours of toil. In truth, the sound of music is always in the air. For hundreds of years, the strict cast-iron laws of the Brahmans condemned the whole body of musicians to occupy a low position in the social scale. Today, the music of India is undergoing a renaissance and it is no more degrading to be a musician. But while taboos have been put aside in Indian music there have also been many changes in the manner in which Indians listen to music. By means of the modern media forms, Indian classical music has spread to the public to a great extent. Concerts are held not only in different regions of India, but also in many countries around the world. How do you analyse all these new changes with regard to the evolution of Indian classical music?

MADHUP MUDGAL (MM): Two stalwarts in Indian music, Pandit Vishnu Digambar Paluskar and Pandit Vishnu Narayan Bhatkande brought about the renaissance in the early part of the twentieth century. Before that, music was confined to the rich and the élite and common people and especially women from good families could not learn this art so easily. Pandit Vishnu Digambar was the first person to look into this matter and he started the Gandharva Mahavidyalaya in 1901 in Lahore so that ordinary people could come and learn the art. Because of him, musicians started getting respect from society. In Delhi, my father was responsible for all this as he started the Gandharva Mahavidyalya in 1939 there. Now the situation is different. During his time, no girl student came and he had to go to houses and request the parents to send their girl children for the music classes. Now lots of people are learning music in different schools that have sprung over the years. Now there are different opportunities available with the role played by the media and especially by the state government, which has sponsored many state scholarships.

RJ: Is the Indian classical tradition of music still based on the guru-shishya method of training, which demands the student to live with his/her master and adopt a life-long attitude of deference and humility toward the teacher?

MM: The situation has not changed. The learning process is still the same, may be the students don't live with their teachers due to the metropolitan way of living, but the relationship of the students with the teacher is still the same. In an institution like ours, everybody doesn't learn for being a professional. Fifty per cent do it as a hobby, 30–35 per cent do it to become teachers, and only three to four per cent do it because they want to make a career out of it and accordingly, we have to give them training. Those doing it as a hobby attend the normal classes but those who want to be professional, for them special classes are arranged.

Western Influences

RJ: Do you think the exposure of Indian music to Western influences has given birth to new forms of musical expression as fusion music or has the invasion of Indian markets by European and American music overwhelmed the native music of India?

MM: No, I don't agree with you. Indian music has stood all the onslaughts of Western influence because of the uniqueness of its taal and ragas, the two distinguishing traits, which are not found anywhere else except in Iran where a reflection of it is visible in the form of *makam*. Otherwise, everywhere else, even in China and Japan, students are learning Western classical music. Though the schools are trying to revive, but the influence is all too obvious. No doubt, new ideas have been experimented with, like in the field of fusion music, but it was there in Indian film music from the beginning in the form of different instruments being used in it.

RJ: The Western curiosity for Indian music started mainly in the 1960s with the hippy ethos, 'raga-rock', and the Beatles, but it eventually turned into a product of mass consumption with Ravi Shankar performing at both the Monterey Pop Festival in 1967 and at the 1969 Woodstock Festival.

MM: Panditji started the evolution. He attracted the Beatles. It was due to his efforts that Indian musicians have started performing outside and earn. Until then they used to perform in concerts for small durations.

RJ: For you it was a positive step undertaken by Panditji?

MM: Yes, it was. Everybody in the world knows Pandit Ravi Shankar.

RJ: Does the current classical/non-classical distinction in India owe much to the influence of colonial European categories of thought?

MM: No, it was there before also. For every fine art, like chamber music in the Western countries, the percentage of listeners is low. For popular and pop music, the percentage of listener has always been high. This is due to the fact that people have different tastes and preferences and there is nothing to feel depressed or disheartened by this fact.

RJ: Musicians in the West regard music in general as an end in itself. However it seems to me that in India, music is considered as a means of devotion and salvation, in a way related to the doctrine of *nama sankirtan* (chanting of the Lord's names). For example, the conception of music in Bhakti reveals levels of relation to the deity as an object of worship, or with Thyagaraja we find the concept that music itself is the ultimate reality and yet never separated from Hindu religion.

MM: When you get into the advanced stage, then it is like that but in the beginning, for the students, it might not be the case. Carnatic music compositions are specially Bhakti in nature but Hindustani music has romantic compositions also. It is said that you go deep into the music and start seeing God but that is only in the very advanced stage. You first start worshipping the raag and the taal and then at a later stage, you feel the spiritual inclinations and maybe some people don't feel it at all.

RJ: What according to you are the distinguishing traits of Indian classical music that distinguishes it from Western classical music?

MM: I would say that the basics are different. It's the melodious structure and the uniqueness is raga and taal. These two characters are the most distinguishing traits of Indian music. Everything is centred on a particular raga in Hindustani music.

RJ: The timing is also important because the ragas are specifically written for different seasons and the time of the day, which we don't find in Western or other classical music.

MM: Yes, I agree with that. Not even in Carnatic music this is to be found. The ragas were performed according to the intensity of the sun. It depends on person to person. Carnatic musicians do not follow this, most of the Hindustani musicians do. I do follow this personally. Even in the Veda there is a shloka, which talks about the raga relating to the intensity of the sun.

RJ: Do you think, these traits of Indian classical music allow musicians to make improvisations, like jazz improvisations?

MM: Yes, because it is very easy to take up a scale and perform. Scale and raag are different. In scale, you can do whatever you want to do but in raag, you can't do whatever you want to do. You have to go according to the laws and the laws are such that once you know them well you are even allowed to break them. It's a beautiful synthesis of law and liberty in our music.

RJ: Has Hindi film music been responsible for the oblivion of Indian classical music among the younger generation of Indians?

MM: No. In fact it's the other way round. Most of the playback singers have learnt classical music before venturing into the arena of film music.

RJ: Do you think that the extraordinary flowering of cable TV and cassette-based popular music has greatly empowered Indian classical and folk music in the battle against film music and Western music?

MM: Because of television, we might lose our folk music. The actual folk music lies with the ladies of the old families. Now because of globalization, everything appears to be the same. The clothes are the same and it becomes difficult to recognize people and we seem to loose our identities. But because our culture is so strong, we survive.

RJ: Could we say that India is at the beginning of a new orientation in the domain of music, where there is the adoption of existing elements of style and their blending with traditional styles?

MM: This is a period of experimentation, with fusion music being very popular. Many new things are being tried. It remains to be seen how successful they are.

RJ: How do you see the changes brought in Indian classical and Indian folk music in the past sixty years. Has it been helpful in the development of Indian music?

MM: It has positive impact in the sense that more people are listening and learning music now than ever before. The only thing is, we are missing out on the classical nuances, and it is becoming more generalized. The special-ness of Indian classical music—we are missing on that.

Prabhash Joshi

Cricket as an Indian Game

RAMIN JAHANBEGLOO (RJ): According to Ashis Nandy: 'Cricket is an Indian game accidentally discovered by the English ... To most Indians the game now looks more Indian than English.' Is this your point of view?

PRABHASH JOSHI (PJ): Yes, it is true that we took it from the English, but then, there are elements in this game, which are closer to the Indian psyche than they are to the British psyche. For example, a test match lasts for five days, something that is not seen in any other game. No festival in India is a one-day affair. The Diwali celebration is exactly for five days. Similarly, Holi starts a month prior to the day when the Holika is actually burnt. It is a festival in which the marginalized of society get the main role to play. Now, Rakshabandhan is the festival of the Brahmans and then there is Dussahara, which goes on for at least twelve days. So all these festivals cut across caste distinctions, and create an ambience in which everybody can participate. Now the élite of the country may have played cricket first, to begin with the British, but it had the participation of the proletarians of this country even in those days when they used to play it in the presidencies, there were people who came to do various jobs and these were the people who would stand at the boundary line and would fetch the ball and give it back to them. At that time they didn't understand the game but still they enjoyed it. This was not the case in England where the game started. There were no celebrations that lasted for a long period. The British gave us both industrialization as well as imperialism. So the atmosphere of England and India created cricket, which was entirely different in essence.

RJ: But the fact is that cricket was much more than just another game to the Victorians. Victorian society glorified cricket as a perfect system of ethics which equated for them the moral excellence and strong character of the English.

PJ: Yes, because it is not the roots that produced the game of cricket in England that are responsible for the creation of this game in India. Indians saw only the British colonizers playing this game. The British had set up a settlement in Calcutta, which was secluded from Indian society. In Mumbai and Madras, the same situation prevailed. The game of cricket was viewed as coming from an alien culture. It was thought of as a recreational activity, which was not a part of mainstream society. The Indians, at that time, participated in the game merely as spectators.

RJ: How is that the Parsi community was the first to take up cricket in India in the middle of the nineteenth century? Are there any famous Parsis today in the Indian cricket team?

PJ: The English thought that the Parsis were not a part of Indian culture and that they came from outside. They wanted to align with them. They wanted a local collaboration with them to rule the country and they thought that the people who would come nearest to them in this pursuit would be the Parsis. All Parsis were sincere. They came to trade in India and settled in the coastal areas. They worshipped the sun god like the Iranians. They became a part of the Indian trading class. The language that they spoke was Gujarati, which was the language of the trading community. Thus the Parsis were looked upon as a community, which could collaborate with the British and help them to rule the country. The ways of the local people were very different from the British and so they thought that if they would have a collaborator whose ways were different from the locals, then it would help them. So the Parsis became the first Indians to play cricket. Parsis are not a society who enjoyed physical activity because they were the people who never did manual jobs. They were not the ones who would go to find jobs in the country as they traded. They didn't react in the physical sense in which the people in Hamilton would have reacted to the game of cricket or the Indians would have if they were the first to take up the game of cricket. So the low caste people in India should have first taken it up because even today, they are the ones who are engaged in the physical work the most.

RJ: So you agree with Ramchandra Guha's bold and revolutionary thesis in his book *A Corner of a Foreign Field* that an unknown Dalit by the name of Baloo was the first great Indian cricketer. It is interesting to review Baloo's life as a Dalit player, because apparently, the Brahmans played with him on the cricket field, but would not dine with him off it. And in fact, during the game's ritual tea interval, Baloo was made to stand outside the pavilion at a distance of his team mates. This shows us how cricket in some sense played a role in both creating a sense of community and a larger sense of solidarity across classes. Is this still the case?

PJ: It is not Baloo as symbol of this. What I am trying to say is that the lower castes or classes that should have enjoyed playing cricket because it is a physical activity were not the classes who interacted with the British in playing cricket. It was the trading classes who first played cricket in India with the British. The Parsis undertook cricket not for the sake of physical pleasure that came out of this game but for the sake of other advantages that flowed from socializing with those who held power. Guha's thesis is more or less a projection of the present onto the past. Cricket today is a passion with all the classes and castes of people in the country who play the game. During those days in which cricket took roots in the country, there was a class of freedom fighters who hated cricket because they thought that cricket was a game of the imperialists who played it only with the rajas and the maharajas, the élite of the country, which was looked down upon by the people because they were the collaborators of the British in the empire. So people of my generation or the people one year prior to my generation hated cricket. I still remember that because of my love for this game, I had to put up with a lot of criticism, even outcasting from the arena of those who were trying to create a national life in free India. They thought that hockey was the Indian game and if you tell them that hockey also came from abroad and that it was first played in Pune in the cantonment, then they would not believe it. They thought it was their game since India went to Germany in 1928 and won there. Do you know that for seven years, during the Second World War, India kept on winning the game? The great players of hockey like Dhyanchand who scored as and when they willed didn't belong to the upper crust of the society. If you look at the first Indian cricket team that went to England in 1972, it comprised of players who belonged to the proletariat. The first captain of the Indian cricket team was C. K. Naidu, who belonged to the Naidu community of Andhra Pradesh and was not a part of the élite of this country. So you cannot single out Baloo. The players belonged to the lower classes and castes because the game of cricket involved physical activity, which could not be performed by the rajas and the maharajas or the Parsis. They played cricket not for entertainment but for other purposes, that is social, economic, and political advantages ensuing from it. The rajas and the maharajas patronized cricket because they thought that by doing so, they would come closer to the wielder of powers. Suddenly, the British too realized that cricket could be a very good vehicle for imperial culture.

RJ: *Lagaan*, an Indian film about cricket and colonialism depicts how the British wanted to subjugate the native Indians through cricket. In this movie, cricket, rather than being a symbol of subjugation, appears as a vehicle of resistance against the British.

This is the irony of history, which turns out to come full circle when Nassir Hussain, an Englishman with an Indian ancestry became the captain of the English cricket team and won the series against India in January 2002.

PJ: It has a history. In 1999, the world cup tournament was held in England and the English team was not only performing badly but not many English spectators were there to see the game. The people who were enjoying cricket then were the people from Sri Lanka, Bangladesh, Pakistan, and India who were cheering their respective teams. This means that the main part of the spectators who made the world cup a festival, a *mela,* were those of South Asian origin. So one of the newspapers in England printed that if they wanted to save cricket then they should involve the Asian community in it so that someday a mother might give birth to someone like Sachin Tendulkar. These were the lines that were written in the paper. It was the time when they decided to bring Asian society into the mainstream of cricket to rejuvenate their own cricket in England. Nassir Hussain was a part of that policy. Not only Hussain, but Monty Panesar, the current great spinner is a Sikh. So the British as matter of policy decided that to keep cricket alive in England they should involve Britishers of Indian or Asian origin in the game and they were the people who gave new blood and enthusiasm to the game.

RJ: What are the main issues of Indian cricket that Indians are obsessed with?

PJ: There are two things we should try to concentrate on. The British used cricket as an instrument of imperialism. Now whatever you use as an instrument of imperialism can also be used as a mechanism to oppose it and turn into an instrument of nationalism. So Indian cricket became an assertion of nationalism because while playing cricket, an Indian was trying to prove that he was good, in fact better, at their game. This is how nationalism flourishes. You take the same ground and then compete. The first Indian cricket hero was C.K. Naidu and he became a figure larger than Sachin in that era. In 1928, a cricket team called Arthur Gilligans came to India and played two matches all over the country. They went to Bombay and played a two-day match with the Hindus. The British had divided Indian cricket into many classes or communities and therefore created a ground for sectarianism. This meant that each community, the Hindus, the Parsis, the Muslims, etc., had their own team and competed with each other. When the match was going on, Early scored a century and hit eight sixes. The next day C.K. Naidu hit fourteen sixes and scored 154 runs. This news spread around the country that there is a chap called Naidu who can hit the ball harder than an Englishmen and can hit sixes against them, which not even an Englishmen can do. So Naidu became a symbol of nationalism that was trying to express itself through cricket. The seed of cricket becoming a symbol of nationalisn has something to do with the seeds of communal cricket, which British were trying to spread in India.

RJ: Are women in India playing cricket?

PJ: Yes, they have a national team and they have reached the semi-finals of the world cup. In fact, the highest score scored by a women cricketer is that of an Indian.

RJ: In the past few years, hooliganism has sullied Indian cricket's reputation. Stone-throwing and other acts of vandalism have become increasingly common in Indian cricket games, especially when India is on the verge of defeat. Do you interpret these behaviours as a consequence of what one might call 'cricket nationalism' in India?

PJ: Protesting in such a hooligan way in India has become a way of expressing dissatisfaction with whatever is happening. It is not only with India's defeat that they will do it. They will do it even when police lathicharge them. If cricket is a source of power then there are various groups that become interested in controlling them. If one group is controlling cricket and there is another group, which is dissatisfied with the way free passes have been distributed, this group will collect groups of dissatisfied people and use them to start a small riot and they will blow it up into a big scene of hooliganism. It is not merely defeat that ignites hooliganism. It is not only in cricket. Vandalism in football in Europe is a much bigger menace. So saying that Indians are expressing their nationalism when their national team is defeated is like mis-understanding the whole cricket scenario.

RJ: Would you say that cricket has become an element of cultural globalization in this area of the world? Through cricket, a country can indulge in more inter-cultural dialogue.

PJ: It was an Indian who wanted to globalize cricket. Previously, cricket was only played in the former colonies of the British. It was an Indian called Jagmohan Dalmiya, the president of International Cricket Control (ICC) and Board of Cricket Control of India (BCCI) who introduced it to other nations. The British introduced cricket in the colonies not because of the spirit of the game but as a means to control their empire. Now BCCI is a British tradition and the ICC used to be an imperial cricket conference. If you want to disassociate cricket from its colonial past then you can take it to those parts, which were not a part of the British colonies. So globalization of cricket would mean that you are taking the game to the people who are not a part of the history of this game. Now you cannot take the history of imperialism away from the game of cricket. The British used it as an instrument of globalization and it was only when they realized that others used it as an instrument that the globalization of cricket started. Chappel, the commentator and writer, says that even if the Indian team goes to the North Pole to play cricket, there would be enough Indian supports cheering them because anywhere the Indian team goes, Indian supporters reach prior to them. So it is the Indians who are globalizing the game of cricket. The growing Indian economy supports 80 per cent of world cricket. The world cup is sponsored by those who have business interests in India because, if the Indian team is not playing, there would be no Indian participation and so the largest market will be lost. The European market contributes only a small portion of the spectators and so, to involve Indians so that you can sell your products, you have to take cricket as the first outlet of that. If the Indians are playing in England, you will find that the Indians are getting more support than the British get from the British crowd. The Indians have globalized it, but incidentally, they have come to acquire the biggest market outside China. I would like to make three points in this regard. First, cricket in India is not only a physical recreational activity but is an expression of many other things, including nationalism. Indians came as a world team in the cricket scene only after the game had been thoroughly democratized in this country. The last man belonging to the rajas and the maharajas in the cricket team was before 1971, when Nawab Pataudi became a cricketer, but after that, all the heroes of Indian cricket belonged to the proletariat like Gavaskar, who grew up playing cricket on the streets. He had to play straight because hitting on the sides would have broken the windows of the colony and thus he developed the art of playing straight drive that became his strength in due course of time. Similarly, Tendulkar is the son of a middle class Marathi teacher. So, the whole process of democratization of cricket in India has taken place and the forces of globalization of cricket have come not from England, but from India.